Guided Journey

3. 7. 00

To Helen.
With warmest good wishes
Alan Kern.

Open now the crystal fountain
whence the living waters flow;
let the fiery, cloudy pillar
lead m*e all my journ*ey through:
strong deliverer,
be thou still my strength and shield.

Guided Journey

Some Experiences of a Lifetime

Alan Kerr

Brolga Press
Gundaroo

Cover Design: Graeme Cogdell

National Library of Australia
Cataloguing-in-Publication entry.

Kerr, Alan, 1918 –
Guided Journey: some experiences of a lifetime

ISBN 1 875495 23 1

1. Kerr, Alan, 1918- . 2. Scripture Union.
3. Anglicans - Australia - Biography.
I. Title

283.94092

Published by: Brolga Press Pty Ltd
15 Cork Street, Gundaroo, NSW 2620

Printed by: OPENBOOK Publishers
205 Halifax Street, Adelaide, SA 5000

Contents

Preface

There is a very striking passage in the book of Isaiah where God speaks to His people and to individual believers about His lifelong care for them.

You whom I have upheld since you were conceived, and have carried since your birth. Even to your old age and grey hairs I am he, I am he who will sustain you. I have made you and I will carry you; I will sustain you and I will rescue you.

As our life moves on it is striking to realise how God's good hand has been over us, long before we came to know Him and how He has sustained us through all the vicissitudes of life. We are reminded that Daniel spoke about *'God, in whose hands our breath is and whose are all our ways ...'*.

For me, Alan Kerr, writing at the age of 80 years, there is special significance in this truth because my early life was uncertain. My physical weakness was a constant source of concern to my parents and when I was particularly ill around the age of seven the doctors had told them frankly that they could not expect me to see my teenage years. Certainly life at that time seemed to be largely made up of 'bad turns', visits to hospital and time spent in bed, with reading as one of my major occupations. Books and a lively imagination created a world apart in which much of those early years were spent. In the providence of God, the doctors were proved to be wrong and the next problem for my caring parents was to explore how this shy and uninstructed youth would take his place in the outside world and earn his living. This was something which that same gracious God would also take care of in due course.

Acknowledgments

I owe a debt of gratitude to a number of people in relation to this small slice of history. First, to my friends John Prince and Ian Milne for suggesting that it could have some significance, and for persisting in the face of my denials, then to Dr Stuart Piggin who also encouraged me and gave helpful advice. To my grandson Luke Kerr who convinced me that I would need to avail myself of modern technology, then procured the equipment and instructed me in the rudiments of its use. Ron Clough kindly furthered my instruction and then the process was continued by Glen Randle who with great patience and skill enabled me to see the task to its conclusion. To Geoff and Ann Kells for kindly making available their holiday home where much of the original writing was done, and above all to Ada whose enthusiasm and constructive criticism has helped to bring it about. Finally I am indebted to Bob and Mildred Kirk of Brolga Press for their editorial advice and proficient handling of the manuscript in what has proved to be a prolonged process. To all these I extend my very sincere thanks and appreciation.

Alan Kerr,
Mt Eliza, April 1999

Glossary of Abbreviations

Scripture versions:

Authorised (King James)	AV
New Revised Standard Version	NRSV
New English Bible	NEB
New International Version	NIV
A Prayer Book for Australia (Psalms)	APBA

Movements and Organisations

Australian Nepalese Mission	ANM
Melbourne Bible Institute	MBI
Schools Christian Fellowship	SCF
Inter-Schools Christian Fellowship	ISCF
Campaigners for Christ	C for C
Scripture Union	SU
Children's Special Service	CSSM
Crusader Union	CU
Inter-Varsity Fellowship	IVF
Unevangelised Fields Mission	UFM
Australian Pacific Christian Mission, (formerly UFM)	APCM
Church Missionary Society	CMS
Evangelical Alliance	EA
St Andrews Missionary Training College	ST ANDREWS
Evangelical Fellowship of the Anglican Communion	EFAC
National Evangelical Anglican Congress	NEAC
Lausanne Congress of Evangelism	LAUSANNE
Zadok National Christian Study Centre	ZADOK
Outreach International	OI
Bush Church Aid Society	BCA

For you created my inmost being;
you knit me together in my mother's womb.
I praise you because I am fearfully and wonderfully made;
your works are wonderful, I know that full well.
My frame was not hidden from you
When I was made in the secret place.....
your eyes saw my unformed body.
All the days ordained for me were written in your book
before one of them came to be.

Psalm 139. vs 13-16 NIV

When all your mercies, O my God,
my rising soul surveys,
transported with the view, I'm lost
in wonder, love and praise.
Unnumbered comforts to my soul
your tender care bestowed,
before my infant heart could know
from whom those comforts flowed.

Isaac Watts. 1674-1748

-1-

1918 – 1933

Early Days

There were high hopes for a new beginning when my grand-father Richard Thomas Davidson Kerr arrived in Melbourne from Britain in the 1870s. He was to marry Margaret Ann Jones from Wales and they had two children before my father Horace Thomas Davidson Kerr was born in 1888. Alas less than twelve months later Richard died, leaving his widow to bring up the three children. This she accomplished, no doubt with help of friends at the Brougham Street Methodist church, in North Melbourne of which my father was a member and, perhaps, also from the Welsh church which his older sister Alice attended. She was to marry Watkin Williams, a leadlight worker and French polisher, who was later to be known by his nephews and nieces as 'Uncle Wattie'. A man of Welsh eloquence and accent he charmed them with his stories and reminiscences. The eldest son Ernest made his way to Sydney where he married and raised a family with whom we had virtually no contact and whom we never met.

On the 26th of May 1917 my father married Frances Elizabeth Pearce, second youngest of the six children of Alfred Benjamin Pearce and his wife Louisa Jane. Alfred Pearce had emigrated from the United Kingdom as had my paternal grandfather. He used to tell us of the three months journey by windjammer. A man of strong Christian faith and a Methodist local preacher, he followed his trade as a picture framer and gilder, but later in life seemed to have moved into doing some building and development.

Above left: My grandparents, Alfred and Louisa Pearce, 1924.
Above right: Myself, aged six at our Essendon home.

Before World War 1 he built a pair of semidetached cottages at Nos 10 and 12 Garden Street, Essendon. He and Grandma Pearce occupied No. 12 and at the time of my birth my parents lived in No. 10. This was my home for the first six years of my life. With us lived Grandma Kerr, as my father had been caring for her for many years.

After attending the Errol Sreet State School in North Melbourne my dad commenced work with a small firm by the name of John Buncle & Sons which sold agricultural machinery. He often used to tell my young brother and me stories about those days and his employer, Mr Buncle, who did not posses a good memory of his customers. When different ones came in from the country he would expect Dad to prompt him and would say 'Well, well, Horrie, who was I just talking about yesterday?', whereupon Horrie was expected to come up with the appropriate name.

Dad later put his memory and clerical talents to work with the State Government in the Lands Department and for most of his time there worked with the State Rivers and Water Supply

Commission. He was a good organiser with a flair for correspondence and minute taking. For a number of years he was
secretary of the Brougham Street Church and of the Methodist
Churches Cricket Association. Apparently about the time when
my brother Roy was born I attended Sunday School at
Brougham Street, but I have no recollection of the church where
my parents met and married and where I was baptised. I can
remember that we sometimes used to go for a walk in nearby
Royal Park after Sunday School. For me, it is a matter of regret
that I have few memories of my grandmother Margaret Kerr or
of her passing. One outing with her that I do remember was an
occasion when we walked together to the new railway station at
Glenbervie on the day it opened, caught the first train to Essendon and walked back home. I still have the ticket No. 0009,
dated 11 Sept 1922 , by which to remember the experience.

One of my few really clear memories from 10 Garden Street
was an incident which made a powerful impression on me. My
mother was on her knees, scrubbing the floor of the passageway
which ran through the house. Just before this she had spoken
severely to me about some misbehaviour and I was feeling most
unhappy. Shortly afterwards she looked up from her task and
made a kindly remark. Still feeling the rebuke very keenly I said
with surprise, 'how can you be nice to me when you were so
cross?' I learnt a great lesson when she replied with a warm
smile 'because I love you'.

At the age of five I made a brief appearance at the infants
class at the Essendon State School, opposite the 'Windy Hill'
football ground which was to be visited so often in later years,
the scene of many a grand encounter. I do not know how many
days were spent there but I am inclined to think that they must
have been few. My one abiding memory is a most unhappy one.
Leaving the school one afternoon I was confronted by two older
boys who pushed me against the brick wall of the building and
threatened me with their penknives, open in menacing fashion.
No doubt it was fairly harmless but my timid soul was terrified
until at that moment my mother appeared, wheeling Roy in his
pram, accompanied by her sister Lou likewise with her small
son, Frank. The aggressors fled and I was overwhelmed with a
great surge of relief, clearly recalled over seventy years on.

Much happier memories centre around that other field of

conflict on the opposite side of the road, headquarters of the Essendon Football Club. Dad had been a dedicated supporter from boyhood, never missing a match for years on end, rain, hail or shine. From early days he took me to watch the team practising and then later to matches where I would watch, perched quite often on his shoulders, standing under the peppercorn trees near the old score board. After the match I would sometimes be taken into the players rooms to see some of them and to be captivated by the heady aroma of eucalyptus. One day I shook hands with the captain, Frank Maher, and there were other heroes who would greet my Dad and include me in that greeting. Essendon was a leading team at that time and a long-cherished memory is of Dad returning from the 1923 Grand Final against Fitzroy, waving his newspaper as he came down the road to me waiting at the gate saying, 'we won, we won'. No radio of course to give progress scores and results in those times. The Dons were League Premiers in 1923 and again in 1924 and this was the beginning of my lifelong attachment to the team and the game.

Dad's job with the Water Commission often entailed visits to the country to supervise aspects of the irrigation program. Even though these journeys were of short duration he would send me postcards from country towns, some of which I still have today. These always conveyed the sense of love and concern which I was fortunate to enjoy, especially as my health was a source of worry to my parents. Despite the limitations on activity because of my poor physical condition I remember my boyhood as generally happy and secure. My parents were caring and devoted to the welfare of their two sons and the atmosphere of the home was cheerful and loving.

It was my ill health which brought about a move from Essendon to Blackburn in 1924. The doctors had recommended a more rural environment as being likely to bring about an improvement in my condition. My parents therefore purchased their first home, in Whitehorse Road almost opposite the Blackburn State School. It was an attractive wooden cottage on an acre of land which was well laid out in gardens with two dams at the back. This house has long since disappeared from the busy area which this has now become. Here I made another beginning at the school opposite and was immensely pleased and proud to have a school cap and to be put into Grade 1.

Unfortunately, ill health again intervened and the next move was to have my tonsils removed, which took place at Epworth Hospital around the time of my seventh birthday. The experience of being left at the hospital and feeling a sense of loneliness and desolation remains with me yet. After a while it became obvious that the 'change of air' had not been of benefit and now the advice from the specialist was to move away from the clay soil of Blackburn and go out to the hills. My chest weakness, involving frequent bronchitis, pleurisy and pneumonia could no doubt have been much more effectively treated with the drugs and antibiotics which are available today. Seventy years ago the environment was considered a major factor in treatment, combined with such things as keeping out of the night air, never getting cold etc. My parents had a friend who was suffering from TB who had moved out to the open spaces of a new suburb known as Rosanna. As this was considered to be my complaint, the decision was made to sell our nice home and buy land at Rosanna, which was a hilly semi-rural area. They purchased a block of land at 5 Hillside Road and entered into a building contract for a fine new weatherboard house to be built for the sum of eight hundred and sixty pounds and arranged finance through the State Savings Bank. So the pattern of our lives was set for the next few decades and the new location proved to be amenable from numerous viewpoints.

While the house was being erected, we rented a home on Plenty Road, Heidelberg, near the corner of St Helliers Street and began attending the West Heidelberg Methodist Church. In January 1926 we moved into our new home, a big venture for my parents who were financially handicapped, I am sure, by the costs of medical attention for their elder son. In those days there was no government assistance of any kind for them. This new beginning meant that a further effort at schooling was now to be made and I spent a few weeks at West Heidelberg State School in Grade 3 which is quite clear in my memory. Once again, illness interrupted, this time seriously and some time was spent in hospital. The advice given to my parents then was to forget about schooling and to let me try to find my way back to recovery. I was linked to a state correspondence course and did some work with it but the doctor's advice was followed and my formal education ended at that point. I did a great deal of reading however and my father enrolled me as a member of the

Athenaeum library. He brought books home for me regularly and it was in this way that I gained most of my general knowledge. I played a lot of draughts and chess with my grandfather, learnt card games which I played with an English lady nearby and roamed the open paddocks and hills around our home. The pattern of constant weakness and chest trouble continued over the next two or three years with two serious bouts of double pneumonia during one of which I was in Airlie Hospital, Ivanhoe for some time with extremely high temperatures. I think it was at this point that my parents believed that the doctor's prediction that I would not see my teens was about to be fulfilled. They must have experienced a great sense of relief however when from the age of 11–12 a steady improvement commenced. Certainly the home life, the abundance of care and affection and the absence of stress, were factors which helped

Somewhere around this time a new element entered into our home entertainment with the advent of radio, at first in its simplest form. Dad procured a 'crystal set' and we spent hours in turn with an old heavy headphone set on and agonising moments trying to find a good spot on the crystal with the 'cats whisker', to gain audible reception. Not many years later this gave way to a three valve radio receiver with a loud speaker, and then successively more powerful models over the years. These brought in an era of never to be forgotten nights around the fire as we listened to the progress of the Test cricket matches in far-off England. We boys were allowed to sit up to unheard of hours enthralled by the company of neighbours and the exploits of the Australian team.

Another portent of the approaching technological age was the advent of the first long distance aeroplane flights. Grandpa took me one day to Essendon aerodrome to see Bert Hinkler land in his Tiger Moth after his history-making solo flight from England. Kingsford Smith flew the Pacific and slowly the epic journeys gave way to the everyday use of planes which were to become a major factor of life a few years later. Because Dad was the secretary of the Methodist Cricket Association, they paid for us to have a telephone installed so that he could get the weekly results into the Monday papers. Such a modern amenity was fairly rare in Rosanna homes and very frequently neighbours dropped in to 'use the phone', leaving their two pennies for the call in our phone box.

Quite often I would take the calls from the club secretaries, noting down the scores and discussing the teams performances with them. After a year or two of this a motion was put to the AGM of the association that I should be appointed Assistant Secretary, which was duly carried.

Apart from this touch of sophistication our lifestyle was quite plain. Most tradesmen called at the home. We put out a tin 'billy' for our milk each morning, the baker called daily in a horse drawn cart with two choices 'white' or 'brown' in his basket. Grocer, greengrocer and butcher all called two or three times weekly, first for the order and then to deliver it. Our perishable foods were placed in a 'Coolgardie' safe, kept cool by strips of cloth carrying water from a tank at the top down the hessian sides. It was to be many years before we felt able to afford the luxury of an ice chest. Mum's cooking was done on the one fire stove, which usually burned daily, or the gas stove. Laundry was done in a wood-fired copper and in cement troughs and then put through a mangle. Our baths were heated by a wood 'chip heater' later to be replaced by a gas heater as with the gas copper.

We walked to the two or three shops by the Rosanna station for any additional needs and we children went on Saturday mornings to spend our pocket money on sweets at the store. This was at first one penny a week each, in later years threepence, which purchased an amazing array of assorted aniseed balls, licorice straps, boiled lollies, sherbet and the like. On these exciting expeditions Roy and I were often joined by our cousin Joyce Powell, second daughter of my mother's sister Alice who with her husband Jim had also come to live in Rosanna. Joyce was almost my age and we were close companions over these years.

Financial constraints were rarely out of mind for long, especially in the years of the great depression around 1929 – 1933 during which Dad, in common with all public servants, had to accept a cut of 10 per cent in his modest salary. As an economy measure these cuts were general throughout the community and in private enterprise the reductions became more drastic. As the basic wage at the time was less than four pounds a week, frugality was the norm for most people, even for those fortunate enough to have work. Thousands of breadwinners had lost their jobs and had to accept government work for what was called 'sustenance', at the rate of two pounds a week. The social services as we know them today did not exist and it was the churches and welfare organisations which sought to bring relief to the thousands of citizens in sometimes desperate circumstances.

Horace and Frances Kerr were a contented couple with a positive outlook on life who made their home the focal point of family life. Entertainment and social activities were simple, centring on relatives, neighbours and the church community. Games and competitions of all kinds were invented and engaged in with enormous enthusiasm. In the summer we were joined by neighbours for cricket matches in our long backyard which took on a 'Test match' atmosphere, whilst in the winter evenings there were table tennis competitions on the dining room table, 'bobs', tiddly winks and a variety of card games which were a source of much enjoyment.

The high point of each year was the fortnightly holiday at Point Lonsdale, a beach resort on one of the 'Heads' of the bay about seventy miles from Melbourne. These were a regular feature of family life between 1924 and 1938 and took place in February, being keenly anticipated for weeks before. Financially they were remarkably frugal, the chief expense being a rented cottage, usually shared with relatives, at a cost of fifty shillings or maybe three pounds per week. The trip to Melbourne by train and the journey down the bay by the paddle steamer 'Weeroona' cost three shillings and sixpence per adult, half price for children, then the bus or service car from Queenscliff to Point Lonsdale cost another shilling or so. It was all a high adventure and the sense of excitement mounted by the hour as we drew nearer to our destination. On the first afternoon there would be a walk to the beach, then around the 'Point' visiting the lighthouse with its signal station. After that, on to the pier with all the familiar sights and aromas being encountered and bringing a deep sense of pleasure and satisfaction to all. From this we would probably go on to the post office store to order the *Argus* for each day and to savour the rich pleasure of spending the first of our carefully saved pocket money. Then the bliss of fourteen days and nights enjoyment and adventure scarcely exceeded by any other travel or holiday in later days for sheer satisfaction of the senses. Because we usually went with

Mother's sister Lou and husband Frank, there were cousins to enrich the days and share the fun. The nightly games of 'Ludo' and cards between our parents became uproarious and we children listened from our beds always wishing we had been allowed to stay up later. Halcyon days indeed.

As I entered my teens it was clear that my health was improving, there were still some of the 'bad turns' but there was more strength for exercise. I had a bicycle and also began to play tennis with my mother and the ladies of the local tennis club. Dad had joined with some of the local people to form a club and have a simple gravel court built on railway land near the Rosanna station, he became secretary and greatly enjoyed the game. So much so that when they began to play in the Eltham district competition it took precedence over watching Essendon in the VFL. I also graduated fairly rapidly to playing with the men on Saturdays and during the week with anyone available. In 1934 I was proud to be a member of the first Rosanna team to win the 'A' grade premiership.

Another new dimension was opening up with regular attendance at Sunday School and church at St Andrews, Rosanna. After moving to our new home we had attended the Heidelberg Methodist Church, however it was a long and hilly walk so that we boys did not go to Sunday School which was held in the afternoon. When we received an invitation to attend the Church of England Sunday School much closer to home, we went and found it to our liking. I was aged ten at the time and in the first year won third prize for attendance and learning texts. Hearing my name called and going forward to receive this prize was a stunning new experience and the book I received was read and re-read many times and is still in my possession.

Eventually under the good hand of God, St Andrews was to be for me the means of encountering a vital spiritual experience but this came about only slowly over the years. St Andrews was a daughter church in the Parish of St Johns, Heidelberg; virtually in the total care of a remarkable lay minister, Horace Hannah who was the chief inspector of the ES&A Bank. Members of his family were active in the Sunday School as teachers and musicians. After a while my parents also began attending this church rather than the Methodist, chiefly because of the teaching and example of Mr Hannah. I was joined in my interest in the church by my friend from next door, Eric Carter. We were the same age and spent a great deal of time together.

However, my parents were now beginning to face the problem of my future. It was obvious that my health was improving yearly and there was every indication that I should be able to anticipate living a normal life. The doctors said that I did not possess the stamina for a full-time job and in any case I had no qualifications and due to the depression jobs were very scarce. Kindly friends made suggestions to my parents, including the possibility of a small poultry farm or of growing tomatoes in greenhouses. These two ideas were based on the need to keep me in the open air but I must confess that I recoiled in horror from them both.

Who despises the day of small things? ....

Zechariah 4.10. NIV

The unfolding of your word gives light:
it gives understanding to the simple.

Psalm 119.130. APBA

Nicodemus
But tell me why; why did you follow Him? ...
Perhaps it was some miracle He did.
John
It was indeed; more miracles than one;
I was not blind and yet he gave me sight;
I was not deaf and yet He gave me hearing
Nor was I dead, yet me He raised to life.

Andrew Young,
From 'Nicodemus'

-2-

1932 – 1938

Birth of a Business

At the age of 14, in the year 1932, with time on my hands I began to make up a few small wooden items mainly for use in our home, when the thought came that it might be possible to sell something. Actually my first sale was a toothbrush holder, with a rack for toothpaste and hooks for the brushes, lacquered white, which I sold to the kind English lady who taught me card games. She paid me one shilling for it and with this I purchased some plywood from Chas Rouch the timber merchants in Heidelberg and made up some more toothbrush holders plus a few other items and soon began to receive a steady stream of orders through neighbours and friends. I still have the little notebooks recording these early orders and financial transactions. Then began a search for new ideas of things to make and I was encouraged in this by my Dad who brought home small articles from a city wood-turner such as serviette rings, eggcups, ashtrays and the like. These I decorated with pokerwork and painted designs, stain and lacquer. My mother was a good sales agent as she showed my products around to neighbours and so, without really thinking about it, we were by the kindness of God, being given the solution to the problem of finding an occupation.

I have to admit that for the first few months I tended to regard this as a convenient means of earning pocket money and not much else. At the end of the year, having commenced in August the sales had reached something over seventeen pounds, with expenses around ten pounds. However after our

holiday during the early months of 1933 I was much more interested in enjoying and improving my tennis and work lapsed.
Some strong parental urging brought me back to it. When my
grandfather built me a nice bench in my sleep-out and I began
to make up wooden trays and other items to decorate, the little
business began in earnest. We also discovered other sources of
whitewood articles suitable for decoration with pokerwork.
This was a process of burning designs on to the various pieces
and painting them with transparent colours, normally used for
tinting photographs, in the days before colour film.

My pokerwork was done in improvised fashion with steel
knitting needles using corks for handles, these were heated on
the gas stove, a laborious process. This later gave way to an
electric machine, an investment which rather troubled my cautious father. "It's a lot of money, son," he said of the five pounds
which it cost, and it was too, for me; but it was essential for the
growth of the infant business. My Uncle Wattie came out one
Saturday and taught me how to French polish, which was suitable for some of the products. The first staff member was engaged to help with the painting while I concentrated on the
pokerwork and finishing. Gwen George was an unemployed
school teacher and a good tennis player and we had spent many
hours playing singles matches in a spirit of keen competition.
We now worked together well and Gwen stayed with me for
many years as a supervisor.

By the time I turned sixteen my sleep-out had been enlarged
and fitted with more benches and my bed moved to the front
verandah. My brother's bedroom was also being invaded and
used as a storeroom. There, in this makeshift factory with a
small staff of girls I laboured with the poker needle and paint
brush as the demand for 'Kerby Art Woodware' grew.

After doing the rounds of the local hardware and gift shops,
my mother accompanied me to interview buyers at the Myer
Emporium and G J Coles and also a large wholesale firm in the
city. Looking back, I imagine that the appearance of this modest
housewife accompanied by the youth with his little suitcase of
samples must have seemed rather out of place in their buying
offices. Nevertheless, in each case orders were obtained and
repeated, and good links were formed which built up and lasted
for many years. New lines such as breadboards, salt boxes,

hearth brushes, bellows and numerous others were added to the range. These were bought in from manufacturers, and the range grew in quality and style as well as in number, as new customers were added.

At St Andrews Eric Carter and I had now become Sunday school teachers and also we started what was termed the 'Young Peoples Group'. This was largely occupied with social occasions, hikes and outings which were well attended and heartily enjoyed. Regular attendance at morning and evening services ensured that a lot of solid teaching from Horace Hannah was being absorbed, besides which, an affinity was being formed with the Book of Common Prayer and with the great hymns of the church. Eric and I were invited by a neighbour to attend meetings of the Heidelberg Group of Toc H, a religious/service organisation which had its origins on the battlefields of France during the First World War. This movement attracted an interesting cross-section of men; some were returned servicemen, others younger but we were by far the youngest. Some were well-to-do and a few on the verge of poverty, but there existed between them a fine spirit of brotherhood.

All had a desire to serve others and to live by the four rules of Toc H, *'To love widely, to think fairly, to build bravely, to witness humbly'*. These rules made a great appeal to us and not having experienced this type of thinking or fellowship before, I found it exceedingly helpful and in later years felt that the benefit lived on, especially of seeking always to think fairly. Every Toc H group had a 'Pilot' whose duty it was to maintain the spiritual focus and a 'Jobmaster' who allocated various tasks to members. One job which Eric and I shared was to visit patients at the Austin Hospital and also to wheel beds to the chapel for services on Sundays. I also started a library for the patients and can remember making an appeal through one of the radio stations and being deluged with thousands of books! We were accepted into full membership of Toc H when we reached the age of 16, at which point I was elected group secretary and later became a member of the Victorian regional committee. It was a great privilege for us to be accepted by older men and to form friendships which became very significant to us at that stage of our lives.

The year 1936 was quite a momentous one in my life. It began when at the invitation of my friend Wellesley Hannah, who was studying medicine, I attended a house party at the Upwey Convention, a large Christian gathering, held each year in the Dandenong Ranges at the end of year holidays. The house party consisted of a group of about forty students from Melbourne University, staying in a guest house and attending the large convention meetings each day. I was greatly attracted both by the people in the group and the teaching and singing at the convention meetings. Strong spiritual chords were being sounded within and I was seeking to respond but at that point the way forward was not clear to me.

In May I attended a similar house party at 'Marna House', Healesville. This time there was no convention program, simply talks and discussions within the group and on this occasion the way into a personal relationship with God was made clear to me and I made a commitment to Jesus Christ. After some years of listening to faithful preaching and exposition of the Scriptures, only then did the need for personal repentance and faith come home to me. In the goodness of God I sought and received forgiveness for my sin, and the assurance of His spirit witnessing to my spirit that I was indeed a child of God. Those of us who become disciples find our way to this point by many and varied roads, but for each one there is a place of decision and I had reached mine. I was able to sing, as John Newton had done two centuries earlier 'Tis done, the great transactions done, I am my Lord's and He is mine'.

Just prior to this life-changing event I had purchased my first motor car for the sum of fifteen pounds. It was an Essex Tourer about 14 years old and it came from an elderly man in Rosanna. He taught me to drive as I paid him for it in three monthly instalments of five pounds. A friend came with me as I secured my licence (no driving schools then) on June 10th, three days after my 18th birthday. I found deep satisfaction in being able to take my parents for outings, also my Sunday School pupils and of course it served as a delivery vehicle for the business. It was great fun next summer to pack the car and travel with the family down to Point Lonsdale for our holiday instead of train, boat and bus. In March 1937 I joined the Royal Automobile Club of Victoria as a club member and in later years this became the center of many family and business functions and celebrations.

At the end of 1936 the Kerby Art Woodware Co. staff numbered about twelve and our products were well established in numerous Melbourne and Sydney stores, the latter due to a trip I had made in the previous year. By this time the operations had taken up a large part of the family home as workrooms and for the storage of stock. My parents were uncomplainingly generous but it was time to move. We found suitable premises in a Bank of NSW building at 190 Bourke Street, Melbourne where we occupied, at first half a floor, then one whole floor and finally two floors. This we outgrew in two or three years and early in 1939 moved the manufacturing element of the business to a new rented factory at 170-4 Cardigan Street, Carlton.

Business life now developed, selling to wholesalers and many more shops. At seventeen years of age I had made my first business trip to Sydney and secured orders from large firms such as Nock & Kirby, Anthony Hordern and others. Not long after this I was recommended to a man by the name of Vic Deakin to be our agent in Brisbane. He became very successful with our lines and eventually laid the foundation for the first interstate factory in Brisbane. Once the business moved to Bourke Street there was rapid development. A salesman was appointed by the name of Doug Outhred. He was a keen Christian and left the Argus office to work for Kerby.

In 1937 Georgina Bell, a talented lampshade artist joined the firm, starting a new section of the company known as Kerby Art Lighting Co. This quickly developed due to her skills, making shades for some of the top decorators and lampshade departments in the city stores. Soon two girls were employed. This new development came about through Ina and her artistic gifts being introduced to me by a mutual friend, Miss Amy Giddings, a well known artist of china painting who had taught Ina this art. Amy Giddings was widely known as a gifted Bible teacher and for some years from 1936 conducted a weekly Bible class in the Hannah's home at Heidelberg which I attended every Tuesday. Miss Giddings was a member of the Presbyterian Church at Ascot Vale to which Ina and her family belonged. Ina attended a regular Bible study in her home. Many of our friends of later years, including Russell Costello and Jean Knight, were greatly helped spiritually by attending these studies. The coming of these two friends, Doug and Ina into the company was a great encouragement to me because of their different backgrounds

The Kerr family: Horace and Frances with Alan and Roy; 1938.

and their strong Christian faith. It was helpful to be able to discuss and pray about business matters with them.

With the growth of the business, inevitably various problems emerged. The engagement of suitable staff to do the decorating and the supervision of the staff was an ongoing one. Gwen George had continued in this role and now acted as workroom manager. We needed staff with artistic ability and training, so that most of the girls possessed considerable personality and individuality which meant that Gwen did not have an easy task. Added to this was the problem of financing the growth, controlling the debtors and especially of costing. My knowledge of these matters at first was nil and I was learning only from my mistakes. Eric Carter had taken an accountancy course, and kept the accounts for us in those early years, however he was not in a position to give advice as he was working and had little time. My lack of education was a real handicap in this area. I had not even known how to calculate percentages so there was a lot of learning to do. I sought help from a cousin of Mother's who was head of a large company and he put me in touch with a man by the name of Alfred Carter, who ran a baby carriage factory and had good small business experience.

Alf was an enormous help and over the next few years he was to call weekly at my office, guiding and counselling me in the conduct of my growing business. For this he was paid a regular fee but it was small compared to the support he provided. Sometimes if there was no money to pay the wages he would provide it, but always with a strict arrangement for repayment within a few days, which was good for us both. Like my grandfather, he was a Methodist local preacher, much in demand for Sunday School anniversaries. He was also a leading figure in industry matters through the Chamber of Manufacturers. We developed a firm friendship which continued long after our business association ended. I remember attending the wedding of his only daughter, Pat, to the star Essendon half-back, Roy McConnell.

Through Ina Bell I became interested in the Australian Nepalese Mission, a small group of people dedicated to taking the Gospel to the Kingdom of Nepal, a land which was then entirely closed to westerners and also to Christianity. The ANM missionaries lived and worked on the border of Nepal and India and sought to contact Nepali people as they travelled in and out of their sealed country. The leader was a most spiritual and gifted man, the Reverend John Coombe and his brother, Alfred Coombe was the mission's secretary. Alfred requested me to form a youth fellowship to support the mission, which with his guidance we were able to do and it met regularly until the early war years. One of the first members was Alfred's nephew, Sidwell Coombe, then a student at Ivanhoe Grammar School and still a colleague in Christian work today. Another was Howard Barclay, whose parents were active in the mission and he later became a noted international missionary leader. Many of the friendships formed then have continued. Alfred and his wife Sabina were also to be close friends and colleagues in the gospel for the next 40 years. Shortly afterwards I was invited to join the Council of the mission, of which Miss Giddings and other Ascot Vale people were members.

The whole of this ANM group made up a dedicated prayer force for the land of Nepal, when it was not a well-recognised country. I am sure there were also other groups around the world who likewise prayed regularly for the light of the gospel to shine into that land. It was in the 1950s that we began to see answers to these prayers when Christian people were allowed to work in the country in professions which contributed to its development. So medical personnel, engineers, builders began to go, in one sense as missionaries, but knowing that proclamation of the gospel was a criminal offence. They worked together in the United Mission to Nepal and from these costly beginnings came a trickle of national Christians. Many of these believers were imprisoned and punished in various ways for their faith. I have seen reliable figures which say that in 1962 the believers were about sixty in number and in 1997 that figure had grown to over two hundred thousand, with some three hundred churches. A sovereign work of God's Spirit in response to the faith and sacrifice of many people down through the years.

"My son, do not think lightly of the Lord's discipline,
nor lose heart when he corrects you;
for the Lord disciplines those whom he loves;
he lays the rod on every son whom he acknowledges".
...but he does so for our true welfare...

Hebrews 12 5, 6 & 10b NEB

He fixed thee mid this dance
Of plastic circumstance,
This Present, thou, forsooth, wouldst fain arrest:
Machinery just meant
To give thy soul its bent,
Try thee and turn thee forth, sufficiently impressed.

Robert Browning
quoted by Rabbi Ben Ezra

- 3 -

1938 – 1942

Light and Shade

Although most of my business time was concentrated on Kerby Art Woodware Co. I also worked closely with Ina on the affairs of our little lighting company. During this time our friendship developed to a point where in June 1938 we planned to become engaged. We felt that we should share this news with Miss Giddings but we were considerably taken aback when she advised against it at that point. I was twenty and Ina was some six years older and Miss Giddings felt we needed much more time to be sure of our feelings. She urged us to make a complete break with the friendship for one year, which was a difficult test. Our initial reaction was not to accept this counsel but after some prayer and thought we agreed to follow it. Having to work together made this a rather hard road to walk but it certainly brought about a deepening of my spiritual life. We did not meet outside work or discuss the matter again until June 1939 and then decided we were being rightly guided to become engaged on my 21st birthday. We were both of the same mind about our feelings for each other and had come to appreciate the value of Amy Giddings guidance. Looking back we could see it had brought us much benefit and it helped me to realise that there are times in life when one needs to both give and receive hard advice.

Douglas Outhred had married and then feeling a call to missionary service left our employment. He was replaced by a mature and very professional commercial traveller, Walter Polglase, who became a great adjunct to the company. Widely known and respected he put our relationships with retailers on a completely new footing. Should there ever be a complaint about prices, he would say with a most engaging smile 'well of course, it costs the company a lot to employ me' and that was usually the end of the objection.

The staff had also been increased by our first full-time office worker in the person of Ada Moffatt. I advertised the position in *New Life*, a Christian newspaper run by Eric Daley whom I knew well and had received an application which was supported by a glowing reference from Eric himself. His parents were long-time friends of John and Barbara Moffat and when Eric was a student at the Melbourne Bible Institute he used to spend his days off with the family, becoming a great favourite with their two younger daughters, Jean and Ada. He was therefore in a good position to write his reference, which proved to be accurate in every detail. Although this was her first job Ada quickly became invaluable in the office and showroom, relieving me of much time-consuming work.

A year or two prior to this I had purchased two blocks of land at Rosanna, quite close to St Andrews Church and now that marriage was planned for March 1941, Ina and I set to work on thinking about a home. It was interesting that in my youth, when out walking, I often paused and sat on a large rock at this spot which had an expansive view. There were one or two houses scattered on the northern side but mainly just open paddocks for the next mile or so. This was now to be the site of our home and the rock eventually became part of the garden. We arranged with Mr A V Jennings, then a relatively small builder, for his company to design and build the house and this was completed in good time before our wedding.

One Sunday soon after our engagement, I was visiting Ina at her home in Ascot Vale and we heard boys selling papers in the street. It was a special edition of the *Herald* announcing that England had declared war on Germany and that we would also be at war. After the initial shock throughout the nation, strangely, in some ways Australia's life was not greatly changed in those first months. Many men had joined and were in training in the services and we all did blackout exercises, first aid courses and the like. As the proprietor of a business I was at that stage exempt from military service. Eric Carter joined the Air

Force and Brook Hannah who had been ill, took on our part-time accounting work, which suited his condition just then. However with the passing of the months, the gravity of the world situation was borne in upon us all, especially when the bombing of Britain began.

Ina and I were married at the Ascot Vale Presbyterian Church in May 1941, her sister, Margaret, youngest of the four daughters, was bridesmaid and my friend Brooking Hannah best man. Ina's parents were Scottish, warm hearted, friendly and of the highest integrity. I felt myself fortunate to become part of their family. We quickly settled into the new home at 51 Grandview Grove and into the life of St Andrews Church. I was Sunday School Superintendent and Ina also taught. She was secretary of the School's Christian Fellowship which worked in Victorian high schools and I was drawn into that work and took a weekly group at Coburg High School. I also accepted an invitation to become a Council member of Campaigners for Christ, an evangelistic and interdenominational organisation which was doing welfare work amongst the troops. Alfred Coombe was chairman and this movement brought me into contact with Leonard Buck, Ralph Davis and many other wonderful men who were to become close friends and colleagues.

By this time the impact of the war in Europe had become profound, our services were engaged in the bitter battles of the Western Desert and when at the end of 1941 Japan attacked Pearl Harbour the atmosphere in Australia was completely changed. The country called up all its available manpower. I was medically drafted B grade and sent to Second Echelon, an Army administrative unit stationed at Elwood. My brother Roy's infantry unit was preparing for service in New Guinea. As the Japanese advanced on numerous fronts in the Pacific it was clear that Australia was directly threatened. Darwin was heavily bombed, one of the casualties being a brother of a girl on the Kerby staff. 'Impregnable' Singapore fell virtually without a fight and the grim Battle for Britain continued without respite. The outlook was dark indeed. However, the Japanese action had brought the United States into the war on a total basis and the far-reaching effect of this was yet to be seen.

On May 10th 1942 Ina entered St Andrews Hospital extremely fit and well, for some minor surgery, and I had been visiting her and staying with my parents. One morning their phone rang at four o'clock and my father told me the hospital wanted me to go in without delay. As I had seen her only a few hours before it came as an appalling shock to arrive at the unattended inquiry desk to see a note reading 'Ring Mr Kerr– his wife very low'. This was confirmed by the nursing staff who told me that she had contracted pneumonia and was extremely weak. Blood transfusions were called for, to which Ada contributed. However, after a long battle over the next three weeks, Ina died on 6th June with her sister Margaret and I at her bedside, knowing she was with the Lord. Next morning, on my 24th birthday, I read in my morning devotions Psalm 18, Verse 30 'As for God, His way is perfect'. It was a most direct message, which I was able to accept. The sense of loss was still as keen but I was saved from any questioning of God's permissive will, for which I was profoundly grateful. Our dear friend the Reverend C H Nash who was at that time weekend assistant minister at St Andrews conducted the funeral at Diamond Creek cemetery. It was winter but the sun shone beautifully. There is a brick arch over the cemetery gates with a Latin inscription and I asked Mr Nash what it said. 'The gate of life', he replied.

I was able to secure the services of a fine Brethren lady, Edith Chenery as housekeeper and she looked after me wonderfully well for the next eighteen months. Mr Nash became a frequent and welcome weekend guest as he came from MBI to take our Sunday services, and we enjoyed many lengthy discussions and also fine music. Although he never discussed his personal affairs it was known that he had endured a series of severe trials over the years and I think it somehow brought us closer during this particular time in my life. I did not dwell on my bereavement but no doubt he understood that it was a time of testing.

A strange thing happened one day to bring this home to me. It was my habit at lunchtime to walk from our Army location around the Elwood foreshore. On this very cold windswept day, I saw a scrap of newspaper fluttering on the concrete paving in front of me, smaller than the palm of my hand, and for some reason I bent to pick it up. Irregular in shape, the only words decipherable were 'when God wants to prepare His soldiers for service He tests them in the front line'. It looked like a piece from a daily newspaper but there was no clue to the context, however I could not help feeling it was something the Lord wanted to say to me, and I found it very strengthening. This is the first time I have ever mentioned this little incident. There are two verses in God's word which describe how I felt in those months. 'It is good for a man to bear the yoke while he is young. Let him sit alone in silence, for the Lord has laid it on him'. (Lam. 3.27–28).

Always fond of music I found it a great solace and companion and my record collection grew rapidly. I also expanded my theological reading and discovered CS Lewis, whose first Christian books were just then reaching our shores. For the next decade or so he continued to speak most powerfully to my heart and mind and I remain one of the multitude who would count him as a major influence in their Christian formation.

*By day you led them with a pillar of cloud, and by night with a
pillar of fire to give them light on the way they were to take.*

Nehemiah 9.12   NIV

*Whenever the cloud lifted from above the Tent, the Israelites set
out;
wherever the cloud settled, the Israelites encamped.
At the Lord's command the Israelites set out,
and at his command they encamped.*

Numbers 9. 17–18b   NIV

*The CSSM did another thing for me: it broke my tongue-tied
shyness.*

*Much against my will Jack insisted on my getting up on the beach
pulpit and giving an 'object' talk at one service. I have forgotten
what it was I talked about and it only took about two minutes.
What I do remember is my knees knocking against each other,
unnoticed by the audience because a high wind was flapping my
flannel trousers. That was the first time I had ever spoken in
public. I was to do so many more times on that beach in the coming
years. I can think of no better preparation for a preacher than for
him to learn to throw his voice towards two or three hundred
people, while there is a high cross wind blowing and the surf is
dashing down on the pebbles twenty yards behind him. Once you
have mastered that trick no public platform will ever frighten you.*

Canon Max Warren General secretary of CMS
UK 1942–1963, in *Crowded Canvas.*

- 4 -

1943 – 1948

New Beginnings

During my time of service with Second Echelon the business continued to function on a reduced scale under the supervision of Mr Polglase. Phyllis Thompson was head artist, Brook Hannah kept the accounts and Ada Moffat ran the office and maintained liaison with me by telephone. The army kept me fully occupied six days a week but normally I had Sunday off and was able to function as SS superintendent. At the request of Campaigners for Christ I had commenced a monthly 'newsletter' type of publication which was sent to all of the servicemen and women contacted in our 'Everymans' huts who wished to receive it. This contained news, stories, anecdotes, bible study and quotations put together with a special view to helping new Christians. My Dad helped with the typing of my written material, and I attended to the printing. Campaigners mailed it out and the circulation eventually built up to three thousand. This continued for thirtysix months. Hundreds of letters were received in response and most of these were acknowledged. A complete file of these newsletters has been preserved. I was told only recently that an army unit also has them on file in their archives.

In August 1943 I was discharged from the army as medically unfit and I became honorary general secretary of Campaigners, giving about half-time to that task. This brought me into a close working relationship with the Director, Leonard Buck, who had been working amongst RAF personnel in Malaya. He was wonderfully preserved from hazardous situations in Singapore to return, after the fall of that city in February 1942, on a ship which was bombed twice as it sailed the Indian Ocean. At that time Len had a wholesale business in ladies fashions but during the whole of the war it saw little of him.

Many thousands of troops were being trained in camps around Australia for the Pacific battles ahead and Campaigners were busy building 'huts' and finding welfare officers to staff them. It was a large and demanding task for the members of the Council, who were drawn from different denominations and widely varying walks of life. They were men with heavy responsibilities, already under pressure of work in their own vocations, with many of their staff in the services. I greatly enjoyed the job of helping to keep the organisation going at the centre, working with Florence Capener the capable office secretary.

The Executive met weekly under the chairmanship of Alfred Coombe, a businessman, senior partner in John Sanderson, well known shipping agents and wool merchants. He was an excellent chairman who certainly kept the secretary on his toes. Like my father he was a first rate shorthand writer, so that my minutes had to stand up to the notes he kept on his agenda paper. It was a high powered group and the meetings, always conducted against the clock, usually left me exhausted, with a splitting headache. Leonard was constantly finding new challenges and wanting to open new centers. As the war effort reached its peak, so did ours and hundreds of men were finding Christ and thousands a 'home from home' at Everymans huts, particularly in North Queensland where much of the training was concentrated. We also had crowded Everymans centres in the heart of Melbourne, Sydney and Brisbane for the benefit of troops on leave or in transit.

A few months before I was discharged from the army a letter had reached me from Reuben West with an invitation to join a small council recently formed to establish the work of Scripture Union in Victoria. This movement originated in the UK last century, and was dedicated to providing Bible-reading notes and also doing evangelistic work amongst children and young people. Active in Victoria at the turn of the century, it had fallen into decline and died. In the late 1930s there were moves to recommence the movement and a small group of interested people was drawn together. The Reverend Ronald Bevington was sent to

Australia from SU England and he began to work in Victoria, just prior to the war. I remember being at an Easter camp he ran at Queenscliff, which must have been in 1939. After the outbreak of war Ronald joined the naval forces as a Chaplain and was posted to HMAS *Perth*. Sadly he lost his life when the *Perth* was torpedoed in the Java Sea. Rueben West, a *Hansard* reporter, continued some activities and during the war years ran a monthly CSSM 'squash' for children at his Mont Albert home.

The Scripture Union was a worthy cause but I felt at the time that there were enough commitments in my program and decided to decline their invitation. However, I discussed it with Mr Nash, expecting him to agree but to my surprise he said 'Alan you must do it. Others have done it for you and now it is your turn to do it for others'. The tone in which this was uttered and the familiar slight tremor of his nostrils seemed to leave me with little choice. I did not carry the conversation any further but sent in my acceptance and began to meet with the little group under the chairmanship of the Reverend J B Montgomery. Little did I think that this decision would have a major influence on so much of my later life.

Some years later I discovered from Mr Nash himself that he had worked with the Scripture Union, serving on beach mission teams in England in the 1880s and editing the first editions of the *Boy's Magazine*. I sometimes wonder whether he had been responsible for suggesting my name to Rueben!

Whilst I was working in the army, Ada used to prepare detailed Kerby reports for me and in 1943 we began to meet weekly for dinner to discuss matters needing decision. During the winter of that year I felt increasingly drawn to Ada and discovered that my feelings were reciprocated and the outcome was that on November 2nd 1943 we were married at Holy Trinity Church, Hampton. It was a small, quiet wedding celebrated by Mr Nash in his inimitable style, with a delightful discourse on Psalm 128. Only family members were present and the ceremony was followed by afternoon tea at the Moffat home. We left for a brief honeymoon at Mt Macedon and had to change a flat tyre in St Kilda Road en route.

In some ways this marriage was a big step for Ada, having been brought up in a rather exclusive Brethren assembly and knowing nothing of life in other churches, to move suddenly into my Anglican orbit. This she did very graciously and happily in the friendly atmosphere of St Andrews and of life at Rosanna in general. She came into my life as a marvellous gift from God and I was overwhelmed at His loving kindness. A replacement was found for the office and Ada was soon involved in a busy round of activities centering on 51 Grandview Grove which was to be the hub of our family life for the next thirty-seven years. The business was prospering at this point and we were grateful that it enabled us to make some significant gifts to Campaigners for the heavy building program which was being undertaken.

A few days after returning from our honeymoon we were approached by an Air Force officer named Harvey Carey with a suggestion that we should help him run a Children's Special Service Mission (CSSM) beach mission at Dromana during the coming holidays. I said, 'we know nothing about beach missions'. His response was 'you are on the Scripture Union Council and this is part of the work you should be doing'. At this stage our small Council had concentrated only on promoting the Bible reading notes and some children's rallies. Harvey was a medical specialist from South Africa where he had been a voluntary worker with SU and had led holiday missions on the beaches there. His challenge to us was 'you find the team and a place to stay and I will lead the mission and show you how it is done'. The newly married couple agreed and with about five weeks to go we gathered a team of sixteen young men and women and went to 'Bayview House' Dromana at Christmas time to await Harvey's magic touch.

We were not to be disappointed; he was a thorough teacher. Each day he came from the Air Force camp at Somers to brief us and to lead the activities of the CSSM. We were plunged into building sand pulpits, decorating them with texts, leading choruses, taking Keenite classes, playing games, running sausage sizzles, lantern processions and all the rest. We received an enthusiastic reception from the children and had a never-to-be forgotten time together. We were all learning and teaching at the same time. I came to understand later that this is a part of the simple genius of SU. Thousands of young people in various countries participate in similar missions every year. They learn to work as a team with others, to organise, to speak to strangers about the gospel, to prepare talks and to receive basic leadership

Beach Mission Team, Dromana, 1943–44, with leader Harvey Carey, bottom right.

An 'Everyman's Hut' in Northern Queensland, 1944.

Listening to a talk at an 'Everymans' Centre.

training whilst they are bringing the good news about Jesus to girls and boys. Wonderful!

Harvey had to move on but he had done his work well and the following year two teams went out and the year after that there were four. These were forerunners in Victoria of the hundreds of beach missions to take place over the next half-century and beyond. The same postwar growth occured in other states, especially in NSW where the tradition was much older. The successful foray on to the beach at Dromana galvanised the Victorian SU Council into action. The fulfilling work on the mission teams brought a stream of enthusiastic leaders and learners into the movement and before long we were conducting twelve or more missions each summer and still growing. I had the opportunity of leading seven missions over the next few years, opening up new sites at Sorrento, Rye, Apollo Bay and Portarlington. At the latter Ada joined me with our young sons Howard and Russell. We stayed in a caravan which we towed to the camping ground where the team members were located and it all worked very well. This was the year when we began to do a regular puppet show, which found me desperately writing the daily episode after breakfast each day so that it could be typed and rehearsed in time for the afternoon beach meeting. It was a tremendous hit and the two main characters lived on for some years in other missions. This was to be my final mission, as life thereafter became too crowded and time needed to be made available for the family and other demands.

I was deeply grateful to Mr Nash and Harvey Carey for first causing me to be involved with CSSM and Scripture Union since taking part in these missions helped me to overcome, to a considerable extent, my feelings of intense shyness at any kind of public appearance. A few years earlier I could not have even begun to imagine myself leading choruses and telling Bible stories on a beach pulpit with such carefree animation.

Although the business was handicapped by shortage of materials, expansion continued. Most of my time was devoted to Campaigners but I made it my special task to try and find alternative supplies of timber. Through Alf Carter we joined the Furniture Guild and the Chamber of Manufacturers, which enabled us to obtain quotas of plywood. Knowing that in Queensland there were ample quantities of white pine for our

At left: Ada and myself in Martin Place, Sydney, 1944, and above at Coolangatta, c. 1947.

breadboards, rolling pins and other kitchen products I was able to arrange to have these items made for us in Brisbane. As many of them were being finished and packaged in Melbourne for sale in Brisbane it was decided to manufacture locally for the Queensland market. Vic Deakin, our agent, arranged for a nearby family to set up a small workshop. Grace Goon from the Melbourne factory went to Brisbane to instruct in design and decorating. The enterprise grew quickly and moved to a bigger factory in Bardon, which also became the centre of despatch to Melbourne.

In Tasmania we had sometime earlier appointed Mr Ian Boss-Walker a wellknown Christian leader in Hobart as our agent. In late 1944 Ada and I enjoyed a tour of Tasmania by car and spent some time with Mr Nash who had gone to the beautiful old church of St Georges, Battery Point, Hobart. He was acting as temporary Rector pending the return from the war of his son Laurence, as incumbent. This visit also gave us the opportunity of stepping up our business there and at the same time we were able to interest Ian in the work of Scripture Union and when a Tasmanian Council was formed, he became the very zealous chairman for a number of years.

A high point in March 1944 was the visit of the Scottish born General Secretary of SU New Zealand, Dr John Laird. We had heard much about him and he proved to be helpful beyond our expectations. He was a medical doctor who had been called of God from his home country to the work of the movement in NZ, an outstanding spiritual leader, wise and yet humble with a personality which quickly endeared him to all he met. He pointed out to us that in Victoria there were three movements doing the work of evangelism in schools, beach missions and Bible reading notes, all of which was done in NZ by one body, the Scripture Union.

A weekend Conference had been arranged at Dromana where he was able to speak to about thirty leaders from the Crusader Union, Schools Christian Fellowship and CSSM-Scripture Union. He shared his insights as to the nature of the work being done and his belief that it would be more effective if we in Victoria were one body. It would help us to focus on the wider needs and make for better use of our resources and people. During the weekend Dr Laird also gave three Bible studies which made a deep impression on all present. God spoke to me personally from what he had to say on a verse in Jeremiah 45 verse 5 "seekest thou great things for thyself, seek them not". I had been asked to chair this conference and the discussions were open and friendly but it was evident that these new ideas would call for a good deal more prayer and discussion before such a union could become possible in our part of the world. Shortly after this I was appointed chairman of SU in Victoria, and this meant that we were able to keep these ideals before us. SU had set up a small office with part-time help, but at the conference Miss Doris Embery felt called to offer for this position full-time and her subsequent appointment represented a great step forward.

Early in 1945 I travelled to Sydney and Brisbane on business and also took the opportunity of attending to the interests of Campaigners and SU in both cities. This presaged a pattern which was to become very familiar in future years, of combining business travel and Christian work. At the end of March I was back in Sydney for a conference of Campaigner council members from the five states. Following this I went on to Townsville with Len to see something of our activities there and on to the Atherton Tablelands, where we had four very busy Everymans centers. I was there when the news came of the death of President Roosevelt. The war in Europe was drawing to a close and in the Pacific great forces were gathering for the final assaults.

While I was absent on this journey my father became ill with a heart attack and although he lived until my hurried return it was not possible to converse with him. He died on the night of May 10th in his home with my mother, Ada and I present. I felt his passing intensely, he had been a lifelong helper and encourager to me. A gentle man, his home and family and his quiet faith had been at the centre of his life, and he died at the age of fifty-six. For the last few years he had worshipped at Ivanhoe Baptist Church where he had some very good friends and through them his faith had been greatly strengthened. In the fashion of young people I had thought of him as elderly and was initially surprised when a much older friend of his said to me, 'You know, Horace died very young'. In later years I came to see these things in a different light: I suppose each generation does the same in its turn. My brother Roy was given a compassionate discharge from his unit in Bouganville and returned home to live with mother.

Little more than a month after this, joy came to our home with the birth of our first son, Howard Ross Davidson Kerr, at Airlie Hospital, where I once had a close encounter with death. It was disappointing to think that Dad had not lived to see his grandson. Ada had arranged to learn all she could about mothercraft and spent her first week out of hospital with Howard at the Truby King organisation, located in the war years at the Riversdale Golf Club. Ada's eldest sister Mary had married Stan Daley who was serving with the RAAF in England, where he flew many missions as a Lancaster bomber pilot, and they had a daughter, Robin. The next sister, Jean who is also older than Ada, had married Reg Deeble a few months before this and within a year or so had a son Rodney, so that the three firstborn cousins are all quite close in age.

The business continued to grow, especially owing to the lack of merchandise available for the retail stores in the war years, but was continually limited by the lack of raw materials, the most important being timber.

The one major solution we had to the timber problem was Brisbane, but even there supplies were limited. This Brisbane

Ada with our first son, Howard, in 1946.

venture became so important to the whole business that a year or so later at the end of the war we leased a former munitions factory at Rocklea to enable us to meet with the demands. Mr Norm Knudsen was appointed factory manager and items were made there for the Melbourne factory also. Adequate supplies of timber, even in Queensland, were still a problem for the next few years. Another venture to overcome the shortage of material was a partnership I formed with a business friend, Tom Taylor. We set up a company named 'Hollyoak', making certain of our fancy-goods items from thick heavyweight cardboard instead of plywood. This firm also made advertising showcards and did silk-screening which was Tom's specialty and built up a nice business, but after two or three years I gave up this connection as time was not available for me to match Tom's contribution.

One of the special benefits of working with interdenominational organisations is that one serves alongside people from across the whole spectrum of the Protestant church and occasionally the Catholic church. Each tradition has something to teach, some emphasis to understand. This process began for me with Toc H, where the membership was apt to include quite a mixture of beliefs and unbeliefs! The Australian Nepalese Mission was very missionary minded and rather 'fundamental'. From them I learnt something of a concern for those living in spiritual darkness, 'having no hope and without God in the world'. Campaigners was a well-rounded blend, except for an absence of other Anglicans. Methodists predominated, and I always felt at home with them, then there was a solid block of Baptists, some Presbyterians, quite a number of leading Brethren plus a few other groupings. Of course Campaigners were without exception, strongly evangelical and biblical and this conferred the unity which was always present but most marked in their prayer meetings. Joining in these very frequent and vital gatherings was a new experience for me, and from Campaigners I learnt a lot about the power of expectant faith.

Now I had entered another world, that of the worldwide Scripture Union movement. All of the biblical and evangelical beliefs were present but in a significantly different cultural setting. Once again all denominations were actively represented, but with more Anglicans, especially in Sydney. Again there were lessons to be absorbed as to how to work happily in unity with a wide diversity of viewpoints and gifts and this was most valuable. Also in the Scripture Union there was a great emphasis on maintaining a strong relationship with the church, the movement regarded itself as 'a handmaid to the churches'. All of these insights proved valuable for me to build on in later life.

One of my special friends in the postwar years was the Reverend Basil Williams an Anglican from NZ who was serving as General Secretary of the Inter-Varsity Fellowship and during his frequent visits to Melbourne he usually stayed at our home. He was always a welcome guest; with his wide theological knowledge he had a great deal to teach us. He was, like me, a lover of good hymns and lent me books about them and he also had a great sense of fun. Ada used to refer to baby Howard as her rosebud and one day she came in to find him sitting on the floor surrounded with rose petals scattered by our guest. A few years later Basil was to serve as General Secretary of SU in NSW and we were to work together closely for a time. He answered many of my hard questions and helped to stabilise my theological position as a Biblical Anglican, sorting out areas of uncertainty and bringing me to a place where my convictions satisfied both heart and mind.

The dropping of the atomic bomb over Hiroshima brought the war in the Pacific to a close very quickly, but left the world pondering what fearful things future hostilities might bring upon it. Nevertheless there was general rejoicing and relief that after six years of conflict there was peace, of a kind. It was impossible however not to think of millions of lost lives, and of relatives and friends and millions more for whom life would never be the same, for homes and families bereft of loved ones. For the church and for Christian work at home there was initially a great benefit, with the return of trained and disciplined men and women into the ranks of congregations and ministry. SU shared in this, gaining some mature leaders, amongst them Bruce Lumsden, Russell Costello, Bruce Morton and many other similarly gifted people. This ushered in a period of rapid growth in the mission outreach assisted by a strong training program, SCF camps likewise expanded greatly.

After the war Campaigners continued with some of the Everymans huts and city centres but the council decided to concentrate on general evangelistic activities including city meetings and radio evangelism. Major John Robinson, on leaving the army became General Secretary, and Colonel Walter Coombe also joined the staff. They began a program of bringing overseas evangelists to Australia. John Robinson commenced 'This is Life' monthly Saturday night rallies in Collins Street Assembly Hall, which ran for a number of years, and resulted in many hundreds of conversions. It would be a fair comment that there was little emphasis on evangelistic endeavour in the mainline churches during these years and this was a large part of the reason for these activities. Campaigners was entirely a lay movement and, I feel, largely an expression of frustration with the lack of church based evangelism. Over the next two or three decades this situation was to change, especially with the coming of Dr Billy Graham.

As a part of this general forward thrust it was agreed by the Campaigner councils in the five States to become a Federal body. As the secretary of the largest and founding Council, I was given the task of attending to the administrative side of this arrangement and was then asked to become the Federal secretary.

For the next twenty years, besides attending to correspondence, agendas and minutes I was also responsible for arranging the annual Australian council meetings. These were residential gatherings held over holiday weekends and usually in very nice locations out of Melbourne or Sydney. At the earlier ones it became customary for the Reverend C H Nash to join us and give bible studies, perhaps better termed addresses, when drawing on his varied experiences he would range far and wide, delighting and edifying his hearers.

We sometimes invited friends and supporters to join these gatherings and one of these was Charles Davis, the father of Ralph, one of our key members. Charles Davis was the head of the leading transport company, Mayne Nickless. He had started his business on the wharves in Sydney and was a tough hard-bitten leader in a tough industry. He was a heavy drinker, spending most nights at his golf club, and had been for a long time the subject of his family's prayers. It was a wonderful occasion when at a 'This is Life' rally he responded to an appeal from the evangelist, Dr Hyman Appleman. It was more wonderful still when there was clear evidence of a radical change in his life. Now he attended our Federal gatherings as a special guest and I have unforgettable pictures in my mind of him sitting, Bible open on his knees as he drank in some of those memorable talks from 'The Chief', then of the two of them in the garden, walking and conversing about the things of God.

In June 1947 I became involved in a new venture in Christian outreach. This was a monthly luncheon for businessmen. A small committee was drawn together, including some Campaigners and we met monthly to plan the functions. When I first discussed this with Alfred Coombe, with the request that he should act as host or chairman of the functions he said, 'Alan, if you are going to do something like that, then it must be done with verve, it must be well done'. A remark that remained helpful to me through the years.

Well, it was well done. We made the venue the Victoria Banquet Hall in the centre of the city which provided a very fine meal with excellent 'silver' service. We presented splendid speakers from business and the professions who spoke of their Christian faith in the context of their vocation. Good quality invitations were printed each month and members were urged to bring non-Christian guests. The average attendance was a hundred but often there were lots more. Our approach was low key, the only audible prayer was a simple grace to begin the meal and the only time in twenty-five years that we sang was when Charles Davis gave his testimony and in his husky old voice invited all to join him in singing 'He lives', which to their credit they did nobly. Many of the addresses were simply outstanding and made a profound impression on those present. I later succeeded Alfred as chairman and Ridley Kitchen became secretary. Then after a number of years he succeeded me. The group was known as 'The Christian Business and Professional Mens Luncheon Group' and functioned for twenty-five years. It was a most satisfying form of Christian witness, ideally suited to involving one's contemporaries.

Soon after the war it had become obvious that plans should be made for the growth of the business. We were very happy with the premises and location in Cardigan Street and decided to ask the owner to add another story to the building, which he did. In the meantime we carried on in no less than four temporary places. The work took much longer than anticipated due to problems of supply and it was a year before we took possession of our fine new factory. It was planned that as a contribution to the work of SU, Kerby should make available at no charge a nice office for their growing field staff, under the leadership of Spencer Colliver.

In this factory we now manufactured a range of some two hundred different articles of household woodware ranging from small hand-painted gift items to breadboards, coathangers and soiled linen baskets. The lighting business still continued for a while but it was not easy to find the skilled staff needed for the high-class of work we did. We were selling our products across Australia and had sent some shipments to a Dutch firm in the East Indies (now Indonesia). In the late forties however, with the advent of plastic kitchenware products and attractive gift items coming from overseas, sales began to turn down. A natural development for us was to make small items of kitchen and nursery furniture, and so began a slow move into the furniture industry. It should have been quicker but I was reluctant to give up the type of business on which the company had been built over fifteen years and we did not have a suitable plant for making larger furniture. We did operate a small factory making

The factory at 170 Cardigan Street after rebuilding.

up our wooden articles in a building off Little Lonsdale Street in the city, but it was quite unsuitable for mass production of furniture.

Eventually the changes occurred, out went our artists and our fancy wrapping departments and in came the machinery and the timber for kitchen cabinets. A very capable factory manager, Alan Johnston, took over the task of establishing and building up production. Modular kitchens were just coming on to the market and at the first 'Ideal Home Show' held in Melbourne Kerby won first prize for its model kitchen layout. Our feeling for design and colour no doubt helped, and from then on Kerby Kitchens became an established name in the market. From kitchens we moved into bedroom items, wardrobes, chests and beds, selling mostly single pieces, and this became the pattern of the Melbourne business for the next few years.

Another little personal venture was to commence an afternoon open-air Sunday school at a housing settlement at Fishermans Bend. I had two or three young assistants but no one to help with the speaking and after two or three years this was dropped. About this time I joined another council involved in witness to the 'outsider' by the promotion of Fact and Faith Films. These were a series of remarkable films, based on nature and the created world, produced by Dr Erwin Moon of the Moody Institute of Science in the US. These superb films all had a very clear Christian message presented in a popular format and they reached a wide audience. Chairman of this committee was Jack Garrett, an engineer. Ron Clough, the secretary, worked in an office set up in the Kerby building at Carlton, arranging showings and providing the projection services. In the days before TV these films had a strong appeal in schools, churches, clubs and organisations of many kinds. My next-door neighbour was an electrical engineer with the State Electricity Commission. He was not a churchgoing man yet after I introduced him to these films he became an enthusiast for them. He had an excellent projection outfit and over the next few years he screened Fact and Faith Films hundreds of times for social clubs within the SEC.

That year there was a breathtaking VFL Grand Final football match when Carlton defeated Essendon by one point, kicking a splendid goal from the boundary in the last minute of play. I was seated right behind the player and my heart sank as I watched the ball sail between the posts. In this year also we enjoyed our first of many family holidays with Ralph and Dulce Davis, just a few days at a house in Sorrento where the owner cooked all the meals for us, a very pleasant arrangement.

In November 1947 Ada's mother, Barbara Moffat died unexpectedly after an operation. Like my father she died when she was still in her fifties. We were not even aware of any life-threatening illness, nor do we think there was one. Barbara Moffat was a woman of strong Christian conviction and character with a deep love for her Lord and these qualities were evident in the family life. Christina, Barbara's sister, had spent much time in Barbara's home. She now sold her business, a cake shop and cared for Barbara's husband, John. Christina, Aunty Mac as she was fondly known, was also very helpful to us over the next few years in minding Howard at times when Ada was ill or we were away,

One beautiful Spring day in September 1948 I went to the

Mayne Nickless office in South Melbourne for a lunchtime committee meeting with Ralph and others. Just as it finished a 'phone message came through for me to say that Ada had been injured in a car accident and would I come immediately to the Eltham-Warrandyte Road. Ralph speedily drove me out and it was an anxious search along that stretch before we came across our green Vauxhall tourer off the road and down a bank where it had hit a tree. Ada was still there, a doctor had attended to her and she was waiting for an ambulance, with a smashed knee but as usual in a crisis remarkably calm and self-possessed. Three-year old Howard had a severe blow to the head but otherwise seemed to be all right. Ada was six months pregnant at the time.

A skilful surgeon at St Vincents Hospital removed the broken knee cap and did what he could to give Ada a workable knee. After being hospitalised for several weeks, she returned home to await the new arrival. Three months after the accident, on December 12th our second son Russell Humphrey Kerr was born at Airlie Hospital, Ivanhoe, thankfully sound and well and we were grateful to God for this and for the addition to our family.

Not long after this we were to make a major change in our church membership. The new vicar appointed to St Johns, Heidelberg, was not sympathetic to the ways of St Andrews, nor it seemed with our strong biblical emphasis, and he was making numerous changes. No longer having responsibilities in the Sunday School, we were still seeking to accommodate ourselves to the new regime, when I receivedan invitation to lead a boys bible study group in St James Church, Ivanhoe, the parish adjacent to Heidelberg. They had in the Sunday School there a good number of teenage boys but no leader, and it seemed right to accept, but I was concerned about taking the further step of leaving our church. To me that represented a major move which I could not lightly take.

I consulted Mr Nash and he wrote me a lengthy letter from Tasmania indicating qualified assent but suggesting it would be good to await his return from Tasmania to discuss it fully. This was not feasible and in the event, feeling it was right, we moved, with the result that we became members of the Parish of St James, Ivanhoe. It was soon evident to us that this was the right course. Ada taught a Sunday School class and this became

Leading a Beach Mission meeting at Rye, 1949–50.

the parish in which our family grew up and where we were to worship and serve for the next thirty-three years. I enjoyed leading the class for a number of years and after a while the senior girls joined with it. There were many fine people in the parish and we quickly made lots of friends.

Dick Linton, a local chemist and optician was Sunday School superintendent and with his wife Gwenyth, soon asked me to consider conducting an Inter-Schools Christian Fellowship 'drawing room meeting' at their home, which I was happy to do. They had three sons and a daughter and the eldest, Bob, acted as games leader while I led the singing and gave some of the talks. Usually we had guest speakers and I was able to invite quite a lot of my Campaigner and SU friends along for this purpose and for some years these meetings were crowded and very popular and in them a number of boys found faith or grew in faith. This format of monthly Saturday evening meetings was much used at that time. Ada also commenced a similar meeting for girls at another home in the area which continued for some years. These gatherings later gave way to a rather different style of mixed study group which we held at our home on Saturdays.

One time I undertook the rather daunting task of taking this group of teenage boys and girls for a weekend at what was then the Crusader camp at Toolangi in the mountains about nine miles from Healesville. It was the Labour Day holiday in March and we had century heat for two of the days. The young people were in extremely high spirits and it took all I knew to keep things on a even keel. We went for a hike to the fire tower on a nearby peak, an open structure which had a ladder going straight up to the 100 foot high outlook platform. Some of the group immediately began the climb and urged me to join them. I have no head for heights, except within the security of an aeroplane but in a spirit of thoughtless bravado I set to. Before reaching a dozen rungs up I knew it was a crazy mistake and said I had better go back. Others were coming up behind me and they would not hear of retreat. 'Go on Mr Kerr, you'll be all right'. At about 30 feet up I was distinctly not all right, I had looked down and my stomach did a somersault, but the worst thing was the effect it had on my limbs. Such was the weakness of my arms, I felt I could not physically grip the rungs. The boys sensed my plight and became helpful, 'You'll be O.K. Mr Kerr, just keep looking up and take one rung at a time'. It was good advice and I tried to take a grip on my feelings as well as the ladder and the ascent continued and the platform finally achieved. The worst thing was that I had to get down again, however in the Lord's goodness this was accomplished despite my acute feelings of nausea and weakness. It is always a good thing to acknowledge one's limitations, a lesson I have been slow to learn.

Daily program at the Dromana Beach Mission.

ARE YOU ON HOLIDAY?
SO ARE WE!
LET'S SPEND IT TOGETHER.
LOOK FOR THE RED C.S.S.M. BANNER

EVERY DAY (Except Sunday, —
  10.30 a.m.—Games.
  11 a.m.—Keenites.
  11.30 a.m.—A Dip (wet—not "lucky").
  2.30 p.m.—Building the Sand Pulpit.
        (Bring spade, buckets and flowers.)
  3.30 p.m.—Beach Meeting.

EVENINGS—
  Watch out for Specials. Announcements will be made at Beach Meetings.

SUNDAYS—
  3.30 p.m.—Beach Meeting.

WATCH FOR—
  January 1—Our Birthday—the 77th—Surprise.
  January 5—Sports Day.
  Also Competitions, Sausage Sizzles, Text Modelling, Pirates' Picnic, etc.

Leader:
Flight-Lieut. HARVEY M. CAREY, M.B., B.S., B.Sc.
Assisted by a Party of Workers Drawn from the 'Varsity, Business and Professional Life in Melbourne.

Praise be to the Lord, for he has heard my cry for mercy.
The Lord is my strength and my shield;
my heart trusts in him and I am helped.

Psalm 28. 6 NIV

God moves in a mysterious way,
His wonders to perform;
He plants his footsteps in the sea,
And rides upon the storm.

Ye fearful saints fresh courage take,
The clouds ye so much dread
Are big with mercy, and shall break
In blessing on your head

Judge not the Lord by feeble sense,
But trust him for his grace;
Behind a frowning providence
He hides a smiling face.

From *Light Shining Out of Darkness:* Wm. Cowper,
1731–1800

-5-

1949 – 1954

Unexpected Changes

In 1949 Melbourne experienced a severe polio epidemic, hundreds of people were affected and many died. One of those was our neighbour Ern Mitchell, at the age of twenty-nine, leaving his wife Bettie with three young children. Bettie and I had been friends since Sunday School days and our hearts went out to her in this sad situation. At that time Ada became unwell and feverish and was confined to bed. One afternoon she remarked to me that she felt so weak that her hand would not pick up her handkerchief. Alarm bells rang within and in a very short time our doctor had been called, then an ambulance and Ada was admitted to Fairfield infectious diseases hospital with polio. Ada's father and Aunt were soon with me to help with the boys and there were some anxious days as we waited to determine the extent of the illness.

I cannot remember how long it was before her condition stabilised leaving both arms and one leg affected, fortunately not her lungs. These were difficult days as little Russell was only seven months old. He was not happy about being bottle fed and it was a problem getting him to eat or drink anything. Through some friends I was put in touch with a Christian girl from the country, Pia Gigliotti, who was willing to come and care for us, which she did very well although Russell was a great concern to her. It became common for me to return from work with Pia saying 'he has not taken a thing all day'. It made for lots of broken nights for me and the situation improved only very slowly as Russell was obviously greatly disturbed by his sudden weaning and Ada's absence. She, meanwhile had been transferred to the Austin Hospital where we able to visit her and so the slow process of rehabilitation was begun.

Pia was an immense help and got along splendidly with Howard who seemed always to be his usual affable contented self. 'Pa' Moffat and Aunty Mac came quite often to take him for outings which Pia and I also did at weekends. In December, after almost six months in hospital Ada was able to return home. Her right arm was severely affected besides other weaknesses. It was necessary for her to sleep on a frame but gradually she was able to move about. Pia expressed a desire to return home and we were able to replace her with another country lass, Ruby Brown, who was also extremely helpful.

In July of that year I was going to Brisbane to collect a new Holden car that Vic Deakin had obtained for me. This car was the first model fully made in this country and a long waiting list of would-be customers existed in Melbourne. Ada and Roy accompanied me and we stayed with the Knudsens, while Ruby cared for the boys at home. Mona introduced Ada to a physiotherapist friend and his treatment proved so beneficial that it was decided that she should stay for a time to try and regain more movement in her arms and leg. It was a difficult decision and not the best for the boys as Russell was once again separated from his mother. Roy and I drove home in the new car and Ada remained in Brisbane for a further three months and certainly benefited from the treatment. I took little Russell with me to bring her home and on the return journey we three travelled the Sydney–Melbourne sector by sea on the *Orcades*. The new Holden was registered with an SU number plate, SU 459. In the CSSM chorus book No 459 was 'Members of the Scripture Union'. The new automobile was much admired by all and enjoyed by the family. At the end of this year Ruby left us to be married and Ada was once again able to cope with running the home. Despite some permanent incapacity, she did this with characteristic courage and calm and we, no doubt, failed to fully realise the effort required.

With Alan Johnston as a very vigorous and capable factory manager the Cardigan Street plant was running very smoothly during these years. The products had improved in quality and variety and Kerby had become a respected supplier within the industry. The company, now known simply as Kerby Furniture, was profitable, still manufacturing basic household furniture and kitchens in Victoria but in Queensland had moved to more sophisticated products. I had been elected to the Council and then to the Executive of the Victorian Furniture Guild, in those days a very strong manufacturer's organisation. Kerby exhibited regularly at the Annual Guild shows and I was also often involved with retailers in judging window displays and design competitions.

Making furniture meant we needed new sales representatives and we were fortunate to have secured the services of Howard Carey, well-known in the trade, who gave us much valuable advice. Also we appointed our first country representatives. Walter Polglase had retired and died just a month before my dear friend Vic Deakin also died suddenly. I went to Brisbane for his funeral, feeling a great sense of loss. He had been a loyal man for the company since beginning with our novelty items and the years had seen us become close and trusted friends. I appointed Norm Knudsen as General Manager, a position in which he rapidly developed. Initially he needed guidance in commercial matters and I began to spend much more time at the Rocklea factory.

With our steady growth however, I was conscious of my own need for help in attaining more understanding in matters of finance, administration and organisation. My ever helpful friend Ralph Davis introduced me to a chartered accountant, Mr Lindsay Yeo, who was a partner in a well known practice in Melbourne. Lindsay was a director of a number of companies and becoming well-known for his business acumen. A Methodist with a warm, friendly personality, he played cricket, was a fine church organist, and for good measure supported the Essendon Football Club. He agreed to join a small Board of Directors which I was keen to set up and soon after this accepted my suggestion that he should become chairman. I found that being the one with most of the ideas and enthusiasms did not help me to be a good chairman. It was better to have someone objective to guide our discussions. The other members at the outset were Ada and Norman Knudsen. Lindsay became a valued personal friend, an enthusiast for the company, and a source of great strength and wisdom in the years to come. He was friendly and patient, with much expertise gathered from the wider world of business, which he was always willing to share. Ada and I had no doubt that his presence with us was a good gift and a blessing from our Heavenly Father.

We were at the time selling a fair amount of furniture in Tasmania but as the freight was prohibitive it was decided to set up a factory in Hobart. To do this we took over a small joinery business which was functioning in a narrow three story building on the fringe of the city. One of the employees, Chris Wharmby, applied for appointment as manager and Alan Johnston and I interviewed and accepted him. He was a well-trained cabinet maker and joiner from England and proved to be absolutely the right choice and added to this was the fact that his wife, Mary, was a capable and efficient office manager. After some time spent in the Melbourne factory learning our designs and methods Chris set to work. The third Kerby factory was successful in making a profit from the outset and it went on to become a major supplier of contract and household furniture throughout the island. Mary's clear and reliable accounts were models of precision, appreciated by the Melbourne office. It added another regular journey to my travel itinerary.

The Brisbane factory had entered into furniture very successfully with 'occasional' items, china cabinets and trousseau chests. The latter were a very popular item in the culture of the fifties, and our designs sold well throughout the State. We began to trade under the name of Rocklea Manufacturing Co, so as to identify ourselves as a Queensland entity. This was important as antipathy towards the southern states was strong at all levels in the years following the war. In order to try and buy timber I had once travelled to north Queensland and found a very suitable supplier. After discussing a contract to make regular shipments to Brisbane he happened to look at my business card. 'Are you from Melbourne?' he asked. 'Yes I am, but the timber is for our factory in Brisbane', I replied. 'I'm not selling timber to b--y Melbourne', he said, 'the deal is off', and he meant it. I returned empty-handed. In both centres the shortage of timber and plywood was restricting output, so in consultation with the Forestry Department a dipping plant was installed at Rocklea, enabling us to treat and use timber which was not otherwise suitable for furniture.

All of this called for factory expansion. A second building

next door was secured in which to place new machines and an excellent skilled staff was being built up by Norm Knudsen, himself a superb craftsman. The range of furniture widened and Rocklea began to make a name for itself in the industry. The production manager, Mort Allen, had worked in large factories and was competent in mass production techniques which reduced costs and made the business much more profitable than Melbourne. I found myself spending increased time there with Norm and his staff in finance, production management and the planning of new lines.

The Melbourne Cricket Ground has a firm place in the affections of a large proportion of Melburnians, and I am one of those who have enjoyed many wonderful events at that famous arena. My dad was a member of the MCC and this meant that in my boyhood there was free admittance to sections of the members stands for me on his 'ladies tickets' until the age of sixteen. I became a keen cricket watcher after the age of twelve. The train fare to Jolimont was seven pence and a bottle of soft drink was four pence, (after claiming the one penny return). By taking sandwiches from home I could watch a whole day of Shield or Test cricket for less than a shilling. Added to this was the opportunity to seek autographs as the players moved about the members pavilion. I could also take my friend Eric when he was free. Together we watched the Test match on that fateful New Year's Day during the 'bodyline series' when in front of a capacity crowd Don Bradman was bowled first ball by Bowes and a shocked unbelieving hush descended on us all. Bradman more than compensated for that over the years by treating us to many happy hours of run making. The 'Don' was a special hero of mine. Just about the time I was setting out in my little business I read an account of his youth. He said that he was extremely shy but he discovered that if you did not have confidence in yourself you could never expect others to have confidence in you. This simple statement met a need within and did wonders for me from that time onwards.

There were also football Grand Finals over the years. I have already told of losing one in the last few seconds in 1947. In 1966 I was with Leonard Buck, a Collingwood supporter, when the same thing happened to his team at the hands of St Kilda. Campaigner colleague, John Nash and I set off one fine day to watch Essendon play North Melbourne in the 1950 Grand Final.

In those days one simply went to the ground and paid to go in. At least until that day that's how it was, but our grief and remorse knew no bounds when we found the ground full and all gates shut. We compared our fate to that of unbelievers shut out of Heaven! The Dons won and we saw the last quarter when they opened the gates to all. After that I always made sure of a seat and have been a spectator at almost all Grand Finals over the last fifty years.

A very different spectacle, or series, was that of the Olympic Games in 1956. It was our pleasure to have Norm and Mona Knudsen staying with us for this notable occasion. They were two unforgettable weeks and we all revelled in the experience which seemed to bring a new aura to our city, and certainly left another indelible impression of the MCG in our minds. One other unusual one which remains in the memory was the final meeting of the Billy Graham Crusade in 1959, mentioned elsewhere. In due course my own membership of the Club came along and it has been most convenient for me that a few years ago this became the home ground of the Essendon football club. There have been many changes over the seventy years since I first made the acquaintance of this great arena and yet essentially, the atmosphere remains the same.

During the fifties Ada and I enjoyed a number of holidays with Ralph and Dulcie Davis, sometimes with the children, other times just the four of us. These were very enriching occasions. We relaxed well in each others company, having many common interests and we spurred each other on in the faith. Ralph had become very much involved in the work of Scripture Union as a member of the Council and his influence was particularly helpful in bringing about the eventual amalgamation of ISCF, the Crusader Union and the SU. We had also been together in Campaigners since the war years so that there were always matters of common interest to discuss.

In the year 1954 there was expansion on the home front as well in the other areas of business and Christian work. A large sunroom was added to the house and the third block of land which I had been unable to afford when building the house was purchased and a tennis court was laid down. As well as providing pleasant recreation this became a playground for the boys and their friends. More importantly there was an expansion in

Ralph Davis,
Basil Williams and
Alan Kerr, c. 1953.

the size of our family, with the arrival three days before Christmas of our third son Marcus Andrew Kerr. Russell was initially disappointed about this as he hoped for a sister but I am sure this was short-lived. From an early age Marcus suffered from asthma and there were two or three urgent trips to hospital for treatment. Likewise there were many nights when Ada had little sleep being up so often trying to relieve Marcus of his coughing and shortness of breath. We were grateful to be recommended to a clever German doctor, Mr Pickhart who, with diet and rather unusual treatment improved his condition a great deal. Due to this Marcus recovered more quickly from asthma attacks and without many antibiotics; nevertheless the condition has persisted over the years.

There was a further addition to the household, part-time, when Lister Hannah the eldest son of Welles and Barbara, CMS missionaries in Tanzania, arrived from Africa to stay with us and to attend Geelong Grammar School as a boarder. Our arrangement with his parents was that he should spend all vacation times with us for a few years and this worked well. We did not know at that time that we were caring for a future headmaster of that great school.

The God who created the world and everything in it, and who is Lord of heaven and earth, does not live in shrines made by men. It is not because he lacks anything that he accepts service at men's hands, for he is himself the universal giver of life and breath and all else. He created every race of men of one stock, to inhabit the whole earth's surface. He fixed the epochs of their history and the limits of their territory. They were to seek God , and, it might be, touch and find him; ...

Acts 17, 24–27a NEB

O God, Creator, Saviour, and Guide, we thank you that you have created all people in your image to seek after you and to find you, and have sent your Son Jesus that we may know you as the only true God.
Look upon the people of our world in all their need, and forgive us for our failure to show your love and proclaim your truth.
Enable us, your servants, to speak your Word with all boldness, while you stretch out your hand to show your power, through the name of Jesus Christ, our Lord and Saviour, Amen.

Colin Chapman. Prayer at Lausanne
Congress Manila, 1989

- 6 -

1954 – 1959

Widening Horizons

For a few years SU occupied a small office in Flinders Lane but as the activities grew, so too did the premises and workload for staff and voluntary workers. After SU merged with Crusaders and the Inter-School Christian Fellowship, fulfilling John Laird's vision, I had stepped down as Chairman and became Honorary General Secretary. This was now proving too heavy a load and the movement needed a full-time worker in this role. I considered the possibility of selling the business and doing the SU work full-time. The idea appealed to me and I mentioned it briefly one evening at a Council meeting.

Next morning I had a visit at my office from a senior and respected member of the Council, Mr JO Sanders, Director of the China Inland Mission, who said that the Lord had given him a message for me. It was a verse of Scripture; 1 Corinthians 7.20: 'Let every man abide in the same calling wherein he was called'. Oswald felt I would be of more benefit to SU and the Christian cause generally by staying in the business, therefore I should devote myself to that. After a few more words he was off, leaving me rather surprised but grateful to him for his concern. After a few days I came to the conclusion that this was God's purpose for me and put the matter of full-time Christian work out of my mind. This message was in fact consistent with my earliest convictions that the Lord wanted me to be in business but doing Christian work and the Scripture that Oswald quoted was very much to the point. 'JOS' also said he felt I should seek an interest and play a part in overseas missions, something which

Ralph Davis had been saying for sometime. My reply then had been that the schools and beaches of Victoria were the mission to which I had been called. However this did not satisfy Ralph, who said I should set an example of wider interest. He certainly set a fine example, for besides involvement in the Methodist Overseas Missions he gave much time to his work as a Council member of the Borneo Evangelical Mission.

Not long after this Oswald invited me to become a member of the China Inland Mission Council. I felt no call to this and had to decline although I knew this would disappoint him and some of my friends. However before long I was to join the Council of the Unevangelized Fields Mission (UFM) through the invitation of my friend, Leonard Buck. He was chairman of the mission and particularly involved in their work in New Guinea where they had some thirty pioneer missionaries. This immediately came to me as God's call, which I knew should be accepted. To return to the outcome of the SU need, Ray Averill, a fellow member of the Portarlington team, a gifted and enthusiastic young man, was appointed to the full-time position and served the movement with distinction for many years.

In 1954 Dr John Laird, who was now SU General Secretary in London made his second visit to Australia. His first visit ten years earlier had left a deep impression on many people in the movement. He had spoken then of the desirability of the three separate organisations in Victoria merging and in the intervening years this had taken place. Now he was seeking something far bigger. He was hoping to bring about more cooperation between the SU, ISCF and Crusader Union in all the States. At this time they were operating quite independently of one another. Two years earlier a conference had taken place at Mt Macedon, Victoria which resulted in the formation of an Australian Advisory Committee but little had come from this. Now with the coming of John Laird a large conference on a scale not even considered before was held at 'The Grange', Mt Victoria in NSW. In attendance were council members, senior leaders, and staff workers from all over Australia. This was organised by Basil Williams who was at that time SU General Secretary for NSW. I had been asked to take the chair at this gathering, which met in a spirit of unity and anticipation. John Laird gave a series of inspiring Bible studies, and put forward his vision for a united work across Australia. He said that as he flew across our country he noted all the farming properties with their own dams and he saw this as a good illustration of a 'waterhole mentality' evident within our separate movements, whereas he felt we should be thinking in terms of sharing a broad stream. He proposed that we should seek a new spirit of interdependence with a vision for the whole of our country. A Federal council should be formed to comprehend and guide this work, to give cohesion and do some planning on a national scale.

The atmosphere was most congenial and the delegates were much warmer to this suggestion than we had expected. After a long and careful debate the conference agreed to these proposals, although some had reservations about the expense of Federal meetings. In those days interstate travel was relatively uncommon, especially for Christian organisations. Dr Laird then told us he had a gift of one thousand pounds from a friend in the UK which could help with travel costs in the early stages.

I was asked to leave the room while the Conference discussed the choice of office bearers. It was over an hour before John came to me in my room to say 'they all want you as chairman but a few people feel you may push things too hard'. And then with a kindly smile he said 'You see Alan, you are driving through life so fast I think you need to learn to stop now and then and pick a few flowers on the way. But you are the man for the job and we all believe that'. It was typical of John that he could so gently and deftly administer a rebuke, which was no doubt justified. With this warning and assurance I accepted the position and sought to heed this advice especially in my relationships with staff members.

I certainly received whole-hearted support as the first chairman of SU Australia and our meetings had a good tone from the outset. It was decided to invite Colin Becroft, successful General Secretary of SU in New Zealand to accept a combined post of General Secretary for New South Wales and the new Australian Council, which happily, he did. This brought about a period of close and enriching collaboration with Colin for the next six years before he moved to commence the work in America. It is pleasing to record that the Federal concept functioned well from the beginning. We had annual council meetings with small executive sessions through the year. Some splendid representatives were appointed by the states and we quickly

Our three children, Howard, Russell and Marcus, early 1956.

developed an ethos and worked well as a team, skilfully organised by Colin.

Ada received much pleasure, friendship and blessing from a ladies fellowship group which met at Jane Buck's home for twenty-one years. There they shared and discussed various aspects of home making, bringing up children, the role of wives and mothers as well as receiving spiritual teaching and encouragement. Many of these spiritual talks were given by Mrs Sanders and Mrs Kidner. These gatherings were held monthly with an average of thirty ladies attending from many parts of Melbourne. During the early days of the war Leonard had led a prayer meeting in his home for Campaigners. These powerful gatherings continued every Thursday night for many years and gave rise to the ladies meetings.

Just a few months after joining UFM I was approached by Archdeacon Kidner, General Secretary of the Church Missionary Society in Victoria asking if I would consider accepting nomination as Deputy Chairman of the Victorian Committee with a view to becoming chairman in due course. It seemed strange coming so soon after joining UFM and my first inclination was to decline. However it seemed to be borne in upon me that this was from the Lord and so within one year I went from no missionary commitment to having two, both fairly weighty. A situation I always put down to Ralph's prayers! Each of these involved two meetings each month plus consultations and for UFM I had agreed to act as Candidate Secretary. CMS called for a much greater learning process. It was a world wide mission with some two hundred Australian missionaries and it took me ages to learn what all the initials and acronyms meant, apart from discovering what they actually did and getting to know the missionaries.

Before long I found myself chairman of the General Committee, a post I filled for ten years. It was a large body in those days with an average attendance of over forty, more like a public meeting than a committee. When the secretary Archdeacon Kidner retired I was involved in finding a new general secretary and home secretary. Two excellent men filled these positions, namely, Reverend Ronald Marks and Reverend Kevin Curnow. Within a short space of time the aggregate age of these three officers had been halved! Being chairman I became a Victorian delegate to the Federal Council which then met in Sydney twice a year under Archbishop Mowll's chairmanship. I was to remain on the Federal Council for about thirty-seven years, during which time it was my privilege to work closely with Bishops Jack Dain and Don Cameron, Archbishops Hugh Gough and Marcus Loane, Bishop John Reid and many other wonderful men and women. I also served on the Federal executive, the Policy committee, and was involved over the years in choosing four Federal General Secretaries as a member of the nominations committee. CMS was my first official work for the Anglican church; I enjoyed it and it became a great blessing to me.

For some years after joining the Council of the Unevangelized Fields Mission I served as candidate secretary which involved considerable time interviewing prospective missionaries. It also meant setting up procedures and bringing in new forms for the use of applicants. We were anxious to avoid the costly mistakes of sending unsuitable people to the field and better screening procedures were necessary as the mission grew.

In 1956 I made my first trip to Papua New Guinea for the Mission. This was a memorable time for me in many ways. It was the first time I had been out of Australia. It was my first time in a new culture and my first experience of mission work *in situ*. I travelled to Port Moresby by flying boat, continuing on after a few days to Daru Island in the Fly River delta and there joined the mission vessel *Maino* and made the acquaintance of Stan Varidel the skipper, who also served as field accountant. We sailed up river about 60 miles to the mission HQ at Wasua, a native village with a cluster of mission houses and buildings which was to be the scene of the Annual Field Conference.

The M. V. Maino *transported personnel and supplies for thirty years.*

I stayed with the field director George Sexton and his wife Ranee, an intrepid couple who had worked formerly with the English UFM on the Amazon River in Brazil. From their house, built in local fashion, I looked across the brown waters of the Fly, at this point about five miles wide. To collect the missionaries for the conference the 'Maino' would travel hundreds of miles up the river. I was delighted to learn that I had been deputed to travel with Stan and the journey was one that lives in my memory. For several days we sailed, just the two of us, conversing, reading, eating our simple meals and anchoring each night a few metres offshore. The broad expanse of swiftly flowing water, framed with almost unbroken walls of jungle, the steady beat of the engine and the tropical heat induced a sense of relaxation which was both calming and satisfying. I read both volumes of *The Brothers Karamazov* on the trip which somehow seemed to suit the situation.

Stan placed me at the wheel of the boat from time to time with a simple instruction 'Fix your eye on some distant object such as an especially tall tree for a landmark and steer steadily for that. At the same time keep a sharp lookout for floating logs and other debris which could damage the vessel'. In later life I found this a useful rule. We must have our distant goals if we are to achieve progress yet at the same time we must be aware of the more immediate dangers which may bring us undone.

The Fly is a great river, one of the largest in terms of the volume of water discharged daily into the sea. It rises from the

*Left: Papuan mother and child; Right: Papuan teacher and pupil at
an early Mission school.*

heights of the Star mountains, just a few miles from the source
of another mighty river, the Sepik, which flows north while the
Fly travels south. It is navigable by quite large vessels for about
a thousand kilometres and I think we were some eight hundred
from the mouth when we collected our most distant missionaries. We gathered the rest of our passengers, family by family at
various points on the return journey and travelling much faster
down stream reached Wasua with a full complement. Before
many more years were out they would all be flying to conferences in a matter of hours.

There was much to be gained and enjoyed over the days
which followed, as I entered into the hopes and aspirations of
these dedicated men and women. Difficulties also, but they
were positive and practical in their approach to the task they
had taken up. It was comprehensive; they were preachers and
teachers, educators and healers, concerned for the whole of the
lives of the tribespeople to whom they had come in response to
the call of the Spirit. These tribes frequently numbered only
about a thousand people, sometimes more, others even less.
Some were head hunters and warlike, others gentler in disposi-
tion, all hearing only at this stage of their history of the living
God and His Son who came to be their saviour and Lord. In

those who embraced the message the change was unmistakable, to meet them it was obvious and to talk and pray with them as fellow believers was an experience to remember.

For the second part of my visit after the conference, I travelled with Leonard Buck, mission chairman, from the lowlands to our newer areas in the Southern Highlands. Tari at 5500 ft was the centre for work amongst the Huli people, stocky, aggressive and mentally sharper than the lowlanders. A characteristic of this large tribal group is their love of colour and ornate hairdress, often adorned with bird of paradise plumes. Apart from that and a necklace, just a few leaves around their waist. One such paid me a visit during breakfast on my first morning there. He had with him a fearsome looking club with a stone ring at the end and greeted me with a volley of words, which my host explained was to tell me that this was his killing stick. It seemed to me that for them fighting was perhaps the equivalent to a weekly game of football or cricket in our culture. On Sunday I sat in the church service where every man had either a spear or bow and arrow in one hand. They were all seated on the ground down one side of the assembly, with the women on the other, when word appeared to come that an enemy raid was imminent. Suddenly, half of the church was deserted when the men all took off as one to confront the invaders. This was, of course, at the beginning of white influence in the area, which had only been opened quite recently.

From Tari we flew in a small single engine plane across the mountains into what was then Dutch New Guinea to the capital, Hollandia. Setting off on this flight I had the first of many experiences of the delays which make up the pattern of visual flying in PNG. That morning the clouds did not lift as quickly as expected and despite two or three efforts the pilot was unable to find the 'Tari Gap' to get out of the valley. Muttering 'better a living dog than a dead lion' he was forced to return and we had to wait another day. Dutch New Guinea was a new initiative for the mission which was searching inland for suitable sites, prior to commencing a work there. With us on that flight was Charles Horne, one of the pioneers of our Papuan work in the 1930s who was to become the Mission leader in this new field. There were no inland airstrips at that time and we flew over the rugged terrain and dropped mail and some food for our small advance party. This was an area which was to witness within a few years a most remarkable movement of God's Spirit when UFM and another two or three missions saw thousands of Dani people turn to Christ within the next two or three decades. These fierce-looking men, with matted hair and faces and bodies smeared with pig fat and soot, would become smiling and loving followers of Jesus and their wives likewise. A glorious transformation.

In 1957 I made my first major overseas trip which occupied four-and-a-half months travelling around the world. After years of reading and dreaming about England and other countries and continents, this was the time when I first experienced the reality. Nothing failed my high expectations. It was a superb and wonderful adventure. It combined business openings and factory visits, Scripture Union and Church Missionary Society contacts and an enormous amount of personal sightseeing. I was fortunate that one of the older generation of travel agents, Ron Bailey of Sydney, planned my trip in which I travelled over 80,000 km, to twenty-five countries, staying in sixty-three different locations.

In America there was a great deal to be learnt about furniture manufacture, new methods, new materials and new machines, as I visited factories and furniture marts in many cities. This learning experience continued in England, Scandinavia and Germany, where more factories and furniture exhibitions were visited, forty-six in all, and many notes and reports compiled. It was brought home to me how we were far behind many of these plants with their modern machines and techniques and that we needed to upgrade and improve if we were to develop as a company. I also gave thirty-five talks, visiting places like mission hospitals, churches and schools and this was also part of a mind-stretching, learning process.

Travelling via New Zealand gave me the opportunity to meet with the UFM Council in Auckland which was to prove useful in future days. A further UFM contact was in Seattle where I spent a weekend with parents of one of our missionaries. I had with me a set of slides from my PNG visit and showed them and spoke at a service. They were so delighted that they presented me with the projector, a new automatic model, so that I could show others. It was not feasible to carry this so they packed it and sent it home for me. I did in fact use those slides a great deal on the trip; they always made a great impact as New Guinea was very little known in the West in those pre-TV days.

Arriving in London I met with the SU Council and spoke to them at their invitation. This august body was the one to which we in Australia were responsible, along with all other branches of the movement. One could not help but feel that this all male, middle-aged group of Londoners were, for all their goodwill, remote indeed from the schools and beaches of Australia and NZ. When, in praying for me there was a reference to 'our brother from the colonies' this impression deepened. Individually, they were concerned, Godly men, and many of them were to become my close friends in the course of time. However, it was my strong feeling that this was not the body which we could look to for world leadership of a dynamic youth movement.

With John Laird himself, it was completely different. He was a man with the world on his heart and was conscious of the problem. I stated my conviction that we needed an international group or body of some kind to oversee development. John proposed that I go to Zurich to talk this over with Armin Hoppler, the Swiss secretary. I went first to Locarno and Lausanne and then Zurich and stayed with a Swiss staff worker, Ernest Aebi for a most delightful day or two and then on to Winterthur to meet Armin. Although now a full time SU staff member he had been in business on his own account and I suppose that helped us to get on famously from the outset. We held many opinions in common and in particular the need for SU to have a world council. Perhaps even more than us, the Swiss SU disliked having to consult London about so many things. These talks laid a foundation for John to begin thinking and planning for a conference in England in 1960 with invited representatives from other countries. Up to this time SU England was the sole authority in the SU world.

Quite apart from these satisfactory talks I relished every aspect of my time in England. I had read so much about various places that I felt I already knew them, and like most visitors I fell under the spell of London. I loved the sense of history, the beautiful buildings, the concerts, parks, shops and so much else. I did a lot of driving, visiting people and places. One country visit was to the home of a Campaigner contact Lt General Sir Arthur Smith who had spoken at meetings in Australia.

He was Chairman of the Officer's Christian Union and also, at that point, the Evangelical Alliance, which was in part the reason for my visit. After a pleasant dinner and talk he said, in military fashion, 'Kerr, you will take your bath at 8.10 in the morning'. I made sure that I was on time as was the bath, already run for me, and then breakfast, followed by devotions. All of the household retinue came into the dining room, cooks, housemaids, gardeners, fourteen in total, sitting in respectful silence, whilst the General read and prayed. It was like a scene from one of my books.

I also had the great pleasure of a meal with John Stott, my first meeting with him, and a night with Jack and Edith Dain, which was to bear unexpected fruit before long. Two nights were spent with Alfred and Sabina Coombe in Edinburgh at Sabina's family home, when they generously spent time giving me my first glimpses of Scotland.

I returned home via Africa, Pakistan, India, Thailand and Malaysia, staying with many CMS missionaries. East Africa was then living with some of the benefits of the colonial era, integrated services, and a fine railway that ran from the centre to the coast, and I travelled freely and comfortably throughout the three countries; Uganda, Tanganyika and Kenya. Especially enjoyable was a night and day trip by steamer across Lake Victoria from Bukoba to Mwanza. In Tanganyika as it was then, two highlights were staying at Mvumi with my friend and mentor from boyhood days, Dr Wellesley Hannah and his wife Barbara, and then at Bishopscourt in Dodoma with Bishop Alfred and Marjory Stanway, people from whom I had learnt much. The Bishop's efficient and Godly administration was in evidence throughout the diocese. It was easy to fall under the spell of this great continent, the expansive views, the wild life, distinctive shapes of the trees etched against the horizon, colours of the sunrise and mountains and the vitality of the people all held a great appeal.

From there on to the crowded cities of Asia provided an enormous change. It was interesting finally to arrive in Malaysia when that country was celebrating the first anniversary of the coming of "Merdeka" (freedom), their release from colonial rule. Lester Pfankuch our newly appointed SU worker drove me from Kuala Lumpur in leisurely fashion down the peninsula to Singapore, during which time I gained my initial insights into

A relaxed evening with the Brisbane management team one month prior to the opening of the new factory; Norm Knudsen is third from left.

the nature of the calling the Movement faced in that region which I was to visit so many times over the next two or three decades. During the whole of this almost five-month-long odyssey I had excellent photographic opportunities and the resulting attractive slides helped to give many people at home a wider vision of the world and diverse Christian activities in far-away lands.

During my absence the Queensland factory had been enlarged and I was eager to see the new layout. It was not to be; during a welcome-home gathering on the night of my return we received a phone call from Norm to say the factory was burning down. In fact it was completely destroyed. This meant I had to leave almost immediately for Brisbane to find temporary factory accommodation and begin planning for a new building. Over the ensuing months a splendid three-acre site was procured from the Queensland government and plans drawn up for a new building. Having seen so many fine factories overseas gave me a vision of what should be built and what new machines were needed. Twelve months exactly after the day of the fire the splendid new factory was opened by Mr Frank Nicklin,

Premier of Queensland. This enabled the branch to go further ahead in terms of efficiency and profitability.

During my time overseas I had taken the opportunity whilst in New York to contact members of the Billy Graham organisation at the suggestion of Campaigners, to inquire if Dr Graham would consider visiting Australia. I was received with courtesy and warmth by Mr Walter Smith a senior member of the team and met briefly with Billy and other team members. It was the time of the momentous campaign at Madison Square Garden and I was invited for the two nights to sit on the platform, there observing for the first time the impact of the great evangelist's preaching, with hundreds going forward each night. It was a new experience and quickened my desire to have Billy come to our country. He made it clear that this could only happen if there was a combined invitation from all of the mainline churches. This was something actively discussed in a number of quarters and in due course an official invitation was forwarded from the Archbishop of Sydney on behalf of the churches of Australia. Alfred Coombe also paid a visit soon after I did and this too helped to bring about a decision by Dr Graham that the team would have a major campaign in Australia in 1959.

For this purpose committees were set up in the participating States and each of these had an Executive and Finance Committee and conferred with members of the team who came to advise and prepare the way. I worked on the Melbourne Executive, which included representatives of all churches, and I think also on the Finance Committee. It was a time-consuming task but we all felt richly rewarded when the campaigns in each city greatly exceeded expectations, in the numbers attending and in the spiritual impact. I often pause and look at the photograph which hangs in the MCC pavilion showing the scene at the final meeting of the Melbourne campaign when 130,000 crowded that great arena, spilling out onto the playing field.

On that Sunday afternoon I had taken a friend from our church and his life was completely changed after he responded to the appeal. In time the blessing from that decision was to spread right through his family. Some of the meetings were held at the Royal Showgrounds where Ada and I went one night accompanied by our fourteen-year-old Howard. It rained steadily throughout the meeting as we sat out in the centre of the ground huddling

Dr Billy Graham in 1959 with His Excellency the Governor of Victoria, Sir Dallas Brooks.

under umbrellas listening and when the appeal was made Howard was amongst the hundreds who went forward. These were stories repeated countless times, and for many years after 1959 one kept coming across people, missionaries and clergy who had made their commitment to Christ during that wonderful campaign.

One day, travelling on a plane I found myself sitting next to a retired schoolteacher, who was a Christian. We talked about missions and I spoke of my interest in the APCM. He asked if I knew a teacher of a certain name who worked with them in PNG. I said that I had known her for years, one of our most respected and diligent missionaries. He then told me how he had counselled her one night in 1959 in a small hall in outback NSW where the Crusade message was being relayed by landline. No large crowd, no 'atmosphere', just the message from the evangelist and the work of the Holy Spirit in the heart of this young woman sitting in the bare country hall. Knowing nothing of the church or the gospel, her life was radically changed in that two-hour encounter. This was typical of the stories which one has encountered from those stirring days.

During the sixties and seventies, theological seminaries and mission boards all found that a large percentage of their applicants came as an outcome of the Crusade. Reflecting on those days my outstanding memory however, is of the atmosphere which prevailed within the community at the time and during the months which followed the visit of Dr Graham. It was a topic of conversation almost everywhere I went. At Furniture Guild meetings, in stores, in banks and factories men and women were eager to discuss not only the campaign but the issues of faith and morality which emerged as a consequence of it. There was an openness to spiritual matters which could only be described as remarkable in my lifetime. Of course there were cynics and scoffers but they were very much in the minority. The press, so often cynical in these matters, was most supportive.

I had one personal experience of the media interest. Before the meetings in Melbourne began Billy and two of his team members had expressed a desire for a game of golf. I was asked if I would take them to my club one morning and with great secrecy we set off early from their hotel and were enjoying the game for the first eight holes. As we approached the ninth green, which at Riversdale is alongside the road leading to the clubhouse, we discovered a swarm of photographers and reporters who descended on Billy and that was the end of our game for the day. Photos, reports and comments made the front page of all the dailies that evening and next morning.

One of the key workers on the Graham committee in Sydney was Bruce Ogden, son of a gifted Christian, Claude Ogden, who owned one of the largest and most successful furniture factories in Australia. Bruce and I had a lot in common and it was not long before he proposed that Kerby should market their very popular CRO dining and office furniture in Melbourne. This became a very successful venture, although it put me out of favour with my colleagues on the Council of the Furniture Guild as they felt I was a traitor to the cause of the local manufacturers. It is interesting to think how insular we were in Australia even in the post war 1950s. I had already observed this in Christian work such as SU, Campaigners, CMS and also UFM. and knew that these state barriers were a legacy of the past which could have no place in a modern nation. Later the same process would have to be repeated at an international level, as we learnt to think and operate globally.

Some time before, I had decided to eliminate beach missions and similar activities from my summer holiday period in order to spend them solely with the family. However, we had not been successful in finding suitable locations or rented houses. With the approach of Christmas 1959 I inserted an advertisement in *The Age* setting out my requirements for a rented holiday home. and in the goodness of God received a very suitable answer. So it was we came to spend the first of many vacations at 45 Rosserdale Crescent, Mount Eliza in Mr Charles Ovenden's flat and garden on the cliff overlooking Ranelagh beach. This home continued to see us as holiday tenants for many years before we built a holiday house of our own at No. 8, a few doors away and were later to make our permanent home at 37–41. That one simple advertisement had a great influence on the subsequent shape and style of our family life.

During 1959 Kerby purchased five acres of land at Thomastown twenty kilometres from Melbourne on which to build a new factory. Unfortunately, due to a severe national credit squeeze this project had to be postponed for quite a long time. In 1960 our long and happy relationship with Alan Johnston, factory manager, terminated when he and our accountant, Keith Cree, left to start their own business together. This was a heavy blow and came at a bad time for me.

While waiting for the Thomastown site to be developed we rented a factory at Arthurton Road, Northcote and located the showroom and office at 284 High Street, Northcote, in a large former furniture store with an upper floor warehouse. By this time we were importing rattan furniture from Hong Kong, a result of one of my trips there. The next two or three years proved very difficult ones for the Melbourne factory operation. We were not making a profit under the new manager, and missed Alan Johnston sadly. Only the agency products, CRO in particular, and the rattan kept Melbourne afloat financially during that period. We had employed Sonia Preston to take care of all design aspects of our operations and it was she who designed an attractive selection of furniture which we named the 'Spring Valley' range. This helped to turn Melbourne around and was successfully taken up in the other branches.

It was 1963 before the new building at Thomastown commenced and it was opened in 1964. Meanwhile a fine large new factory was built and opened at Glenorchy, Tasmania, and in it that branch continued it's steady profitable progress. Kerby had now established themselves as one of the island state's leading manufacturers with their products featured in all stores and a growing contract business as well. Over the next few years we were to fit out the bedrooms in virtually all of the large hotels and motels built in Tasmania at that time. Chris Wharmby became a member of the Furniture Guild Executive as Norm Knudsen had also done in Queensland.

Things had moved along at home with Howard commencing secondary schooling at Carey Baptist Grammar, Kew. Howard joined the SU group at Carey, was on the committee and involved in all of their activities. This included attending ISCF camps in the holidays, which were a great help and encouragement to his spiritual life. Each of the boys in their time at Carey benefited from these camps with their many and varied activities and indeed from the school itself. Also a strong formative influence in their spiritual development was their participation in the Parish Youth Fellowship at St James, Ivanhoe, eventually under the leadership of George Farrington.

When Howard completed matriculation Ada and I gave him the choice of doing architecture at university or of taking up an apprenticeship at the Brisbane factory. Howard decided on the apprenticeship . After a useful two years he returned to work at the Melbourne factory, and did a design course at the Royal Melbourne Institute of Technology. After this he applied for and was awarded a scholarship to work in America and England.

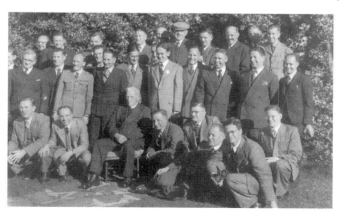

An annual conference of Campaigners for Christ in the early 1950s. The Reverend CH Nash seated and Mr Charles Davis at the back, wearing cap.

Forget the former things; do not dwell on the past.
See, I am doing a new thing!
Now it springs up; do you not perceive it?

Isaiah 43.18,19a N.I.V

Every human organisation has within it the seeds of its own decay.
It must, therefore, re-examine itself or be re-examined from outside
from time to time.
If it is to survive it must be reborn. The sixteenth century reform-
ers understood this when they took as one of their mottoes for the
Church the words Semper Reformanda *— always needing to be*
reformed.

Dr John Laird

In the year 1652 when throughout England all things sacred were
either neglected or profaned this church was built by Sir Robert
Shirley Bart, whose special praise it was to have done the best
things in the worst times and hoped them in the most calamitous.

Inscription on a stone tablet
in a Yorkshire church

-7-

1959 – 1965

'Old Jordans' and New Ways

In 1959 at the request of the Australian SU Council I visited New Zealand to discuss with the leaders there the possibility of establishing a Council of SU in South East Asia to initiate and oversee the formation of the Movement in the countries of that area. Due to the initiative of Cecil Johnston from India, who drew our attention to the opportunities in this region, we were already supporting our first staff worker in Malaysia and Singapore. Now our plans were encompassing Thailand, Indonesia, Japan, Hong Kong, the Philippines and beyond. The NZ council responded readily and warmly to our proposals and we were quickly of one mind on the matter. At their suggestion we decided to recommend that such a body should be known as the 'ANZEA' Council, which stood for Australia, New Zealand and East Asia. It was agreed that the first meeting would be held in Singapore when delegates were en route to England for the international conference which was to be held in 1960. It was also agreed that Asians should form the majority of members on this new body as speedily as feasible.

The Reverend Tony McCutcheon had taken over Lester Pfankuch's job in Malaysia after the latter took up a teaching appointment there and it was decided to request Tony to be the General Secretary for this new entity. He readily agreed and took up the challenge of our regional plans with enthusiasm. This involved identifying likely people in each of the countries, spending time with them, seeking to share his vision and to implant in them a desire to actively engage in evangelism and discipling of young people in schools and churches. He was helped in this task by Colin Becroft who visited the countries involved. They performed their work well and with God's guidance and blessing gathered a number of exceptionally gifted men and women who became the nucleus of the committees and councils in Singapore, Hong Kong, Bangkok, Kuala Lumpur and Tokyo. These included the Reverend Junichi Funaki of Japan, Professor Khoo Oon Teik and Dr Lawrence Chia of Singapore, the Reverend Peter Young and Mr David Boler of Malaysia and many others who became part of a vital family of faith within Scripture Union.

Our first meeting took place in April 1960 when the Council was officially constituted and plans laid for the first year. I was elected Chairman with Colin Becroft Secretary and Tony McCutcheon Regional Secretary, all subject to the approval of SU in London. The oneness of spirit which emerged from these discussions was most encouraging to me and it foreshadowed the very close bonds which were to exist in our work together over the years ahead. It was agreed that the Council would meet at the same time next year and that a small Executive would maintain contact meanwhile. After the meeting the delegates to the international gathering departed for London. Colin and I travelled together, enjoying brief but memorable visits to Israel and Lebanon, staying in what was then the attractive city of Beiruit and driving up to Baalbeck, and then visiting Athens.

So we came to London and another new development which was to become a major factor in our lives over the next two decades. It had its beginning in a Buckinghamshire village during a delightful warm and sunny week in May 1960. Following the earlier thinking and discussions about the need for the SU movement to set up an international base, rather than the London Council and office carrying responsibility for the world-wide movement, Dr Laird prevailed upon the London Council to agree to the calling of a world-wide conference to discuss the future development of the work. This convened at a Quaker conference centre known as 'Old Jordans', a most delightful setting with a history going back to the time when their religious gatherings suffered oppression and persecution in the 17th century. Twenty-three delegates gathered, representing twelve countries and all of the major SU Councils at that time. We once again had reason to acknowledge the masterly and spiritual leadership of John Laird in his presentation of the issues and his opening up of the Scriptures. SU in England was already in its ninety-third year, and he stated that "Old societies, like old men, can easily become set in their ways, stiff in their movements, and vision and insight can become dim by reason of age... Can a society be born when it is old?" he asked and we all inwardly answered in the affirmative. SU could be reborn by the power of the Spirit.

English chairman Mr Derek Warren, a lawyer, led most of the sessions and skilfully guided the discussion day by day. Initially not all the delegates found themselves in agreement with the concepts which were emerging but eventually under the Spirit's guidance we became of one mind. So we were led to the formation of an International Council with responsibility for the oversight of the conduct and development of the work worldwide. The London Council graciously declared itself willing to hand over to this new body the rights which had been theirs from the birth of the movement in 1867. The decisions made around that conference table in 1960 were to prove seminal in the life of the movement, opening up a period of remarkable expansion. John Laird had often reminded us that causes which in the providence of God begin with a MAN and grow to become a MOVEMENT are always in danger of turning into a MACHINE and ending up as a MONUMENT. Mindful of this truth, as we sought growth we also prayed that the Holy Spirit would keep us as a 'movement'.

At the outset, the new council comprised Derek Warren, Chairman, Alan Kerr, Deputy-chairman; Armin Hoppler, Secretary, John Laird, and Colin Becroft, with Robert Ewan of England as Treasurer. It was agreed that we would meet at least once yearly, endeavouring to do so in the various countries where SU was at work, but watching how the travel costs fell on members. This meant a new travel commitment of both time and money for me as I was the most distant member. This I was prepared to accept as it was such a strategic and necessary step for SU. In the goodness of God it transpired that it often became possible to fit this in with commitments for business travel which arose in later years.

A major new initiative agreed by the Old Jordans gathering was to establish SU in the USA. Mr Stacey Woods, American director of the IVF strongly urged such a move and promised support. The outcome was an invitation to Colin Becroft to take

Founding members of the S.U. International Council, early 1960s.
From left: PD Warren, AT Kerr, Dr JM Laird, CK Becroft and A Hoppler.

up this challenge and after due consideration, he accepted. This move had implications for Australia and the new ANZEA region, of course, as well as for Colin and his family. Another decision of the 'Old Jordans' conference was the adoption of a regional pattern for development based on that proposed by Australia and New Zealand for SE Asia. We had suggested that our two countries be responsible for the growth of the work for the region from Indonesia in the west to Japan in the north including at that time Malaysia, Singapore, Hong Kong, Taiwan, Phillipines, Borneo, Thailand, PNG and Pacific Islands, under the supervision of the regional council which we termed the ANZEA Council. This regional plan was seen as the key to orderly development and control and six regions were planned, each containing at least one member country of some experience. It was pleasing to have the plans we had made in Singapore a month earlier approved and made acceptable as a pattern for our future international growth.

Not long after my 40th birthday I shared with John Laird the opinion that I felt it to be God's guidance that the following ten years were to be given to developing the business, although this need not mean that my participation in Christian work would diminish. He concurred in this and in my conviction that for many men the forties could be years of their peak achievement, or at least of their endeavour. The introduction a few years earlier of Mr Lindsay Yeo to the company was bearing fruit. He was becoming increasingly well known as a director of a number of large Australian companies, and had a great deal to contribute to us. The board had grown in numbers and Lindsay led it well. He had introduced regular monthly meetings with reports, planning, and careful scrutiny of the accounts and was eager for progress. His ability and experience had begun to play a vital part in the expansion which we had hoped for in the sixties and I wanted to fully support him. It was through his help that finance was secured to eventually build the new Melbourne factory and also paved the way for new factories in Hobart and Adelaide. In the years ahead he was to continue steering the company well. He helped Kerby to run a private firm in public company style. I am sure there were many occasions when he was disappointed with my frequent absences due to Christian commitments but he was invariably cheerfully supportive and positive.

My conviction that it was a time for growth in the business heightened the ever present problem of balancing this with the increasing demands of the honorary tasks which it had seemed right for me to accept. I had a firm belief, strengthened since Oswald Sander's talk with me, that my calling was to be a Christian worker in a business situation. This meant that overall the Lord's work was to have priority, but that He also meant me to give of my best in the world of business. It was necessary to look to Him constantly for the wisdom and grace to discharge this dual commitment and of course make time for the all important responsibility of home and family.

During the years of working with Campaigners and Scripture Union I felt increasingly the desirability of finding a way for evangelical Christian movements in Australia to speak with a united voice on some issues. Colin Becroft was another person, who coming from New Zealand, perceived the same need. In Australia many Christian movements almost seemed to be in competition, and interstate rivalries were strong, with very little concern for consultation. We felt that a movement similar to the Evangelical Alliance in Great Britain could be valuable, so after consultation with the English body an Australian EA was established. We decided that this body should be governed by an Australian Council with State branches subservient to it being set up as the movement grew. We were seeking to avoid the problems caused by State branches developing differing policies, however the problems of distance and the expense of travel in our large country were real and difficult to overcome.

Many Christian leaders were interested and pledged their support and in April 1957 a Council was instituted, planning to meet alternately in Sydney and Melbourne. Alfred Coombe was the first chairman, Mr Justice Richardson of Sydney his deputy and I was secretary for a time. Bryan Bayston, a Melbourne lawyer, was one who saw the possibilities, and gave strong assistance. After a slow beginning this movement now makes a valuable contribution to the Christian cause in Australia, especially through its missionary section.

George Farrington was a business man with a strong desire to exercise a Christian ministry amongst young people. He came to St James, Ivanhoe, as a part-time staff member and quickly developed an excellent youth work. This experience caused him to feel a great burden for the underprivileged youth of the whole district, not simply those who came to our church. One Saturday morning he shared with parishioners Dr John Solomon, David Woods and myself his vision for a 'drop in' centre in the heart of Ivanhoe. The outcome was that we decided to constitute ourselves as a committee to bring into being 'Open House'. We would seek for suitable premises and gather a group of prayer partners and supporters. I agreed to act as chairman for an establishment period, which lasted three years, when John Solomon took over that role. David was treasurer for many years and eventually chairman, succeeding John. With typical generosity and dedication, George gave up his electrical contracting business entirely to commence this youth work full-time. With his wife Muriel and a band of volunteers he secured a shop in Ivanhoe and 'Open House' was born. It provided recreation, a coffee lounge, Bible studies and counselling. Due to their resolute devotion to the task the center grew, staff and properties multiplied and their ministry touched the lives of thousands in the ensuing years. This movement of sacrificial service expanded to other ministries with older people as well as young and after thirty years continues, a work of God's grace.

The memorable conference back in 1954 which brought into being the Australian Federal SU body had also suggested that

Colin Becroft of New Zealand should become the General Secretary in NSW and act also as Secretary to the new Federal body. This far-sighted move quickly began to bear fruit. Colin, just old enough to have seen war service, possessed a keen mind, good theological understanding and splendid organising ability. He speedily applied himself to the re-building of the work in NSW, and at the same time set about making the Federal concept real. His experience as successor to John Laird in NZ had equipped him well for the Australian task and I greatly enjoyed watching him at work. He made heavy demands on all who worked closely with him, which could have been irksome if we had not been richly rewarded with a sense of achievement. Many things were happening to realise the vision John Laird had glimpsed and put before us in 1954. We could only admire Colin for his dedicated and professional work, and give thanks to God.

When he left our country in 1961, to apply himself to the enormous challenge in the United States he was able to look back on six years of solid progress. We, for our part wondered how we would fare without him but even at this point his careful planning was in evidence and he introduced David Claydon to succeed him in both state and federal areas. Only twenty-four, David was new to the work but he obviously possessed ability and academic qualifications. At first we missed Colin with his wisdom and experience. However, before long all came to appreciate David's spiritual qualities and commitment. I found that we worked together very effectively and with the passage of years our friendship deepened.

A project which occupied our minds in the early sixties was the establishment of a wholesale book-selling company which we called 'Emu Books'. This agency, later to be known as Bookhouse Australia Ltd was fostered by David Claydon and myself and began in a small way with the support of Dr Paul White, Harold Knight and others, as a partnership between Scripture Union and Inter-Varsity Fellowship. It's objective was to increase the circulation and availability of good Christian books, many of which were not being offered for sale in Australia at that time. Emu gradually secured agencies from many of the leading Christian publishers overseas. Later it led to the development of ANZEA Publishers Ltd, to encourage Australian writing and publishing, as a separate entity under the chairmanship of Phillip Knight, an engineer. Phillip, a longstanding

Pondering a knotty point with Colin Becroft.

friend, who had been associated with SU beach missions in Victoria, now lived in Sydney and was the owner of a flourishing construction company.

Bookhouse Ltd underwent several changes of location as stocks increased and required more space. The books were sold to Christian bookshops throughout the country which in the seventies numbered over eight hundred. The Board met monthly in Sydney and as in SU, David and I worked together harmoniously in this enterprise and we were fortunate in obtaining the help of splendid board members, including a most dedicated treasurer in Jack Clingleffer, interestingly enough, one of the contacts from our work in Malaysia now living in Australia. I remained chairman of the company for some eighteen years at which point it was agreed that Bookhouse and Anzea Publishers should merge, with Phil Knight as chairman. Regretfully, due to serious ill health, it was necessary for Phil to resign and two years later I resumed the chairmanship until 1987 when Geoff Kells took office, with me, at his request, as deputy chairman. For a large part of this time Bookhouse traded well and paid a share of its profits to the two movements responsible for its commencement. In later years, due to severe competition in the trade, and the increasingly high cost of books, the company struggled to remain profitable, and to the deep regret of the whole industry, after an unhappy venture into retailing, in 1994 it had to close its doors. In the meantime, I understand the total number of Christian bookstores had come down to under three hundred.

In 1963 I became a member of the Anglican Evangelical Trust. This is a Melbourne body which manages certain trusts and legacies for the benefit of Christian work. One of its major assets was a large home in East Melbourne which was once used as a training home for deaconesses. This was to prove significant for the Church Missionary Society as it's Federal council had long-term plans for a training institute for missionaries. As Victorian chairman, I was particularly keen that this should be located in Melbourne. Since CMS tended to be so strongly Sydney oriented it seemed to me that a Federal function in Victoria would be beneficial. I had discussed this idea with Archbishop Mowll and also Marcus Loane, and had even addressed the NSW Council on the subject but at that point there seemed no likelihood of CMS agreeing to a such a college being located in Melbourne. The old uncertainties and reservations about Melbourne died hard.

It is instructive to consider the manner in which God uses small, apparently random, happenings in weaving His designs. As a member of the appointment sub-committee of the Federal body I was at the meeting in the early sixties called to nominate a new Federal secretary, effectively the Chief Executive Officer of the Society. Several names were discussed but none seemed right when one member said 'I have heard about a man in England who is well spoken of, his name is Jack Dain, does anyone know him?' No one else did and the proposal may have died right there except that I was able to say that I had spent a night at his home and found him most impressive. He was the administrative head of a large English-based Mission and widely respected. The decision was made that I should write to ask if he would consider an invitation to the post. Jack still enjoys telling this story. My letter arrived at his office and he scarcely gave it a serious thought but at the evening meal he said to his wife Edith, 'I had a letter today from Alan Kerr who showed us the slides of New Guinea'. It was said with a chuckle, simply as a matter of interest. 'Really, what did he say?' 'He wants us to go to work in Australia'. Another chuckle. 'Oh Jack, that would be nice!' Then Jack tells how they discussed the idea and before they retired to bed that night he knew that he would be accepting.

Lots of things had to happen before it all became a reality with Jack and Edith and their four daughters landing on Australian soil. We soon knew that this was God's appointment and a new day dawned for CMS Australia. His noteworthy service ended all too quickly when Archbishop Gough made him an Assistant Bishop in Sydney and his gifts were made available to the whole church. However, those six or seven years filled with constructive thought and action were very fruitful and brought the Society out of its pre-war past to a point where others could move forward to the challenges of the eighties and nineties.

Just one area in which his influence was effective was the matter of a Federal training college. Jack strongly supported such a move. When it was proposed that the proceeds of the former deaconess house could be made available by the Evangelical Trust in Melbourne this carried the day. A beautiful old home in The Avenue, Parkville was purchased, next door to Ridley College. and the Trust provided the funds for a new accommodation block to be built in the grounds, entering into an agreement with CMS for its long-term occupation.

So it came about that in 1964 St Andrews Hall opened its doors, with the Reverend Dr Francis Foulkes as its first principal. Francis was a New Zealander, a Rhodes scholar, and with his wife Marjorie served as CMS missionaries in Nigeria. Their appointment to St Andrews was Jack's initiative. I served as chairman of the college for quite a few years and therefore had the pleasure of working with this gifted man, Francis, whose scholarship, humility and gentleness left a deep impression on all who knew him. This provision for pre-service training and orientation studies, marked a big advance in the work of CMS, just one of the many benefits and reforms brought about through the advent of the Reverend Jack Dain as Federal Secretary.

It is interesting to note that amongst the first candidates to enter the College were David and Jean Penman of New Zealand, bound for Pakistan. A few years later David served as Principal of the college before returning to New Zealand to take a large parish. From there he returned to Australia to become at first a Bishop and then Archbishop of Melbourne.

I find it interesting to reflect on my early association with this wonderful society. When I became State Chairman some of the Victorian leaders warned me to beware of the NSW hierarchy as 'they always want everything their way'. Some of these men referred to were friends of mine through Scripture Union but they likewise shared with me their concerns about Victoria as being 'a little theologically unsound'. To a point these comments represent the longstanding differences in the doctrinal stance of each. However many of these fears and hesitancies were swept away as Jack's influence began to permeate. He was instrumental in reducing the size of councils and committees, cutting down meeting times, and bringing in residential Federal council meetings which enabled us all to see our main tasks with greater clarity.

In 1960 another business venture arose from my desire to move into modern, top-class furniture. On my second overseas trip I put a proposition to an American firm, Herman Miller, to be permitted to manufacture their furniture under licence in Australia. This firm was famous throughout the world for high quality design and products in office furniture and seating for commercial use such as airports, government buildings, libraries etc. In 1961, after a visit to Melbourne by Hugh DePree, the chief executive, it was agreed and they recommended that we should get in touch with Dolph Bohren an experienced tradesman, who worked for the firm in Switzerland. In 1962 Dolph and his family arrived and set to work making our first products. Early in 1963 the range was launched in Melbourne and Con Boeve from Herman Miller, USA, visited for this occasion.

In 1964 the whole operation was moved to the new factory in Thomastown. The high level of quality and prices went against the venture, as the Australian consumers and government departments seemed not yet ready to pay for this prestigious furniture, and progress was slow. Herman Miller is a remarkable firm, their designs are world famous, they have high ethical standards, some brilliant people and they were very helpful to us. It transpired that the owners of the company were Christians and the founder Mr D J DePree, I discovered on meeting with him, was world president of the Gideons. After working at this for some years we did not achieve the leadership that was necessary and we eventually received permission to sell Herman Miller to another Melbourne manufacturer, Aristoc Pty Ltd, who were well established in this market area.

1964 was a year which saw many changes in the Kerby Group. The fine new factory at Thomastown was completed at the beginning of the year and the Board met for the first time in the new offices in February. The minutes of the meeting tell us they inspected the new factory and administrative areas and expressed their pleasure at the excellent standard of the new facilities. For the first time in more than three years all of Kerby Victoria, with Herman Miller, were coming together under one roof after being in four different locations. However many new problems appeared and needed to be dealt with. Some machines were not adequate. It was difficult to get qualified factory staff at Thomastown and the level of factory management was an ongoing difficulty. Much time and effort was spent wrestling with these problems and it was not surprising that financial results for the year were disappointing. This was not helped by the fact that we then lost the CRO agency which had brought in a steady income. This was partly due to Kerby's success, as CRO's furniture became so popular, that they decided to set up their own factory in Melbourne. Although the 'Elite' brand of furniture from Sydney that we used to replace it was useful, it did not posses the style and sales appeal of the CRO range.

1965 saw a determined effort to lift the whole performance of the Kerby Group. A management conference was arranged for March, attended by twelve key men. This was held at Mt Eliza in the home where we spent our holidays. Following this the Melbourne factory began to get busier and Ern Rothschild was appointed as factory manager for Kerby, relieving Dolph Bohren who had been managing both Herman Miller and the Kerby factory for the past year. We had been gaining quite good sales in Adelaide and this led to us looking into starting a factory there. After investigating possibilities and advertising for a manager, Ron Ironside was appointed and a small factory building found and operations commenced.

*Then I said to the nobles, the officials and the rest of the people,
'The work is extensive and spread out, and we are widely separated
from each other along the wall. Wherever you hear the sound of the
trumpet, join us there. Our God will fight for us!' So we continued
the work....*

Nehemiah 4.19-21a NIV

*Now understand me well. It is provided in the essence of things,
that from any fruition of success, no matter what, shall come forth
something to make a greater struggle necessary.*

Walt Whitman

- 8 -

1965 – 1970

Increasing Tempo

Although for the past twenty years my workload had been quite heavy, 1965 seemed to mark an increase in the tempo which was to go on steadily for the next fifteen years. The factories were bigger, staff larger, sales higher and financial exposure greater and all this made the burden of management substantial. Travel increased and there were demands on my time from many different quarters. Although I was able to shed a number of smaller Christian activities and committees, new and larger ones took their place. Chairmanship of SU Australia and of ANZEA both involved a lot of consultation and travel including twice-yearly visits to Singapore. Since the advent of Jack Dain the workload on CMS Federal council and executive had increased, likewise UFM, now renamed Asia Pacific Christian Mission (APCM) was expanding rapidly.

While all of these may have seemed an unreasonable burden on top of the demands of business, I never felt it that way, chiefly because I believed that I was fulfilling my calling, and there were unexpected benefits. Often the Christian meetings acted as a kind of therapy after some of the difficulties of business. This was true in a general sense but sometimes it was quite specific. One instance comes to my mind as typical. During one of the most difficult times with the Victorian branch we had worked very hard and were hoping for better results. Late one afternoon our accountant came to me with some devastating news, the latest accounts were the worst yet. After all the effort and higher hopes, I felt absolutely crushed and sick at

ANZEA SU Leadership Conference, circa mid-1960s.

heart. Then it was time to go to the city for an APCM meeting. Len was away and I had to chair the Executive. I drove from Thomastown feeling numb, not knowing how I was going to cope. We were meeting for dinner as usual and when I entered the restaurant my colleagues were enjoying their meal, in high spirits. I was quickly caught up in the mood and we went on to have a long and fruitful meeting. Driving home late that night I was thinking over some of the events of the evening when suddenly the memory of the Kerby situation came flooding back to me. Now I saw it in a different light, plans and possibilities began to fill my mind and by the morning I was able to arrive at the office poised and ready for a renewed attack.

After serving for some twenty-five years with Campaigners for Christ it was evident to me that my role had been completed and I should retire from that movement, which had been a source of much spiritual strength and inspiration. However newer responsibilities such as the Anglican Synod and Diocesan Council together with Ridley College and various other committees made increasing demands on time and thought. There was also a growing number of social contacts with the business and Christian world. Hospitality, always a pleasure, became more constant and meant that frequently guests were staying in our home, also there were numerous functions to attend. In 1964 and 1965 I made extensive overseas trips through Asia, includ-

S.U. ANZEA office bearers, mid-1960s.
Left to right: J. Clingleffer, Treasurer; J. Robinson, Secretary; A.
Kerr; Prof.Khoo Oon Tek, Co-Chairman.

ing the Canton Fair in China, to London for SU. and Chicago for Herman Miller. The 1965 trip also included Taiwan and Japan and a lengthy journey to PNG visiting the Highlands and staying for Field Council, and added to these were the many interstate trips. For many years I had been interested in thinking and speaking about the subject of time and making the best use of this limited resource. I felt that I had learnt a lot about how we can improve our use of what is given to us. Now the necessity was laid upon me to improve my performance and really put my ideas into practice.

At the end of 1964 Howard returned from Brisbane to find a new wing had been added to the house. This consisted of two bedrooms, a bathroom and gallery, also a new carport and entrance at the side of the house. Shortly after this he started work at the Thomastown factory. In 1966 Howard celebrated his twenty-first birthday with a very pleasant occasion for family and friends in one of the function rooms at the RACV. Later that year came Russell's eighteenth birthday and it was agreed that in 1967 he should enter the new university, Latrobe, which was being built only a few miles from our home. That year saw Marcus commencing at Carey in year seven. Ada was not able to take him on the first day as she had slipped on the back lawn and broken her leg, and I was away, so Russell escorted his young brother to his new school. In 1966 we broke for one year the sequence of family holidays at Mt Eliza to travel instead to Benora Point on the Queensland border where we enjoyed time with the Knudsen family, who were at their beach home at Fingal. Prior to this holiday Russell had arranged to 'hitch hike' to north Queensland with Keith Stebbins, a friend from Carey. It was a strange feeling, one Ada did not relish, depositing the two boys on the highway out of Coolangatta and wishing them a good trip. A sign of changing times, as today we would probably not consider approving such a mode of travel. In the event the boys reached Cairns and returned safely, reporting a successful and interesting trip.

The years of 1964 and 1965 were difficult, not only for the Melbourne business but the whole of the group encountered problems. However, as the economy improved in 1966 so things took on a much brighter note for the Kerby group. The Brisbane factory made their first successful move into dining-room furniture, manufacturing tables and chairs, whereas previously they concentrated on buffets and cabinets only. Chairs are one of the most difficult items of furniture to make. The wooden members are often slim yet they must be strongly constructed as they are habitually badly treated, especially when people tilt them back and rest all their weight on the two back legs! The company's products were sound and before long they were involved in plans for extensions to the factory, setting up an excellent conveyor production line under Mort Allan's supervision.

At the same time the small factory in Adelaide was expanding rapidly, driven by Ron Ironside's enthusiastic management. During the course of the year a second factory was purchased at Magill, north of Adelaide, for the manufacture of dining room furniture. This building was alongside one of the State's most famous vineyards, a very pleasant sight as one stepped outside. By this time Adelaide sales were exceeding those of Hobart. A new company, Kerby NSW was registered and began selling furniture in Sydney from the Brisbane and Melbourne factories. At this point it was simply an agency with a sales manager.

Melbourne was also experiencing better sales but still finding it difficult to make a profit, and some senior personnel resigned.

In these circumstances I was asked by the Board to accept, for the time being, day-to-day management of Kerby Vic. Because of this I did not attend the SU International meeting that year, the only overseas journey being a visit to Singapore for the ANZEA Council. I confess that I was reluctant to miss the SU meeting, not because I thought they could not manage without me but I had a feeling that I was backing down on my principle of giving priority to my Christian commitments. Nevertheless I had to heed the Board's special plea. I can only remember two occasions when they actually articulated what I am sure they often felt, that I should give more time to the company.

I have already related how I believed that the Lord made it clear to me that my Christian ministry was to be exercised through, and alongside my business activity. During this period in the mid-sixties and again later there were particular times when this created a very real tension which I had to face. It was important to be loyal to the Board and our executives and that I should give of my best for the Kerby group. At the same time there was a strong sense of commitment to fulfilling the Christian activities which I had accepted. I rejected the idea of just attending to these when it was convenient. Each of them had only been undertaken after prayerful consideration and some had been laid aside when it seemed my task was completed.

Although some of my friends and staff colleagues urged me to curtail my Christian interests, I felt very strongly that it was right to continue trying to balance these demands of family, business and Christian work. I think the roots of this conviction lay in the belief I had, given my dubious health in early years, that God had preserved my life for a purpose and therefore my priority should be first to seek the Kingdom of God. I felt His purpose for me was to be involved in industry and yet at the same time to be channelling time, energy and finance into the affairs of the Kingdom

At all times I was most fortunate in having Ada's full support and a wise and understanding chairman and friend in Lindsay Yeo. Interestingly, I discovered that as I aimed to exercise discipline in one of these areas the others also benefitted, although I should confess that not always did I achieve the desired balance.

With hindsight, it is plain that there were times when I was in the wrong and my sense of priorities was astray.

At the end of a very busy year in 1967 I was able to note in my diary that we had seen the best achievements for a long time. The business had continued to forge ahead, results were good and prospects bright. Management and decision-making showed improvement and particularly pleasing was a major financial reconstruction which had been carried through by the Board. This had the effect of using all the group's assets to greater advantage and it released new funds for onging expansion.

A noteworthy personal experience for Ada and me was an eight-week overseas journey commenced in April 1967. This was Ada's first visit to Europe. The main objective was to attend the Centenary celebrations of the SU movement in London followed by an enlarged meeting of the International Council in Switzerland. On the way home there was an expanded ANZEA Council meeting in Kuala Lumpur, which in itself was significant. The seven years since the setting up of the regional Council had seen striking developments and we had every reason to give thanks to God and to the gifted people who under His good hand had made these things happen.

The celebrations in London included a reception at the House of Commons, a fascinating all-day tour of historic London arranged by John Laird and a crowded Centenary meeting at the recently opened Festival Hall. There was also an English SU conference at Swanick, Derbyshire. The Children's Special Service Mission was founded in the year 1867 when an embryonic children's mission was held on the beach of Llandudno in Wales by Josiah Spiers, a public servant with a heart for evangelism and for children This became an annual holiday event and led also to children's evangelistic meetings in the cities. Later came the Bible reading notes and all the activities which make up the movement known now as SU. The great strength of SU is the impressive way in which it utilizes voluntary workers, training and equipping them for witness and service. It has the highest standards and after all these years, by God's grace remains true to it's biblical foundations. Many thousands of people around the world today are engaging in Christian work of one kind or another because of the influence of this movement on their lives at some point.

After London there was a visit to Paris and then to Lausanne for the International Council and Conference where the opportunity was taken for a larger body to survey progress since 'Old Jordans'. There were adjustments to be made and deficiencies to overcome, nevertheless it was obvious to all that the most remarkable growth had occured This must have brought a sense of great thanksgiving to John Laird as he was now approaching the time which he had set for his retirement. Ada was greatly charmed with Switzerland and not without reason. A lovely farewell to this beautiful country was two days spent at the SU property above Lake Locarno before flying to Spain to meet up with Norm and Mona Knudsen in Barcelona. Norm had already been abroad for the company but this was a long service leave holiday. We spent two pleasant days together, sightseeing and even attending a bullfight, which Ada declined. Leaving Europe Ada and I flew to the US where most of the time was spent at the vast Furniture Mart at High Point, North Carolina and then in San Francisco. After two days in Honolulu we went to Auckland for a brief stay with the Deebles. Returning home I then had to speedily visit all the interstate factories and pick up all the threads of the business once again.

Shortly after this trip Ada was hospitalised at Cotham Clinic for surgery, the removal of a malignant skin cancer from her face and for the reconstruction of her right cheek under the skilled hands of Mr John Hueston. Then I had a brief Kerby conference in Queensland, one day was spent at the Brisbane factory and two at Broadbeach. These management conferences were now a regular annual fixture from which we all derived much benefit. They also served to remind our enthusiastic State executives that we were an Australian company and to preserve us from insularity of mind or spirit.

That year also saw Joe Yawson, an SU leader from Ghana, arriving to work in the Melbourne factory and receive further training. Joe was employed in the furniture trade in Accra and came to us through inquiries he made from Armin Hoppler. He stayed with us in our home for some months and then his wife Josephine also came to join him and they rented a house, eventually remaining for three years. Joe was an influence for good

Joe and Josephine Yawson, now living in Takoradi, Ghana.

and a fine Christian witness in the factory and also at St James. We were pleased to know this experience was valuable to him to the degree that when he returned to Ghana he was able to start his own company, and rename his youngest son Alan Kerr Yawson! The bonds of affection were very real and some years later we paid a visit to the Yawsons in Ghana and were welcomed with great warmth and I was widely introduced as Joe's 'father'.

When I became a member of the UFM council in 1952 most of my attention for the first few years was focussed on my task as candidate secretary. This in itself occupied a lot of time interviewing all candidates in depth, and attending to the documentation and contact with home councils. However after I had visited PNG a few times and had met with the councils in New Zealand and Sydney it became obvious that the Mission had a great need of restructuring to meet the demands of growth and the expectations of the council members. The Victorian body was also called 'The Home Council', in that it made the policies, handled the money and ran the mission.

The main work of the State councils was to recruit new candidates and gather prayer and financial support. Only the Home Council made decisions on accepting the candidates. This dated back to the mission's beginnings in Melbourne. However many of the members of this group were elderly and some extremely conservative in theology and decision making. Regretfully they also shared a distrust of most ideas which emanated from outside Melbourne. When I travelled to meet the other councils it was to find members deeply committed and highly responsible who felt most frustrated at not being able to share in the planning for the work of the mission overseas. Naturally, they disliked being told what to do by a Melbourne secretary without having the opportunity for debate.

The New Zealand council was particularly strong, including some of Auckland's leading Christian businessmen, and it was clear that it was an urgent necessity to set up a governing body comprising members of the major states and NZ. This idea was at first an anathema to the Melbourne council and even to the chairman. However after visiting the Field council it was clear that the missionaries also felt this was a pressing need. Eventually it was agreed there should be an interstate conference and this was held in March 1967 with New Zealand members also present. It was a highly successful event and in the light of good fellowship and mutual understanding many of the objections to a national council were swept away. My experience with similar situations in SU and Campaigners over a decade earlier proved helpful.

With strong support from New Zealand and NSW, the Federal council became a reality. All of this meant that from this point on I became deeply involved with the life of the mission. Leonard Buck and I worked very happily together, as we had done in Campaigners. At the beginning some of the Victorian Council members were uneasy about my Anglican connection, likewise a number of the more conservative misionaries who were also dubious of the business aura. I had to adjust to feeling that I did not really belong as I was not fully accepted, and this troubled me. One night my loyalty was tested when at the end of a prayer session one council member voiced strong criticism of the Archbishop of Sydney (Dr Howard Mowll) for taking part in a meeting of the World Council of Churches. However Len invariably gave me total support and in the light of the superb work being done by the mission, these small personal considerations had to be put aside. Once the mission councils were unified, giving us a broader constituency, this problem faded away.

As Len had me appointed Deputy Chairman this meant that

the leadership role often fell on my shoulders, as he was frequently absent on other activities. About this time we began to put forward the idea of 'Team Support' as a means of financing the work of the mission. Ron Clough, who joined the staff in the sixties was strongly in favour of this, as he had been with the Federal Council moves. Despite early opposition it was ultimately adopted as mission policy. It meant that each missionary would (in cooperation with the mission) need to raise their own support before proceeding overseas; some difficulties but many advantages.

Thinking about my now fairly heavy commitment to missions I reflected back to my friend Ralph Davis telling me that I should have a missionary interest and become a member of a mission council. My reply then had been that SU was my mission, but Ralph insisted that an overseas mission interest should be part of my life. A view I did not share at that time. Within two years I was a council member of CMS and also UFM and became increasingly committed to both of these bodies over the next thirty years. Pondering this in later years brought me to the conclusion that the most likely way to develop an enthusiasm for missions is to be able to experience something of the actual work at first-hand, which I was fortunate enough to do. If that is not possible, then meeting and hearing lots of missionaries is a good substitute. In 1967 and again a few years later I was invited to give the missionary address at the Melbourne Synod. First-hand experience of life on the mission field and of mission administration stood me in good stead on these occasions.

Howard's marriage to Andrea Buck in January 1968 was a family milestone, and a pleasant side effect was that it gave us a family link with Jane and Leonard. Howard was now able to take up the Victorian Overseas Foundation scholarship he had won a year earlier. With Andrea he travelled to North Carolina to work with the White Furniture Company at Mebane. This was an old established firm owned by a Christian family which manufactured high class dining and bedroom furniture. I had first made contact with them when I visited their plant on my journey in 1957. Howard and Ann were well received by the friendly and generous folk of the area particularly those in the church they attended. It was an experience they richly enjoyed

Howard and Andrea's wedding in January 1968. Seen here with their parents.

Russell's marriage to Joan Holdsworth in April 1970.

and they travelled quite widely before going on to Europe and England the following year.

Meanwhile Russell was well into his studies for an Arts Degree at LaTrobe University. There he met Joan Holdsworth from Mortlake whom he was later to marry. Both Russell and Joan were amongst the initial group of 450 students at LaTrobe, many of whom later became prominent in political and public life. Russell was active in the Christian group there and through him Joan also became involved. Marcus was enjoying his early years at Carey Grammar School and an improvement in his health.

The rising tide of the Kerby Group affairs was continuing and at the first Board meeting of 1968 a number of new projects were put forward. Also the audit for the previous financial year showed a satisfactory group profit. Almost all of the factories were busy and requesting new items of plant and building extensions. Preliminary figures for the first six months of the next financial year were already well ahead of budget with record sales in some factories. Even the difficult Victorian branch was doing well and earning a steady profit, which was thankfully a nice change. Early in February I visited Perth to try to find a warehouse or store for the goods now being sent from the Melbourne and Adelaide factories. My report to the Board stated that warehouse rents were high and transport cost likewise. Perth was an exciting market and my belief was that we should start manufacturing there. The Board gave qualified approval and on a visit in April, I made arrangements for the purchase of land and the building of a factory. The Board decided it would be a good strategy to find a manager within the group. After some discussion the final choice was Des Kenna, factory manager of the Hobart branch. By August Des and his family had taken up residence in Perth and on November 26th the splendid new factory on a five acre site at Maddington was opened by the Minister for Industrial Development, Mr Charles Court.

Kerby WA Pty Ltd was the first of our companies to have all its financial affairs completely independent of the groups normal bankers. This came about through what I believe was the very direct guidance of a caring God. I had found the task of financing the building difficult and it appeared that we would have to rent. As I walked along a city street in Perth after an unsuccessful interview, a large neon sign caught my eye, 'Rural & Industrial Bank of WA' and I was prompted to change my course and visit a bank I had never heard of before. One hour later I was seated in a spacious office overlooking the Swan River enjoying afternoon tea with the Chairman of that bank. He had just promised me his full support in financing, not only our building but also our plant and trading requirements. He was as good as his word, became a great friend and we were closely identified with the R&I bank for the rest of our time there. Never at any other time have I experienced such a speedy and satisfactory major financial transaction.

Des entered into his task with great enthusiasm, from the first month his production exceeded budget and the branch went on to become very successful. Looking back, it was an interesting sign of the company's growth that a project that was not even thought of in January could be completed and in production by the end of November.

My overseas trip that year to attend the SU Council in London included a visit to Kuwait to ascertain export possibilities. There was some interest, but they were close to the fine factories of Europe and it would be difficult to break in. We did in fact mount a kitchen display at a trade fair a few years later but without success. On this first trip I had a very bad chest infection and felt so weak I seriously wondered how I would get out of the place on my final day. I had over the years became fairly used to coping with these 'off' times but Kuwait is one that remains in my memory. At such times, and they were quite frequent, I have found the Scripture 'As thy days, so shall thy strength be' to be very meaningful for me. These words were part of Moses' blessing on the tribe of Asher, nevertheless I share the conviction of believers through the ages that promises such as these are the heritage of all who put their trust in God and His Word. The rendering of these words in most modern versions is 'your strength will equal your days' and I can only say that this has most often been true for me. Nevertheless it is my responsibility not to make unreasonable demands on my constitution.

With some effort and the Lord's help I did get on to the plane from Kuwait and went on to Germany to buy plant for the Perth factory and then to the US for a brief visit with Howard and Andrea at Mebane. I also made trips to PNG and Singapore, and then to Bangkok for an East Asian Christian Council as a delegate from the Australian church. The year ended on a strong note when the Tasmanian company secured their largest contract to date for units in the Strathgordon township. Mr Tom Spencer, then company secretary reported to the Board that the profit for the year ending June 30th 1968 would be the highest to date.

On the family front 1969 was a significant year. Howard continued to work with the White Furniture Co. in Mebane. Russell began working with Kerby Vic. part-time and Ada and I, accompanied by Russ and Marcus made a major world tour. This was something I had been hoping to do for a while and it seemed that the time was right. Again we were indebted to Ron Bailey for some excellent help in planning and we set off via Port Moresby in Papua New Guinea. This gave the boys at least a taste of the country I was visiting so frequently and a glimpse of missionary work. In those days no passports were necessary for Australian visitors to PNG, so when the day came for us to fly out from Moresby we got out our passports and discovered that Ada's had expired! It took some very good work on the part of our missionary friends and the Australian Commissioner to produce a new one in the few hours remaining before flying off to Hong Kong.

There the boys greatly enjoyed the sights and the shopping, especially Russell who loved the bargaining but did not always come out on top! We went on to Delhi, staying at a hotel like a palace and then to Israel. Ron had planned for us to spend a few days in the Arab quarter in Jerusalem and for our driver guide there to be an Arab Christian, who gave us some good insights. Then, when we went for a couple of days to Galilee, he had a Jewish Christian guide for us. On my previous visit with Colin we had to do a lot with non-Christian guides and it was so much better to be escorted by understanding and pragmatic believers, not to mention a car for the whole family.

We all appreciated the privilege of absorbing something of the atmosphere of this ancient land, and it certainly provides another dimension to one's reading of the Scriptures. We stayed in the Arab section of Jerusalem and with our Arab guide were able to gain some understanding of the Palestinians' plight, which has of course worsened immeasurably since those days. Like many others, we found the accretions to the various significant sites in Jerusalem disappointing and for that reason found the quiet of the hills of Galilee and the Lake brought us closer to the days of our Lord and the gospel stories. I think it may be rather different today.

In Rome we saw more ancient sites, some of them magnificently impressive. It is a city to stir the blood and quicken the imagination. We hired a car and drove for several days to Pisa and other ancient cities and then to the Riviera. From the coast we drove north through France to Locarno in Switzerland where we stayed at the SU guest house at which our International Council met. Once again it was nice that the boys were

*With the family at
Jacob's Well in Israel.*

able to meet the men with whom I was so closely associated in the wider work of SU.

We had arranged to rendezvous with Howard and Andrea at Salzburg in a certain restaurant at 8 pm on a specified date. They were travelling from the USA to Britain where Howard was going to work at another furniture factory. The timing was exact and we had a good reunion for a few days before both going off in different cars and different routes for England. The boys were always rather inclined to smile at my enthusiasm for England in general and London in particular, however after our time there I had a feeling they were well on the way to sharing it. We stayed in the heart of the West End and enjoyed a splendid time there and returned home via New York, Niagara, the Canadian Rockies and Honolulu. During the trip we noticed that Russ spent quite a deal of time reading and re-reading, it seemed, certain letters from Melbourne. It was therefore no great surprise to anyone when he and Joan announced their engagement a few weeks after our return, which was a source of much pleasure to us all. Three months later we celebrated his twenty-first birthday.

It was in 1969 that the APCM, formerly UFM, set up a separate organisation which later took the name Pasuwe Ltd. standing for Papuan Supply and Welfare. Its objectives were to provide general supplies to missionaries in isolated places; to train young nationals in business management, and by opening trade stores to make profits to be distributed to church and community causes. This was mooted in the first instance because we could see that one or two missionaries who were really dedicated to pioneer evangelism in the new Highlands areas were spending a great deal of their time in arranging supplies for these isolated locations. It seemed to us that this type of work could be better done by a person located in Port Moresby. From this, developed the idea of supplying the national people as well and then of small trade stores where local people could receive training in management. It could also be of benefit by enabling them to purchase basic needs at fair prices. In the absence of roads all transport was by air or sea and prices tended to be high. The Mission was bound by its own Constitution not to engage in trading and this led us to set up this entirely separate entity incorporated under PNG law. The concept was to draw a Board of directors from Christians in Australia, missionaries and the national church, in equal numbers.

The first Directors meeting was held at Wasua in February 1969 when I was elected chairman. George Turner, vice chairman and treasurer and Dudley Deasey, secretary. In July we interviewed Alan Pugh, a Victorian with retail experience in G J Coles & Co. Ltd for the position of manager and he was appointed at the Board meeting which was held in August. This began a pattern of two meetings in PNG each year which has continued through the whole life of the company. Alan and Judith Pugh took up their work in Port Moresby with enthusiasm and the small company grew rapidly. Although Judith had two teenage daughters and a son she managed to also work in the office and later opened the first store in Port Moresby. Once, the missionary force had to manage with a very rudimentary supply line but with the growth in imports from Hong Kong and Japan and the increasing sophistication of the market, Pasuwe was soon involved in carrying a wide range of merchandise for them. As we began to earn profits the Board was able to make grants along agreed lines to causes in the realm of education, health, community and church life. In ventures such as these I was always keen that we should use our giving to 'make things happen which would not otherwise happen'. The Board adopted this dictum as a guiding principle.

Another new responsibility which I felt it right to accept in this year was election to General Synod, the senior body of the Anglican church in Australia. This was a task which I came to enjoy very much, it's meetings ran for a week but only once in four years. Later I was made a member of the standing committee as well as the executive and the finance committees and all this did involve more time. One reason I found this enjoyable was that it meant rubbing shoulders with men and women of differing churchmanship, many of whom I came to appreciate very much and some whose closer friendship I valued greatly. Working predominantly amongst people of 'evangelical' convictions is a privilege and it is where I normally wanted to be; but it did me a lot of good to perceive other viewpoints and to understand and appreciate the differences brought about by background, training and experiences. Perhaps this is one of the reasons why I find that I am now a good deal more tolerant in some matters than in my younger days, but always providing biblical truth is held to be paramount.

I also served on the committee organising the second visit of Dr Billy Graham to Sydney and Melbourne in 1969. The effect of the Crusade in Melbourne was markedly less than the one a decade earlier. The fact that Billy was now regularly on TV was one explanation but there was also a striking difference in community attitudes to religious matters than even just ten years before. In fact, looking back now over the changes in culture during my lifetime, one realises that the sixties were the decade which saw the most dramatic shift toward what has become the post-modernity of today. Standards of behaviour, family values and much more all began to be radically affected. However in Sydney, where to their credit, the churches did a great deal of preparation, the second Crusade had a much wider impact than in Melbourne, but it was chiefly amongst church people.

Although life on the home front was always busy with my frequent absences, nevertheless Ada and I managed regular visits to the opera, ballet and various concerts. Also I still managed to see a few football matches each season. These I discovered to be the best therapy when life became very crowded. During a game of golf I found that walking down the fairway one could still have pressing issues on one's mind, but at a football match, never! That is provided Essendon were playing!

Jesus answered, 'Are there not twelve hours in the day?'
Gospel of John , 11-9 AV

We want not time, but diligence, for great performances; and we squander much of our allowance, even while we think it sparing and insufficient...
We never consider ourselves as possessed at once of time sufficient for any great design, and therefore indulge ourselves in fortuitous amusement...
We must learn to know the present value of single minutes, and endeavour to let no particle of time fall useless to the ground....
Samuel Johnson

All men complain that they haven't enough time. It's because they look at their lives from too human a point of view. There's always time to do what God wants us to do, but we must put ourselves completely into each moment that he offers us.
Michel Quoist

Because a man has a shop to mind
In time and place , since flesh must live,
Needs spirit lack all life behind,
All stray thoughts, fancies fugitive,
All loves except what trade can give?
Robert Browning, *Shop*

- 9 -

1970 – 1973

The Rising Tide

The year 1970 ushered in the major decade in my life so far as Christian and business activities were concerned. It was in these years that I had the responsibility of being chairman of the SU International Council and also chairman of the Asia Pacific Christian Mission. It was a pity that both of these major tasks came to me almost concurrently, as each demanded a lot of time and called for leadership I was not always available to give. As well as this I was also involved with a number of other organisations. At this time they included the Federal Council of CMS; Chairman of Bookhouse Australia; Chairman of the Evangelical Fellowship of the Anglican Communion (EFAC); Open House; St James, Ivanhoe, vestry; member of General Synod, also Melbourne Synod and Diocesan Council and Finance Committee; Ridley College; St Andrews Hall; Anglican Evangelical Trust; Christian Businessman's Luncheon Group and various SU Committees.

Sometimes friends would ask whether I could really keep the affairs of these various movements or societies clearly in my mind and whether I was able to properly serve them. The latter point was not for me to judge. Undoubtedly, one could always do better, but on the former, I seemed to have been given the ability to concentrate well on one thing at a time. When I was at a meeting or involved in the affairs of a particular body or business, I was able to feel that this was all that mattered at that time. Also I tried to make a habit of doing my 'homework' and thinking through issues beforehand.

Much time, thought and planning was given to each of these responsibilities. Travel was constant and during the next ten years I was to average over 100,000 miles annually, a good deal more than a million miles during the seventies. My diary also shows that I managed to read quite a considerable number of books each year throughout this time. From the working notebook I see some interesting resolutions for the new year 1970 and set them down as a matter of interest:

1: Seek to avoid emotional pressures. Relaxed approach, especially watch public commitments. Health vital.

2: A better witness to staff and more readiness to speak of my faith; also to talk more with strangers.

3: In business more creativeness. Convert insight into action.

4: Determine to better economic performance. Be more realistic in approach. Watch marginal ego projects.

5: In Christian work give better value to key things. More leadership for ANZEA, SU and APCM: Ridley may need help. Also International SU.

6: Remember overall, think well, be cautious with impulsive decisions.

I had developed a little system of making up a yearly workbook, which became like a second diary and which went everywhere with me. It was just a large bulky exercise book in which I had a section for each branch and aspect of the business, one for each committee or movement I was on and others for ideas, relevant quotations and comments from my reading, and the type of entry I have quoted above, to keep stirring myself on. Returning from a meeting or a visit to one of our companies I would record notes of decisions and unfinished business so as to be ready for next time.

Roger Putnam joined the group as the designer and to help with the overall concept of bringing into our various branches a common identity. He designed a logo which we began to use on all stationery, brochures, and advertising. About this time the company adopted the title The Kerby Group of Companies. The Kerby Group, for short, and each branch simply traded as Kerby (Qld) Pty Ltd. and so on. A nice seal was created with the letters 'KG' as the chief feature and one of these was placed on each piece of furniture produced. I worked hard at achieving a sense of unity amongst all managers and senior staff. It was for this reason we held annual conferences, when good fellowship was enjoyed, business discussed, plans laid and aspirations fired. In 1970 this conference was once again held at Booth Lodge, Kallista, when major plans for 1971 were shared. 1970 was a difficult year for most businesses and the company's branches were fighting hard to maintain sales. Because of this the directors requested me to once again forgo my usual visit to the International SU council. This was only the second time for a number of years that I had not visited Europe. However the usual brief trips to PNG and Singapore were made. I also visited Indonesia and Darwin for SU and later in the year with Ada and Marcus enjoyed a brief holiday at Hayman Island.

On the 11th April 1970 Russell and Joan were married at St James Church, Ivanhoe, at the early hour of 8.30 am. followed by a true 'wedding breakfast'. It was a relaxed and lovely occasion. One reason for the early timing was to allow them to catch a plane to reach their honeymoon destination at Fingal, near the Queensland border that day. On their return they rented a house in Ivanhoe for some time before later buying their first property, also in Ivanhoe. So the Rosanna household was reduced to three. Howard and Andrea returned home from working in the US and England. Howard commenced work with the Kerby group in the Victorian branch, and they purchased a nice home unit in Heidelberg.

In Autumn of the following year Ada and I were visiting New Zealand for the wedding of our niece Barbara Deeble and whilst there received word of the birth of our first grandson, Luke, born on the 19th March to Joan and Russell. This gave us all great joy. Another significant family event took place at this time. A deposit was paid on a block of land at 8 Rosserdale Crescent, Mt. Eliza, with the intention of building a holiday home in the future. I was battling on the health front in the early part of the year, being confined to bed for the second time within a few months with pneumonia which forced the cancellation of a few activities.

Just before the end of 1970 our Board made a significant new move by taking over a colonial furniture business by the name of Authentic Furniture Co. and during these first weeks of 1971 we were busy absorbing this into our system and introducing the new lines into all our branches. The business was built around the importation of beautifully made turned chairs from Japan which were matched with tables and buffets made in our factories. It was a most attractive range for retailers and also for contract sales to restaurants and the like and it was to bring us big business over the next few years.

April saw me setting off on a five week trip which took me to thirteen countries. This included my first visit to our new suppliers in Japan and also to the firm in California which owned the license on the designs. The factory was in a provincial town by the name of Takayama, at the foot of the mountains which were the source of the lovely oak timber used in the manufacture. This was a long journey from Tokyo and a very interesting one, as was the whole of the five weeks of travel which took me from the East to Europe, then to Ghana in West Africa for an SU meeting, finally to London and Canada. So far as I can remember, the development with Authentic was a final straw in our relationship with the Furniture Guild as they regarded importing as 'beyond the pale', and perhaps it was as well that I had left the Council a few years before it happened.

New moves were being made in Sydney which had begun chiefly as an outlet for Queensland products. A small office furniture company known as Beresford was purchased and for the first time Kerby began manufacturing in NSW, under the management of Graham McAleer. It was also our first venture since Herman Miller into the rapidly growing office furniture market. Management was the subject often under discussion at this time especially in view of Norm Knudsen's desire to retire in two or three years. Various changes were considered. David Woods, Victorian accountant, was appointed as Group accountant and began to bring about a much firmer grip on company accounts. He was shortly to succeed Tom Spencer as Group company secretary. Most branches were now busy again and functioning well except for Kerby Victoria which really had been plagued by a management weakness since the departure of Alan Johnston over a decade ago. This was a cause of much distress and embarrassment to me. I had been able to set up and guide the interstate branches successfully but could not do it on 'the home front'. We had made a number of new beginnings and had tried numerous remedies yet the same weaknesses always seemed to manifest themselves. It was indeed a spiritual and practical 'thorn in the flesh' for me.

1971 was also a year of conferences. Within the Anglican church I had been chairing a small committee which for two years was working towards a major Anglican Congress to be held in September. The inspiration for this conference came from the Reverend George Pearson, a former CMS missionary from Tanzania. He felt that the evangelical wing of the church in Australia needed to follow the example of the English movement known as the Evangelical Fellowship in the Anglican Communion (EFAC), with their 1967 Keele, UK conference. This large gathering had succeeded in bringing evangelicals, clergy and lay people, closely together and establishing them with a new profile in the British church. It had proved of immense and lasting significance marking a renewed surge of biblical churchmanship in the Church of England.

It was George Pearson's vision that something similar should take place in Australia. He virtually had me installed as Chairman, somewhat against my will at first and we gathered a small committee. Before long we were all enthused with the potential, although it took a great deal of persuasion on our part to engender a similar spirit within the wider constituency of the church. Nevertheless eventually excellent plans took shape and in the September vacation of 1971 the first National Evangelical Anglican Congress (NEAC) was held at Monash University near Melbourne, attended by over six hundred delegates drawn from all states. The chief speaker was the Reverend Michael Green from Oxford, supported by many other able men and women in an excellent program. Leadership of the congress was shared between Bishop Clive Kerle of Sydney and myself, demonstrating a nice balance between Melbourne and Sydney and clerical and lay members. Clive and I were old friends and the arrangement worked well.

The congress proved to be a memorable occasion and a milestone in the life of the Australian Anglican church. As I move about Australia it is quite usual to meet clergy who refer to it as a special happening in their experience. I believe it was at this gathering that the question of the ordination of women in the Anglican church was first seriously publicly debated in Australia. We also heard an address from a female Aboriginal writer, on issues of injustice affecting the lives of her people, which was not common at the time. Social concern in general gained a high profile. Michael Green in his studies from Acts was superb and appealed greatly to the younger clergy. We enjoyed having him with us at home for a couple of days – a lively character! Much was owed to George Pearson for his strategic thinking. His enthusiasm was unabated and he began almost immediately talking about the need for a further congress in another ten years time. This did in fact take place in 1981 also at Monash. One of the many benefits stemming from the Congress was that we now had a formally constituted committee of the Evangelical Fellowship in the Anglican Communion functioning in Australia, albeit in modest fashion.

On an altogether smaller scale I had the opportunity of planning and leading the first parish weekend away at Belgrave Heights Lodge for St James, Ivanhoe. Nothing like this had taken place in the parish before, and that brief time of fellowship and learning together quickened the spiritual pulse of many. From that time on it became an annual fixture.

The Kerby conference for this year also took on a higher profile. It was held at 'Moondah' the splendid premises of the management college at Mt Eliza, attended by a larger group than ever before and continued for five days. At this conference I stressed the necessity for unity and harmony as well as clear management objectives and the importance of spiritual aspects of life. There were excellent speakers, good discussions and the event was most valuable.

To round off the year of conferences, APCM for the first time held their Federal council meeting at 'Booth Lodge', Kallista – a very successful event. The fact that we met on Anglican ground may have caused some members of the old 'Home' Council to blanch, but most of these had now gone to their reward, to rejoice with members of the church universal. Very likely they would have relaxed and greatly enjoyed the fine fellowship and the sense of oneness in Christ which characterised these annual gatherings. There is no substitute for dining , walking and talking together in a free and companionable atmosphere, as it is this that enables people to feel relaxed with one another and enriches the business and prayer sessions.

I have found that preparation is a vital factor in running a successful conference. The homework must be carefully done, bearing in mind the main objectives it is hoped to achieve. A comfortable venue, attractive location, satisfying cuisine and a careful balance between work and leisure are all desirable factors and the agenda should so far as possible be drawn up so that there is a logical and emotional progression. Members should be able to sense the underlying purposes and aspirations in order to gain personal satisfaction from the proceedings.

In 1972 there were two major Kerby group conferences. The first of these in the early part of the year was something special, as it took place in New Zealand and was really an experiment which the Board allowed me to try. Planned for General Managers only, it took place in the context of a NZ tour for these men and their wives. This was in recognition of a record company profit the previous year. The tour took in Auckland, Christchurch, Mt Cook, and the actual conference was held at a hotel in Waireki near Rotorua, during which the ladies engaged in other planned activities. The experiment was generally judged to be highly successful, from the business and social aspects, and particularly so because the wives of our excellent managerial team were able to participate. The normal group conference was again held at 'Moondah' with an increased number in attendance. It was a great pleasure for me to have my brother Roy as a part-time member of that conference, as he had joined the staff the previous year.

Ralph Fry, formerly of Queensland and South Australia was now manager of Kerby Victoria and Howard was assistant manager in Hobart. Ron Ironside had left us in order to start in business on his own and Gerry Anconie had replaced him in SA where plans were being made to build a new factory on the outskirts of Adelaide. Two or three years later, after another very good trading result we repeated the idea of an overseas conference and travelled to Penang where we met at the Rasa Sayang Hotel after spending two days in Singapore en route. We also visited two factories which we had begun to use to supplement our stocks of Authentic lines.

On the home scene our family had been enjoying the use Mr Ovendon's flat in Rosserdale Crescent since 1959 and had become very attached to the Ranelagh beach and its surroundings.

As my load became heavier we increased our annual stay from three to four weeks. This quiet time away, with visits to Flinders to share time with Ralph and Dulce Davis at their holiday home and play golf, to read, swim and enjoy time with the family became a most welcome relief from the constant pressure and travel. At a time when so many things in our business were changing rapidly and new responsibilities were multiplying, this holiday was one feature of our family life which did not change.

At our next parish house party it was a great pleasure to have Bishop Alf Stanway as speaker and he gave us a memorable series of talks on prayer. One of these, on the text 'when you stand praying – forgive' I have always remembered. It speaks to me of the need to forgive just as often and as freely as I expect the Lord to forgive me. I have found it enormously helpful. A truth already clear to us in the Lord's prayer but perhaps dulled for me by its very familiarity. The substance of these talks is included in the very helpful little volume published by Bishop John Wilson entitled *Prayer* by A. Stanway. I first met Alf before he went to Africa and over the years we became close friends. Years before this, after his first visit to London, he had said to me as we sat in front of an open fire one winter's night 'Let me tell you some of the things I learnt from the great ones, how they manage to do so much', and he told me how he discovered the difference between delegating (which is temporary) and devolving (which is permanent) saying how it had helped him. Likewise, I found it most helpful, and it became one of the means by which I was enabled to carry a wide range of responsibilities. When, as mentioned earlier, I stayed with him at Dodoma in 1957 I was able to observe some of the beneficial results of his devolving in the diocese of Central Tanganyika, as it was then. Much later on I was to see this again in Philadelphia.

I had been helping Gerald Davis, Ralph's eldest son, working on a small committee with a church newspaper he was pioneering in Melbourne. Although edited by Gerald it was published and printed by a large commercial company. However, in 1972, through various circumstances it appeared that this paper may have to cease publication. Archbishop Frank Woods who was Primate of the Australian Church at the time, approached me to ask if I would try to raise some capital and form a company to begin publication of an Australia-wide Anglican newspaper with Gerald as managing editor. With the help of a few friends it was not long before this came to pass. The company was registered as Church Press Ltd and the paper named *Church Scene*. At first it was published fortnightly, later becoming a weekly. We were able to build up a small but strong board. Bishop Stanway was a member and strong supporter from the beginning, and it was always a cause of satisfaction to Gerald, also to me, that his father, Ralph Davis, took a great interest in the project, helping with good advice as well as capital, although he was not an Anglican. Years before, when Gerald had just left school he had expressed a strong desire to run a Christian newspaper, and Ralph had asked me to see if I could offer him any advice. This I sought to do and may have had a part in directing Gerald's footsteps at that point; in any case we have always enjoyed a close friendship. In company with many others, I still admire the magnificent job he did in establishing *Church Scene*, and his competence in managing it so ably.

I continued as chairman of this company, Church Press Ltd, for twenty years during which time the newspaper achieved an established place within the Australian church, although not without its trials and tribulations. My retirement was marked by a function at the RACV which I deeply appreciated. Archbishop Rayner was the host and each of our sons with their wives were invited guests, together with Board members and their wives. The fact that our family could be present was a factor which made it something special for me.

I was always disappointed that the Church, through its General Synod never saw it's way clear to providing any subsidy or financial support for *Church Scene*, although a few small, more far-sighted Dioceses did give some help. It seemed to me that the paper fulfilled a most important role in keeping our widely scattered National church informed about major issues, trends, and people and events within the body. I found it hard to contemplate the loss of such a vital communication link. There were times when the burden of maintaining the paper's liquidity pressed heavily on all of us. While he was alive, Alf Stanway was a source of help and strength during these times as he infused all of us with his spirit of faith and trust in God to see the enterprise through.

Eventually the Board members became used to living on a

knife edge, acknowledging our continuing dependence on the Lord's gracious provision. Gerald functioned as editor for twenty-five years, when health factors made it advisable for him to step down. Regretfully two years after this, publication ceased due to financial pressures. Very few church papers anywhere in the world operate without subsidy of some kind or another and it seemed to me that our Australian church was very short-sighted in failing to provide at least some assistance.

The new colonial furniture range now involved me in regular visits to Japan and it soon became obvious that the Japanese factories were becoming too busy to supply all of our requirements. Looking elsewhere, I found that similar timbers and expertise existed in Yugoslavia and late in 1972 I visited the charming northern city of Ljubljana and through the state-run organisation was able to find suitable sources of supply. The official appointed to look after me was a friendly middle-aged man whose first name was Boyan. From the beginning he always called me 'Mr Alan' and he was with me from early morning till late at night.

The factories began work at 6.00 am and finished at 2.00 pm, with a break in mid-morning, so our day began at crack of dawn. Around two o'clock Boyan would take me to lunch which would go on until four, we would discuss shipping schedules and orders, maybe do some sightseeing and he would then insist on taking me to dinner in the evening. Food and conversation always seemed to play a large part in my visits to this picturesque country which at that time was still under Marshal Tito.

I once found myself in Ljubljana on a Sunday and discovered no church open, but a perfect gem of an Opera House which was. It was a small scale replica of the classic European design, and the Sunday morning performance was as artistic as it was spirited and satisfying. My counsellor and guide, Boyan, became a good friend. A Catholic, he would sometimes permit himself to speak of the old days and then say in a sad, far away voice 'now, everything is changed'. If he is still living he may be regretting even greater changes.

On my eastern tour that year I also revisited China for the Canton Fair where we bought cheap plywood and hardboard, spending some time there with Alan Pugh who was buying for

Pasuwe. In China one had to deal through a multitude of lesser officials and departments, entirely different to the Yugoslavian system. This impersonal attitude was borne out in their correspondence with all their letters simply 'signed' by rubber stamp with a red star. No doubt things have changed for the better now that they are supplying such a huge volume of merchandise around the world.

When Marcus was in his final year at university and had in mind beginning work with the company in 1973, it was decided that it was a good opportunity for Ada and Marcus to join me on one of these visits to Japan and Taiwan. This was done and they enjoyed some interesting sightseeing as well as the business contacts. We were not to know at the time that twenty years later Marcus would be making many more visits to Taiwan in the course of his own business. Our Japanese suppliers in Takayama were always helpful and courteous and we experienced typical provincial Japanese hospitality, including changing our shoes for slippers at the front door of the hotel; rolling out our bedding on the floor at night and taking Japanese style baths, which go for depth rather than length, not to mention the fine meals. While I was occupied with business Marcus and Ada enjoyed shopping and meeting the people. Setting off on this journey caused Ada some anxiety as we were in the midst of major additions to the Rosanna home with a large section of our roof consisting of tarpaulins. However on return we found all was well and were able to get on with the furnishing of the upstairs section which gave our home a very pleasing new dimension.

The year 1972 saw two further grandsons added to the family. A second son, David, for Russ and Joan, and a first, Fraser, for Howard and Andrea. We began to wonder if there would be any grand-daughters for us.

On the Kerby front numerous building projects were on the board for 1973. A beautiful new factory was in progress in Adelaide due to be opened mid-year. This was built for us by the South Australian Housing Trust and in quality and finish it exceeded any other of the Group properties. Additional land had been purchased in WA and major extensions were to be built, more than doubling the original size of the plant. Under Des Kenna's enterprising management the Perth branch had prospered, being involved in a great deal of contract work for the large mining towns being built in the north of the state.

In Queensland the factory had already grown to use almost all of its land but we planned to build new offices and an upstairs showroom. Likewise in Melbourne a large showroom was built across the front of the factory which included some additional office space and a pleasant new office for the managing director.

In the early part of this year our Board gave serious consideration to proposals from Overseas Corporation Ltd that they should take over our company, merging it with their metal furniture company, Namco. This had some attraction for us as it would provide finance for growth and other benefits. In the event their offers were not considered adequate and were declined by the Board.

The development of the business over the past few years had been extensive and much of this was due to the excellent Board of Directors which gave wise experienced leadership. Mr Lindsay Yeo's influence had grown and he was now serving on the boards of many companies including some of Australia's largest, but still gave unstintingly of his time and enthusiasm. Mr F H (Pos) Rollason and Mr Charles Sandland had wide business experience on which to draw, and together with Norm Knudsen, Ada and me, we made a very happy team. Board meetings were always 'special occasions' and our lunches together afterwards were enjoyable times.

This year was the heaviest yet for me so far as travel was concerned with two overseas trips to Europe, beside almost weekly interstate visits to branches, plus PNG. In April I left for Hong Kong and Taipei where there was an ANZEA SU conference and then went on to Rome meeting up with WA manager, Des Kenna. We spent considerable time together in Germany at the Cologne Fair, then visiting numerous factories and machinery merchants looking at new machines for the extended WA factory. Flying into Rome, I gave Des a little 'run down' on the local currency and warned him that I had found Italian vendors rather expert at the art of 'short changing'. We obtained some money at the airport and set off for our hotel by taxi. As Des handled our bags, I paid the driver. It was dark at the entrance and on moving into the lobby I was mortified to find that I had given the driver a fifty thousand lira note and not the twenty for which he had 'carefully' counted out the change! It was interesting to me that Des on his first experience outside Australia, was captivated by Rome and the old buildings of Germany also. We then went on to Holland and England and returned via the USA.

It was there that Des had another good laugh at my expense. We were late for an appointment in Kentucky and I was tempted by the large powerful car to move a little too fast. We were flagged down by an officer with a cowboy hat and with pistols protruding from very prominent holsters. After admitting my fault and showing my licence, I tried to cut short the lecture about the feelings that the State of Kentucky had for speeding visitors. I said 'Well officer, we have to meet some people in town and would like to move on'. There was a change of tone, 'the position is, sir, that you are under arrest and you will drive ahead of me to the sheriff's office to be dealt with by the law'. Standing to one side and scarcely controlling his mirth, Des was busy photographing the scene. At the sheriff's office we were eventually allowed to leave by 'posting bail' of $100.

Now listen, you who say, 'Today or tomorrow we will go to this or that city, spend a year there, carry on business and make money'. Why, you do not even know what will happen tomorrow. What is your life?... Instead, you ought to say, 'If it is the Lord's will, we will live and do this or that'.
Epistle of James, Chapter 4-13,14   NIV

There are several kinds of power. One is coercive power, used principally to destroy. Not much that endures can be built with it. Even presumably autocratic institutions are learning that the value of coercive power is inverse to its use. Leadership by persuasion and example is the way to build-everywhere.
Robert Greenleaf
in *Servant Leadership*

- 10 -

1973 – 1977

A Major Move

In September 1973 the opportunity arose for the Kerby group to take over PGH Furniture, one of the largest furniture factories in Sydney and manufacturers of the widely known 'National' wardrobe range. We had at one point been the Victorian agents for these wardrobes until PGH set up their own Victorian factory, in similar fashion to CRO. The acquisition would cost $1 million plus picking up all the ongoing costs for the biggest project yet faced by the group. This gave the Board much food for thought and it was deferred for a time. Shortly after the management conference in September, it was felt we should seriously consider the possibility of making this move if financial arrangements could be put in place, which Lindsay Yeo undertook to investigate.

It was arranged for Norm Knudsen and Ada to join me on a thorough inspection of the plant. Norm returned to Brisbane that evening before we had time to discuss the proposal, and Ada and I flew home to Melbourne. Early the following morning we received the devastating news that Norm had died at 4.30 am. from a severe heart attack. With great sorrow I set out the following day for the funeral, to convey our sympathy to Mona, Nancy and Chris and to make short-term management arrangements. Norm was buried on Saturday, September 29th just one week after sharing so much of his wisdom and experience with his colleagues at the conference.

Norm and I had worked together for almost thirty years and had shared many ups and downs. We had seen the tiny Rocklea business grow into one of Queensland's largest and most respected furniture companies. His abilities had a great deal to do with this growth. He was quiet and thoughtful, a strategic thinker and possessed good technical gifts. Norm grew remarkably into the practice of management and was a valued Board member. He was always learning from his experiences and from those of others. The work of building up Kerby Queensland was an adventure which he and I shared together and remains one of the fondest memories of my business career. After a good deal of discussion the Board accepted my recommendation that Norm's son Chris, already a staff member, should be appointed General Manager in an acting capacity, and he was later confirmed in this position. Despite his youth Chris fulfilled the high expectations and justified the confidence shown in him.

A few weeks after Norm's passing our Board made the decision to take over PGH. Largely due to Lindsay's guidance the finance was available, although in 1973 the sum of $1 million loomed far larger than it does today. There was a complication which proved unhelpful. Within the extensive building was a door-making plant, operating separately. This would have added to the price and we did not want it as it was outside our area of interest. It was agreed that PGH should continue to run this activity but after one year this was clearly not practical and we were persuaded to add it to our responsibilities, but it was always an added burden.

A family milestone for Ada and me was our 30th wedding anniversary on November 2nd, celebrated with a dinner at the Hotel Australia together with members of the family and a small number of friends. The following morning I left for Los Angeles to meet with the Authentic people there and after that to London for a meeting of the SU International Executive. This meeting was held at the home of Derek and Ruth Warren tucked away in the country a few miles from Berkhamsted. I had not been in England in November before and always remember from that meeting, a day when the heavy frost lay on the ground all day long, despite the sun shining. From its inception in 1960 the International Council had been a small but closely-knit body. Beginning with only six members it had grown somewhat and was shortly to become much larger, although the executive was small. The gifts of Derek Warren as first chairman, and prior to his illness and death, Armin Hoppler as secretary in addition to

John Laird's wise and helpful influence had given this body a very sound beginning. I had found it a pleasure as well as a great privilege to become chairman in 1972. The work of SU was expanding rapidly around the world and it was an exciting time as well as a large responsibility for the council. In order to keep in touch with as many branches as possible the council met in a different country each year and usually on a different continent. The friendships formed during these years until my retirement in the eighties were greatly treasured and many of them continue. Ada and I have been greatly enriched through our fellowship in SU, a small reminder that 'the Lord is no man's debtor', because we have received far more than we have given.

The year 1973 had been very strenuous and I found myself wondering how I would cope in 1974 with the growth in all areas and now the huge new responsibility in Sydney. This was one of the problems I was pondering when the year opened. I broke a long-standing resolution never to interfere with summer holidays by leaving Mt Eliza almost two weeks early in order to take a health course at the Hope Foundation at Wallacia, NSW. There I spent a relaxing time of diet, exercise and about five or six of these days on a liquid diet, at the same time reading through the six books of Samuel, Kings and Chronicles. This treatment was helpful and I returned feeling fine and at my lowest weight for years. It gave me a good start although 1974 continued to be a battle with bouts of chest infections. Travel and the sharp changes of climate, especially in tropical countries, with air conditioned hotels and buildings, was a real menace for me, as was cigarette smoke on planes and in airport lounges. Thankfully this has now been largely banished from public places.

During the previous year, family links with the company had changed somewhat. Russell had left to enter the teaching profession which was in line with his calling and intentions. In Tasmania, Howard resigned his position with the company to enter business on his own account. Howard and Andrea had purchased a home at Kingston Beach near Hobart and were active members of the local and very lively Anglican church. He commenced with the design and manufacture of kitchens under the name of Kerwood Pty Ltd. However, our youngest son, Marcus, joined the company that year and settled into an administrative role at Kerby Victoria, having obtained his Bachelor of Commerce degree from Melbourne University.

Preparation for the actual takeover of the PGH factory proved to be a large task, with many details covering legal, financial, staff and public relations amongst other things needing attention. The company was well known and firmly established in the Sydney trade and the move put Kerby very much in the spotlight in the state where we were least known. It gave a great deal more work to our small group management team in head office Victoria, especially David Woods, who was now group accountant and company secretary.

One day in April my brother-in-law Reg Deeble was in Sydney and it was an interesting experience to escort him through the factory where twenty-five years before he had worked and been responsible for the installation and maintenance of the kiln drying and pressing operations. I could remember a day when he had given me a tour of inspection.

Shortly after this Jean Deeble was to join Ada and me in a major overseas journey which commenced early in June and lasted for two months. Meeting up with Jean in Honolulu we went to Los Angeles and then to Lima, Peru, after that to Sao Paulo, Brazil for a Latin America SU conference which was most stimulating. There we found a directness and informality in relationships and in spiritual dealings which was a timely rebuke to me personally. Following this we travelled through Venezuela to Barbados for a few days delightful holiday. A beautiful beach but I had a bad chest infection and could not swim! We then travelled on to London where I attended the SU International council, while Ada and Jean took a coach tour to Edinburgh and the Lakes District. We then went to Switzerland for the event which was the main focus of this journey. This was the first Lausanne Congress on Evangelism where three thousand delegates from countries all over the world met for more than a week. I was an Australian delegate and Ada and Jean attended as guests.

The Lausanne movement owes a great deal to Dr Billy Graham who was one of the major figures in bringing it into being. Its main emphasis is world evangelism and in stirring God's people to action in proclaiming the gospel to unreached peoples. Its influence on the growth of mission in the final quarter

A section of the Lausanne Congress, 1974.

of the twentieth century has been incalculable. At this history-making congress we heard many wonderful addresses but none more memorable for me than that given by the aged writer and world figure Malcolm Muggeridge, who had only recently embraced the Christian faith after almost a life-time spent in denying it. He was a masterly orator and this was an occasion which lives in many memories. After further sightseeing in Switzerland we went on to Venice and Rome before returning home. On this, as in all my travels, I kept in close touch with activities at the office and with the various managers.

The development and management of the Kerby group was now becoming quite complex with branches in every state. Each one was making its own distinctive products, although the 'Authentic' colonial range had introduced a product which was marketed by all branches. To some extent it was wise to leave things this way as each branch had found its market niche, and also the different branches possessed varying skills in manufacturing and promotion. But there were benefits in buying and marketing to be achieved through a greater degree of uniformity. At our conference this year we discussed these issues and there was a general desire to pool resources and learn from each other. It was proposed to do this by setting up committees and specialised groups. This came about in the following year, although we had already been holding managers' conferences as well as the annual general conferences. It was interesting that statistics showed that 47% of the Group's production was now in bedroom furniture, 41% dining room, 9% contract and only 3% kitchen production.

One experience which I enjoyed at this point was accepting an invitation to address Marquand and Company's annual conference at Cowes. Marquand's were the accounting firm of which Mr Yeo was the senior partner. I was asked to speak to more than eighty accountants and auditors on 'Making the best use of time'. Apparently what I had to say was well received as over the next few years I encountered frequent references to it. It was a topic to which I had given a great deal of thought, both from the practical or business point of view and also from the aspect of Christian stewardship. The Lord has taught me that we can achieve far more than most of us think possible by careful planning and wise use of time, which is our greatest treasure. It is one resource with which all of us, from the greatest to the least, are equally endowed, twenty-four hours daily. Good stewardship of this inestimable gift yields great rewards.

The year 1975 opened on a sad note when on the 5th January I received a phone call at Mt Eliza from Roy to say that Mother had died after a long period of illness, at the age of eighty-four. Three days later the funeral service was held at St Andrews, Rosanna. I was very conscious of my failure to devote sufficient time and attention to my mother in her closing years, especially since she had moved from 5 Hillside Road into a nursing home. As so often in life, regret comes too late to be effective. Roy and I were greatly blessed in having parents who were so devoted and caring for us. In particular, my bad health caused them much concern and they spared nothing in seeking my welfare. They also did all they could to help with my early business efforts. Mother especially, was helpful with sound suggestions and Dad provided much practical help. Mother's faith was strong, a source of comfort in her later years when she knew so much illness. We were indeed fortunate to have a stable and happy home life, surely the greatest bequest any parents can make to their children.

After being at Mt Eliza that summer we began to make plans for building on our land at 8 Rosserdale Crescent. We appointed architects and briefed them on our requirements. They later presented us with plans for a cedar home of an unusual and interesting split-level design which seemed to fit the purpose and location well. We called tenders by early June hoping the house would be ready for the following Christmas holiday period. Shortly after that we had the pleasure of Os and Jenny Guinness staying with us at Rosanna and over the course of the next few years we saw them quite often. We enjoyed this delightful couple, Jenny, a former *Vogue* model and Os, one of the most stimulating Christian thinkers and writers of his generation. I am grateful for the way in which he has helped to shape or reshape my Christian thinking in a number of areas.

Just prior to the end of the financial year I was entertained at lunch in Sydney by the senior partner of our auditors there, Bill Bowie-Wilson. He took me to the Australian Club, a most appealing venue and I was surprised and nevertheless pleased when a few days later, Bill suggested that he should put forward my name for membership. It did not take long for me to agree, but it took much longer to find the required nine members personally known to me to support the nomination. However these were found and in about three years time I was admitted to membership. This club proved to be an ideal location for Sydney visits and in recent years Ada and I have greatly valued the convenience of having a 'home' in this beautiful city from which we enjoy the views of the Botanic Gardens and the harbour. I am now a life member of the Royal Automobile Club of Victoria, and this together with the Australian Club opens a host of doors to clubs overseas, especially in London. I have always enjoyed the world of clubs and would much prefer to stay in one where possible rather than a modern hotel. Long established clubs in particular have an atmosphere and air of history which I find more homelike and most congenial.

After eight years of unstinting service, Alan Pugh, responsible for Pasuwe's splendid early growth, had returned to Australia because of family commitments and for a time worked with the Kerby group as import manager. He had succeeded in achieving our initial aims in PNG and more. In his place the Board appointed Alan Judkins, an engineer with good management experience. He and his wife Ailsa were New Zealanders who had been living for some years in Australia and together they gave splendid leadership to the growing company, building on the work of the first decade. The Judkins took the company through the period of its most rapid expansion to a point where it had about thirty-five stores and three supermarkets throughout the Western and Southern Highland provinces. Ailsa played a large part in this as she helped to develop our clothing trade. They also identified closely with their parish church, St Martins, in Boroko, and Alan was widely used in Anglican affairs.

During the ten years in which they worked with the Company the Judkin's suffered two armed hold ups in their home besides a number of assaults and break-ins numbering about eighteen in all. One or two of these incidents would have been sufficient to send many people back home but they continued to quietly and diligently attend to the work, showing at all times the utmost composure. An inspiring example to many others during very difficult times. Pasuwe's growth had been remarkable but at this point had reached its zenith. With the opening up of roads into the highlands and better transport everywhere, trade stores proliferated. Pasuwe still supplied our missionaries requirements but in numerous locations they were able to buy locally. Also we were encountering problems in the areas of security and of staff integrity. However each year saw very substantial grants made to causes in the various categories named in our objectives.

At Kerby I was involved in what seemed to be a never-ending round of visits to branches, plus the oversight of the various committees that had come into existence, no less than five. I did not attend all of these but I liked to keep closely in touch. All of this was in addition to the manager's meetings and the general conference. Fitting these in with overseas commitments, apart from ensuring my attendance at major events such as general Synod, CMS and APCM council meetings was like a jigsaw puzzle, however with careful planning it usually worked out. I communicated regularly with all key staff members. Every Monday a bulletin went out from head office giving sales results for the previous week from the branches with a few personal comments from myself. Record achievements and good figures were always especially noted.

Laying the foundation stone for the SU Camp building, Changi, Singapore.

The 1975 International SU council was held in France enabling me to fit in visits to the Cologne Fair as well as Zurich and London. In addition there were the usual two visits to Singapore, Hong Kong and Port Moresby. On one of these visits I had the pleasure of opening the new SU campsite at Kota Kinabalu in Sabah, one of the fruits of regional development under the ANZEA Council. A few years earlier I had performed a similar function in Singapore at a nice camp site on the beach near Changi. Regretfully it was not many years before the land was reclaimed for part of the new airport and I found myself in a Jumbo jet rolling down a runway over our camp site. After a great deal of effort on the part of the Singapore SU Council the authorities made available a new site on Sentosa Island.

The Kerby conference that year was once again at Booth Lodge, the lovely Anglican property at Kallista in the Dandenong ranges. Each year we had as a guest speaker someone prominent in the business world, usually a Christian friend who would also speak about the relationship between faith and business in their experience. On this occasion our guest speaker was Mr Bruce Redpath, then Managing Director of Mayne Nickless Ltd. He gave a most inspiring address conveying excellent business advice and also giving a clear account of the application of his Christian faith to the world of trade and industry. As well as having guest speakers, it was my practice to open all these major gatherings with some personal spiritual reflections and a brief prayer. Although we were about to launch into intensive discussion on commercial matters, it was always my hope that some at least would apprehend that we 'do not live by bread alone'.

At the end of that year we celebrated Marcus' 21st birthday with parties at home and the following night at a restaurant, a reminder for us of the passage of the years. Then Christmas found us for the last time at 45 Rosserdale Crescent. We had hoped to be in our new holiday house but it was not yet completed. During this holiday Marcus left us for an overseas journey which included three months in Switzerland at L'Abri, a Christian training establishment presided over by Dr Francis Schaeffer. Ada and I were to meet him in Greece later in the year.

During those holidays there was to be a change in the leadership at St Andrews CMS training college which was to have far reaching effects in the life of Melbourne Diocese. I went up to greet David and Jean Penman and family returning from the Middle East for David to take up his new post as principal. I had been chairman of the college committee since its inception in 1964 and remembered David and Jean as resident trainees from NZ during that first year. Since then they had been in Pakistan and the Middle East including some turbulent times in Beirut. Through all these years Dr Francis Foulkes had been the loved and respected warden. He had established a sound tradition which has served this institution well. Under David Penman it was to continue its excellent training program, preparing missionary candidates for the reality of service in many different countries. It had long been a vision of CMS to have this type of training and after eleven years we were able to verify the fact that we now had fewer first term missionaries returning home because of personal problems, and a more effective missionary force withal. David Penman was soon to make an impact on the college and well beyond.

During this same summer the Reverend Dr John Stott came to Melbourne to speak at the CMS conference at Belgrave Heights, where he delivered a series of memorable studies on 2 Corinthians. More than twenty years later one still hears references to those talks. I remember Dr Peter Adam saying recently that it was there that he glimpsed just how powerful such exposition of the Scriptures could be, and many of us are also richer for his insights shared in those days. It was a pleasure to have John as our guest at home for two or three days, during which we took him to the Healesville Sanctuary where our woeful illiteracy in the matter of Australian bird life was exposed by this master ornithologist.

In February Mr John Hueston removed a skin cancer from Ada's hand, replacing it with a skin graft from the arm. It renewed our sense of gratitude, too, for his skilful work in virtually giving her a wonderful new cheek some years before. After that came an exciting holiday weekend in March when we moved into our just completed holiday house at 8 Rosserdale Crescent, Mt Eliza. This became the first of many weekends happily spent in this quiet relaxing atmosphere.

In the month of March the Kerby Board met in Sydney to enable its members to observe the manufacturing operations in the newly acquired Sydney factory. This was followed by discussions which Lindsay and I had with a sharebroker regarding plans for the Kerby group to be floated as a public company. In the same month we received a proposal from Mr Howard Silvers that we should take over his wholesale furniture hardware business. This company was a major national importer, holding agencies from many overseas manufacturers, especially of German furniture accessories and hardware. Well known and respected by the trade throughout Australia, Howard Silvers and Company had branches in all states and was administered from a very crowded head office in Sydney. This proposition was still under consideration when Ada and I departed at the end of April for Singapore where there were more ANZEA SU meetings.

From Singapore we flew to Athens, meeting up with Marcus who had completed his time at L'Abri, and enjoyed with him a brief cruise to the Greek islands. The three of us then travelled to Ljubljana in Yugoslavia where we were looked after by my friend Boyan Gruntar. Our various suppliers were all State enterprises and at the end of our visit we were entertained handsomely in Belgrade by trade officials. After a brief time in Zurich, and Copenhagen we went on to London. Leaving Marcus there, Ada and I went on to Africa where we visited our longstanding friends Wellesley and Barbara Hannah at Moshi in Tanzania, and we all drove off on a safari to Ngorongoro game reserve. Driving into the lodge our African driver stopped on the narrow road, confronted by a large elephant. He said it could get angry with us and turn the car over. After a little while it slowly moved off but then pursued the car as we quietly moved on. Wellesley suggested to me that we should take a walk in the dusk before dinner, and seemed surprised at my lack of enthusiasm!

In the morning we woke to a beautiful sight. The lodge was built on the rim of a huge volcanic crater some miles across. The floor of the crater was veiled in mist, only the circling rim, touched by the rising sun, was visible, then the mist gradually rose giving a spectacular 'birds eye' view of the wildlife below. Then it was an unforgettable experience to drive almost 1500 feet down onto the crater floor in a Land Rover with open roof and view close up lions, rhinos, hippos, giraffes, hyenas, thousands of impala, zebras, and wildebeest.

Later we went to Johannesburg, our first experience of South Africa. The SU people were very kind and helpful, particularly one couple who wanted to come to work in Australia and needed a sponsor. They were overjoyed to meet us and eventually came to Sydney with our assistance. As they were working in the schools of the black township of Soweto they were able to take us into a home and to drive us through the area which otherwise we would not have been permitted to enter. This was only two or three weeks before the first serious student riots. Although we had been aware of the hardship caused by apartheid our brief visit nevertheless brought home to us in a very stark fashion something of the terrible injustices prevailing in that country. A few personal experiences left an indelible imprint on our minds and it was not really an enjoyable visit, although it was full of interest, giving us much food for thought. From Johannesburg we flew to Perth and enjoyed a couple of days with our friends John and Moyra Prince, although a lot of my time was spent with Des at the factory.

Marcus arrived home three weeks after us, having greatly enjoyed his experiences and especially his time at L'Abri, which included being one of the cast in the filming of Dr Schaffer's series *How then shall we live ?* A meeting of the Kerby Board on June 22nd made the final decision to proceed with the purchase of the Howard Silvers company. We were therefore immediately involved in arrangements for stocktaking at their warehouses in each state in preparation for the takeover.

On June 24th I attended a meeting in Canberra with David Claydon, Spencer Colliver and others to formally set up a Christian National Study Centre, later to be named 'Zadok'. This possibility had been under discussion for some time and now a committee was formed with myself as chairman, Spencer as Deputy Chairman and David as Secretary. Our objectives were to bring into being a National body which would seek to relate and apply Christian principles to public life, particularly in the realm of economics, science, politics and family. To this end we would appoint a Director who would reside in Canberra and develop a program of seminars, meetings and conferences and also publish papers drawing attention to a biblical view of these issues. Before long we had gathered together quite a distinguished group willing to act as board members and had agreed on a program of half-yearly board meetings in the national capital which was to be the chief center of our activity. The Reverend Dr David Milliken who was at the time living in the US was invited to take up the post of Director, he accepted and duly took up the role in Canberra.

Former missionary schoolteacher Bob Callaghan had now been appointed as the first full-time Director of the Asia Pacific Christian Mission. Leonard Buck had been acting honorarily as Director in a part-time capacity but his time was increasingly taken up with extending the ministry of the Christian Leaders Training College at Banz in the Central Highlands of PNG. He had been deeply involved in this valuable work since its establishment and APCM now needed the undivided attention of one man. Bob's appointment was widely welcomed and he proved himself to be a vigorous leader and made many good moves which advanced the ministry and influence of the Mission. I very much enjoyed working with him, admiring his alert forward-thinking outlook and spiritual vitality. In November 1976 Len officially retired from the APCM and we said farewell and thankyou to him at a splendid function which also marked the 40th anniversary of Jane and Len's marriage.

APCM had its beginnings in Australia in the 1930s as an autonomous branch of the Unevangelised Fields Mission, alongside the English and North American branches. Sometimes workers from those branches served on our fields, under our administration. We had good contacts and relationships with the British Council and exchanged visits but felt we needed to work more closely with our US friends. They were established in Irian Jaya quite close to our area and we should all benefit from cooperation. It was eventually agreed that the US Council Chairman and Director would visit us for discussions and these were carefully planned over a long time. Bob and I would represent our council and so that we would be undisturbed a meeting room was booked at a city hotel.

At the outset of the first day of meeting, our visitors put certain questions to us about the doctrinal stance of our Mission on the question of pre-millenialism. We answered frankly that as in the matter of the mode of baptism, our members and missionaries held differing views which were mutually respected and we worked happily together. They told us that as we did not share their views, making them mandatory for membership, they could no longer work with us. After a brief discussion it was obvious that our attitude of liberty of conscience in what we believed were minor issues was unacceptable, and the meeting was abandoned there and then. Furthermore, they said that their fellowship in working with us in Irian Jaya was at an end.

This demonstrated to us in a graphic manner the rigidity of certain groups in the US with regard to peripheral areas of doctrine. In probably 95 percent of our beliefs we were at one, certainly on all major tenets of the faith, but there was no flexibility or tolerance with regard to any divergence from their views. I remembered that some years prior to this I had paid a visit to their HQ home in the States and that their director, learning that I was an Anglican, had told me I should leave and find a 'Bible believing church'! This came after we had enjoyed an evening and morning of warm-hearted discussion and fellowship. It was somewhat the same on this occasion. Ada and I had already invited our visitors with their wives to have dinner at our home on the final evening and in the event this came about and we had a very pleasant time together.

It was about this time that Ada and I were confronted with a far deeper problem of differing beliefs and much closer to home. This began with the strong desire of Russell and Joan to seek to discover a deeper level of leadership and Christian community. They, with a number of friends were attending meetings on Sunday evenings in the city which they found helpful to this end. In the course of time two or three of the leaders of these gatherings went to Canada where they were attracted to a certain type of teaching emphasising the case for spiritual 'fathering' informing such communities. On return these leaders announced to the assembled group that they felt it should become itself a church, which in order to be strong and pure would not associate with other churches or movements. So that to continue as members of the fellowship they would need to leave their present churches, they would also be expected to give lifelong loyalty and commitment to the leadership of this group.

Over the next few days the choice had to be made as to where their loyalties lay and if they were to continue with the group, with the result that some left but far more remained and pledged themselves to accept this leadership, with Russ and Joan among them. They saw it as a means of strengthening their discipleship; but as the implications began to clarify Ada and I were greatly distressed. There were many issues but two alone made it unacceptable to us. The pledged commitment, first to a man instead of directly to Christ; which meant in time that they tended to accept his pronouncements as God's will for them. Then the exclusivity, which of course was divisive and totally opposed to NT teaching on the church as the body of Christ and 'the communion of saints'. It brought separation from fellowship in movements and churches, in some cases separation from families. A kind of iron curtain came down between us in all areas of the Spirit. We were fortunate that the bonds of natural affection between us were strong and also that Russ and Joan obviously wanted them to remain that way A few times in the early days we sought to discuss some of their viewpoints from our understanding of Scripture but these were always strained and difficult talks and eventually we avoided them. After some time Russell was asked to become a pastor in the church and to move to Brisbane where they had a small congregation. This they did around 1977, with their three boys, Luke, David and Ben, the youngest, who was born in 1975. We were pleased on the one hand to see them enter full-time Christian ministry, yet there was a deep uneasiness about the character of the body to which they had committed themselves.

After retiring from their distinguished service in Tanzania our friends Bishop Alfred and Marjory Stanway had taken up residence at Ridley College, Alfred holding the post of Vice-Principal to Dr Leon Morris. It was a very happy arrangement and after four years the benefit of their experience was evident throughout the college. Suddenly they announced, to our disappointment, that they had been invited to consider a call to move to Pittsburgh in the USA to set up an evangelical seminary within the Episcopal Church.

The magnitude of this task at their stage of life rather took our breath away, but they were sure of God's call, and leaving their home city they went in full confidence of His guidance. Toward the end of 1976 there was opportunity for me to observe their progress. I visited furniture fairs in Italy and Switzerland and then went to Toronto to chair the SU International Council meeting. This gave me the long-awaited experience of seeing North America in the Fall. The rich and mellow colours showering from the hand of the Creator in such abundance came fully up to my long-held expectations. Better still, this journey also enabled me to see the Stanways at work in their new environment and this likewise was deeply satisfying. Early days yet but it was clear that they had won the hearts and the loyalties of a dedicated group and that by prayer and faith a new college was being soundly established. In the days ahead it was to grow into a most significant institution, bearing a strong witness for biblical truth and providing sound training for ministry within the Episcopal church.

A visit to Tari and Samberigi in PNG plus trips to all the branches rounded off what had been a record year of travel and made the summer holidays at Mt Eliza especially welcome, particularly as we were now in our exciting new home at No. 8. Russ and Joan with their family were down from Brisbane and came to spend a week with us. Howard and Andreas' family was a similar size, Ondine and Andrew having been added to our growing list of grandchildren over the last two or three years. Other visitors were Nigel Sylvester from London, International Director of SU, with whom I was now working closely,

I spent many happy hours in the mission field leader's home at Tari, PNG. Here it is attended by a few friendly locals, men of the Huli tribe.

and Dieter Hass from Germany, a consultant in furniture manufacture.

The Kerby group brought Dieter out to visit all our factories and make a report on what should be done to bring the machine shops to maximum efficiency. His advice was very helpful, but because of the enormous gap between the latest European technology and the situation in some of our factories we could not afford to install all the plant and handling equipment which he recommended. We had some excellent machines especially in Perth, Brisbane and Sydney but in many cases they were not effectively linked together or conveyorised as in modern overseas plants. This was one of our constant difficulties in having seven different factories, where the quantities to be processed did not justify great capital expense on conveyors, or very sophisticated high-production equipment.

Quite often we were tempted to feel we could do better with one large and efficient factory, manufacturing for the whole company. Against this was the very heavy cost of transport of completed furniture, in addition to some obvious facts of management, because we had grown as individual branches. Also the local markets varied tremendously from one State to another. Other major manufacturers used to say that they envied our localised set up. Another weakness with our group was the wide diversity of products which to some extent was forced upon us because of the small population as compared to Europe or USA. As an example, Kerby Tasmania was probably the largest manufacturer in the State, but in order to achieve the sales it needed it was forced to make a wide range of products. Not in any of the factories visited overseas did I ever see one with such variety.

We were seeking to overcome this problem of diversity in our large Sydney factory. It was already well-equipped, but we purchased a considerable amount of new plant to set up what was becoming known as a 'flat panel line'. This was particularly well adapted for wardrobes and wall cupboards and any cabinet furniture, but it was difficult at that time to generate adequate sales volume. It would operate perhaps only a few hours each week thereby losing a lot of it's potential value. It was the emergence overseas of high-cost mass production machines, often computer controlled, in addition to the high labour costs in our country which was to pose intractable problems for many Australian manufacturers. For instance, in Sydney we had the technical capacity to produce the colonial style chairs our Group was selling so freely but the finished cost would have so far exceeded the imported product that it was ridiculous even to contemplate it. Coming events were only just beginning to cast their menacing shadows.

When I entered the furniture industry in the late forties, there were in Melbourne a number of large and prosperous factories, usually owned by family companies or individuals. These supplied the major part of all furniture sold in the retail stores, small manufacturers made up the rest. Almost the only imported products available were in the designer departments of big emporiums or in decorator shops. The picture was the same in each state and continued into the early seventies, when the rise of large automated factories in Europe and then East Asia brought about a gradual revolution in our country. It coincided with the steep increase in the cost of labour, and importantly, with the reductions in the prohibitively high import duty in those years. These labour costs affected not only the work done in our factories, but the cost of materials used by us. I can remember the sinking feeling I experienced when researching the cost of veneered chipboard in various countries, to discover even American factories paid only half the price we did for this basic resource. All of this led to the inexorable growth of imports and one by one these industry 'giants' of my early days faded and folded until today they have virtually all vanished. Had I been able to see this trend to imports more clearly in 1973 we would not have taken over the large five-acre Sydney factory of PGH, which we did hoping it would give us the ability to perform at a 'world' level.

This same year brought with it Mort Allan's retirement from the position of production manager in Queensland. The group owed a great deal to Mort, his able planning of the factory production was one of the reasons for Brisbane's high profitability. It was an operation which, for its size, did compare favourably with some overseas. Mort's son, Greg, began to take over his father's role very effectively.

The Howard Silvers company, although profitable was not well organised and there were many complaints from customers. It was necessary to find a new location so we moved to a larger building at Silverwater. Not only did we lose Howard Silvers as manager but the chief accountant retired shortly afterwards and we missed their experience. A new manager was appointed and eventually the company functioned very well. However during 1977 it comprised a considerable extra burden for me and David Woods. Howard Silvers was a very knowledgable man in the hardware industry. In the first year he accompanied me to what was known as the Interzum at Cologne. This was the annual international display of furniture hardware where I met with many of our principals, appreciating the insights and advice I received, as well as enjoying Howard's company and experience.

Or again, if the trumpet call is not clear, who will prepare for battle?

1 Corinthians 14, verse 8. NRSV

Then he (the King) said, 'who shall begin the battle?' He (the prophet) answered, 'You'.

1 Kings 20, verse 14. NRSV

The chairman is not simply the presider over meetings, but must also serve and lead the trustees (Council or Board members) as a group and act as their major contact with the active inside leadership.
Chairmen stand apart from administration, but they are inside. They must be well informed, and, as servant leaders of the boards, they must be influential. But they must also stand outside with some objectivity that allows them to watch and evaluate. There is a subtle paradox in their role – they are both inside and outside.

Robert Greenleaf

- 11 -

1977 – 1978

Chairing and Sharing

The Anglican church in Melbourne, through its Synod brought in a rule limiting the tenure of its ministers in any one parish to ten years. If a parish wished to retain its incumbent for a longer period it had to make special application to the diocese and receive approval. This was rather revolutionary at the time as the average period spent in one parish was much longer. The new rule was judged to be beneficial to both clergy and parishes, and generally speaking I think that is the case. Now the time tends to be even shorter. It so happened that the vicar at St James, Ivanhoe, Reverend Jack Shilton completed his ten years at that point and received a call to another parish. As a result the Reverend Howard Dillon from Sydney was inducted as the new vicar in 1979. He proved an excellent choice and later, after serving in another parish he became Archdeacon of Melbourne and senior adviser to the archbishop of the day. Shortly after he commenced at Ivanhoe it was agreed the church buildings should undergo major renovations, particularly the interior which had been virtually untouched for over fifty years. The vestry appointed an appeal committee and requested me to take the leadership with the objective of raising $80,000. Our Kerby design consultant, Sue Carr, made a big contribution to the planning and colour co-ordination. When the work was eventually done the interior of the church was transformed. Other work on the halls and grounds brought the total to $100,000 which was eventually contributed by the loyal parishioners. Shortly after Howard's induction the Reverend Robert

Dann was installed as the new Archbishop of Melbourne, following the retirement of Frank Woods.

A major event on the family front was the marriage of Marcus to Barbara Kirwan on June 13th 1977. This took place in St Stephens Church, Darebin, close to Barbara's home and was a delightful occasion. It was also a source of deep satisfaction to us and to Andy and Thelma Kirwan as we all knew how well suited Barb and Marcus were to each other. Each of our sons married quite young, like their parents, and we constantly give thanks to God for their wives and the lovely families He has given them.

Marcus and Barbara Kirwan at their marriage in June 1977.

The National Study Centre in Canberra was making progress. The Reverend David Milliken of Melbourne, who had been living in America, had taken up his duties during the year. He proposed it should be known as the Zadok Institute, a name which soon became well known in religious circles. David was an impressive figure, something of a radical but nevertheless strongly biblical. He was an excellent speaker and the Zadok board had reason to be pleased with the way the movement was opening up. Regular seminars were being held and thought-provoking papers published. Board members were drawn from Melbourne, Sydney, Adelaide and Canberra which meant that meetings were not easy to arrange. Because it was a national movement and aimed to influence national life it was agreed that the centre should continue to be located in Canberra and the meetings held there. The pattern was established of quarterly board meetings on Friday evenings, sometimes including Saturday mornings. Later, David Milliken was to be followed by the Reverend Dr Peter Marshall, another excellent appointment. Peter contributed particularly well in the process of enhancing the unity of the Board and building up a team of volunteer helpers. As it happened I was the only member of the board without a university degree or doctorate but we worked together very happily and maybe the touch of commercial experience was helpful. We travelled from different points of the compass for the meetings and at first did not know each other well, also we were breaking new ground. All this called for a special effort on my part to achieve that sense of unity and ease with each other which is so desirable. To do its best, a council first has to find its 'soul' and this process often takes quite some time.

There are some fundamentals to be observed in chairing meetings. I have found that first it is necessary to feel ones way towards the level of formality or otherwise which is appropriate for the particular board, council or committee. Orderliness is important, people like to feel that things are properly organised. They need to know not only what they are about to discuss but why. Agendas which are thoughtfully drawn up contribute to this and I always like to confer with the secretary or person doing this, to ensure a logical flow of discussion, also making sure everything is included.

As chairman, I regard it as a matter of prime importance that the outcome of the meeting is the advancement of the aims or purposes to which we are committed. Good agenda planning helps greatly to this end. At least from time-to-time one needs to introduce the note of aspiration which should stir members to thinking new and perhaps loftier thoughts. Above all the chair person must make it a matter of vital concern that the group should come together in a spirit of harmony, enabling it to work well together, and to enjoy the doing of it. In the case of larger bodies where the board or council has heavy responsibilities one seeks to cultivate a sense of trusteeship. Where the work is of a Christian nature I have come to see the importance of a brief reading from the Bible, accompanied by a very few carefully selected words and prayer, at the commencement of a meeting. Frequently, God speaks to us at such a time.

At the beginning of 1978 I wanted to make a determined effort to deal with some of the complexities which had arisen in the past year. In the business these centred around the Melbourne factory, hardly a new problem, but Adelaide had also run into heavy weather in its endeavours to replicate Brisbane's successful dining room production line. The re-organisation of Howard Silvers in the new premises was not going smoothly and in fact functioned poorly until the following year under a different manager. How often bad situations come about because of the wrong man in charge and how radically they can change when the right one appears. The accounting section was grappling with computer installations and David Woods was feeling the pressure. I was also conscious of the need for excellence of leadership in my two major Christian responsibilities at that time, SU International and APCM.

It did not help that when the year opened I was under something of a cloud due to illness, a chest infection deteriorated into pneumonia. bringing three visits to the doctor during January and with X-rays and visits to a specialist in February. However when the business year opened I was able to get to work but in rather subdued fashion. Undoubtedly the complications of the group program were making the task of management difficult and my lack of energy did not help. During this year Howard was encountering serious problems in his business in Hobart and this was made worse by a large bad debt incurred by a dishonest customer who ended up in goal. The upshot of all this was that Howard closed down his company and took other employment. It was a difficult situation as he had worked hard and put so much of himself into it. I felt keenly for him and for Andrea.

This year I was travelling to Sydney almost every week as this was by far our biggest operation and also the head office of Howard Silvers. By Easter my health had improved but the break at Mt Eliza was welcome. At the end of April Ada and I departed for a meeting of the International SU council in Nigeria. We travelled by way of Amsterdam to Kano, which we remember as the hottest place we have experienced. Flying in, it was like a picture of Bible days, hundreds of square mud-coloured flat-roofed houses and buildings. Fortunately, for the meeting we went to Miango, a cooler place in the hills, where we met at the Sudan United Mission guesthouse. We had a splendid meeting with a memorable series of Bible studies from the book of Malachi given by a young Nigerian, Emmanuel Oladipo, who, as I write, is now the SU International secretary. The building in which we gathered had an iron roof and during a violent tropical rain-storm we had to adjourn our deliberations as it was impossible to hear each other's voices.

From Africa we went to Berganstock, near Lucerne, in the Swiss mountains where we were joined by our friends Ralph and Dulcie Davis for five days. Such times were scarce now with our busier lives, however as usual we had a relaxed and happy time together. Ralph was then Chairman of Mayne Nick-less Ltd, a company which was now spread around the globe and employing many, many thousands. From Berganstock we travelled by car to the town of Weihl in Germany where Ralph had to attend to some business and we had to go on to Hanover. Before parting we had the joy of attending a service with the Sisters of Mary at their Community home in Darmstadt. They

Ralph and Dulcie Davis with Jane and Len Buck, Ada and Alan at the Davis's holiday home at Flinders.

kindly invited us to lunch and escorted us around the attractive property, all built by their own hands. They are a remarkable community; we delighted in their tranquil spirituality and it was an inspiration to meet them. Each of us received a blessing from God during that visit.

From Hanover we flew to Heathrow. I had been keen to visit England, but for no special reason. Ada said, 'Well if we do, lets go straight to the country and keep away from London'. So we hired a car and went direct to the town of Broadway in the Cotswolds. We stayed for a few days at a very old hotel, the 'Lygon Arms'. From there we did trips every day to the charming surrounding villages. One day we enjoyed lunch with Os and Jenny Guinness at a pub outside Oxford and went on to Derek and Ruth Warren for dinner. It was a most satisfying and productive week.

I have found that breaks like this stimulate my thinking and planning faculties. A great deal of my best planning has been done away from home or office and I always had my yearly work book with me in which I made copious notes and lists of things to do. Leaving Broadway we flew to Hong Kong for an ANZEA conference. This was a large gathering of SU people from all over East Asia and was followed by two days of AN-ZEA council meetings. Our dear friend Professor Khoo Oon Teik was co-chairman with me and we shared the leadership of these gatherings, after which Ada and I flew to Penang for three days, then home. Two days later, being the Queens Birthday weekend the whole family joined us for dinner at 8 Rosserdale Crescent, Mt Eliza.

Shortly after our return there was a general managers conference to set budgets for the new financial year. In August Ada travelled with me to Sydney, then to Russell and Joan's in Brisbane for three days where she stayed while I was in New Guinea for Pasuwe. We then spent a couple of days together at Surfers Paradise. It was always good to be with them despite the considerable areas which were, so to speak, 'out of bounds'. The full Kerby conference was again held at Kallista. We were now endeavouring to work in divisions, the two major groups being dining and bedroom, but with joint sessions on matters of general concern.

The wisdom of the prudent is to give thought to their ways....
Proverbs 14 8a NIV

*If any of you falls short in wisdom, he should ask God for it and it
will be given him, for God is a generous giver who neither refuses
or reproaches anyone.*
James 1.5   NEB

*Urwick argued that the only way to deal with muddle and confu-
sion was to begin by drawing up a plan setting out the ideal
structure, and then to fit the personalities into the structure. He
maintained that it was a mistake to begin with the personalities
and then try to make the structure fit in with them, or to try to do
without structure altogether... thus gradually drifting into an
unworkable organisation... He emphasised that the recognition of
the need for an ordered structure is of great importance because it
can make or mar peoples' lives. The Romans in their love of order
had a word for all this. It is in the form of a Latin rhyming couplet
which can be translated:*

> *No high quality avails*
> *Where the rule of order fails.*

Urwick, Elements of Administration, quoted by
John Laird

*We cannot live for ourselves alone. Our lives are connected by a
thousand invisible threads and along these sympathetic fibres, our
actions run as causes and return to us as results.*

Herman Melville, the author of Moby Dick

- 12 -

1978 – 1979

Surprise Development

On August 4th I had an interview which was to eventually change the course of our lives quite dramatically. I received a call from Mr Malcolm Rich who owned a bedding business known as Permarest. They had factories in four States and had been quite profitable. However Mr Rich was well known as one of Sydney's largest punters and had lost enormous sums of money in gambling on racehorses so that his business was at the point of bankruptcy. Some way or other he discovered that Rank Industries, the TV manufacturers, which was part of the world-wide Rank organisation was anxious to move into furniture and white goods. Mr Rich had tried to interest Rank in buying his business but was told they were looking for cabinet furniture. He knew of Kerby and had the idea that if he could interest us in selling to Rank they would take his business as well. He asked if I would be willing to meet with the chairman of Rank to discuss this. I went with Malcolm Rich (in one of his two Rolls Royce cars!) to meet with Keith Russett who appeared mildly inter-ested, but more so in Kerby than Permarest. He said that he would be in touch after further consideration. On September 11, five weeks later, he rang me and said he was very interested in Kerby and would like to meet with me. An appointment was made for the 26th. In the meantime I consulted with Lindsay Yeo who was happy for me to gather all the information I could but of course to make no commitments whatever.

As arranged, we met for dinner at the American Club and discussed our respective companies. Keith was very positive

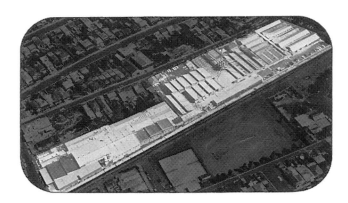

The Kerby factories:
Top: Kerby (N.S.W.) Pty Ltd
Centre: Kerby (Q'ld) Pty Ltd
Bottom: Kerby (Vic.) Pty Ltd

The Kerby factories:
Top: Kerby (W.A.) Pty Ltd
Centre: Kerby (S.A.) Pty Ltd
Bottom: Kerby (Tas.) Pty Ltd

about making a move towards Kerby. However he would only want to do this if he could buy the Permarest company and incorporate it into our factories. During the course of this discussion, I told him about my Christian interests and something of my philosophy of life and work.

The next move was for Keith Russett to meet with Lindsay Yeo and me at the Kerby office in Melbourne when according to my diary for October 10th, 'Proposals were made and agreed in principle. We said we would need to discuss them with our Board and Keith likewise with the English board of Rank. There were also complications with Permarest to be sorted out'. It was two months before we heard from them again and this gave our Board ample time for consideration of all aspects of the proposition, also for Ada and I to think about the personal issues.

My immediate feelings were that I hated the idea of giving up what had been built up over forty-five years. The proposals were that Rank would take a 51% interest and that we should continue to manage the business under Rank's overall direction. I naturally wondered how this would work out from the point of view of my Christian convictions. At our second meeting I had again made mention of the time I spent in Christian work. Against these personal reactions stood at least three hard facts. (1) The business as it stood needed additional capital if it was to move forward, and the move for a public 'float' did not seem feasible at this juncture. (2) Since acquiring the large Sydney factory plus Howard Silvers we had been overburdened with administration and no longer had the control we formerly enjoyed. (3) I was in my sixty-first year and there was no obvious successor ready to help or take over my role. All of this seemed to indicate that perhaps the Lord was pointing the way to a new future.

Nothing happened until early December when I met with the English managing director and a week or two later with the English chairman of Rank. The Kerby board met on December 8 and made the final decisions in response to Rank's proposals and the step was agreed. The main elements of the agreement were that Rank was to take 51% of the Kerby shareholdings with an option of a complete takeover at the end of two years. To achieve this 51% Rank would purchase all of our minor shareholdings outright and then as many of the Kerr and Yeo holdings as needed to make up that figure. The price proposed for the shares we considered to be fair. Of course, for our family much would depend on their value in two years time, when they were to assume total ownership. Permarest was to be purchased outright and Kerby would have the responsibility of restoring it to profitability. I was to have a contract to be Managing Director of Rank Kerby, our new name, for five years.

Later that month Ada and I met with the Rank directors at a dinner at the Union Club in Sydney. The whole plan was to move forward immediately in the new year. So 1978 closed on a rather momentous note with many of us facing a very different future. We shared some feelings of relief and excitement mixed with apprehension and a little sadness. In the last week before Christmas I visited all the branches to attend their Christmas functions as usual and to give them the news in detail. The final business day of the year closed with a dinner for Marcus' birthday together with Barbara and her parents.

The eventful happenings of the past two months gave a special significance to the summer holiday which followed. There was a sense of challenge and excitement as well as uncertainty. I had never worked 'under' anyone except for my time in the army, and what it would be like at the age of sixty-one made me wonder. Something of the task ahead was forecast by the fact that during the first few days of January I had to break into the holidays to make two trips to Sydney. Both of these were brought about by the need to absorb the Permarest bedding business and by problems associated with it.

Shall we accept good from God, and not trouble?
                                        Job 2. 10b NIV

*For I sought the Lord's help and he answered; and he freed me from
all my fears.*
                                        Psalm 34. 4 APBA

Far in the future
Lieth a fear,
Like a long, low mist of grey,
Gathering to fall in dreary rain,
Thus doth thy heart within thee complain;
And even now thou art afraid, for round thy dwelling
The flying winds are ever telling
Of the fear that lieth grey,
Like a gloom of brooding mist upon the way.
    But the Lord is always kind,
    Be not blind,
    Be not blind
    To the shining of His face,
    To the comforts of His grace
    Hath He ever failed thee yet?
    Never, never; wherefore fret?
Fret not thyself, nor let
Thy heart be troubled,
Neither let it be afraid.

                                        Amy Carmichael

- 13 -

1980

Storm Clouds Gather

With the takeover by Rank, four members of the Kerby board had to resign. These were Ada and Howard Kerr, Charles Sandland and 'Pos' Rollason who had each served diligently and well. Lindsay Yeo and I became members of the Rank Kerby board and were joined by Keith Russett, who became Chairman, Peter van de Velde and John Clarke. At their first meeting, held on February 2, it was decided that the Kerby factories in each State should absorb the Permarest firm into their premises, with the exception of Brisbane where space did not permit. Unfortunately all of the best people had already departed Permarest, rendering this a very difficult undertaking and upsetting the balance of the Kerby plants. Seeking to breathe life into what was virtually a defunct company was time-consuming and in some respects fruitless because the type of wire mattress they manufactured was becoming obsolete. The decision to take up Permarest, which had made me uneasy, cast a shadow which was somewhat ominous.

A second sign of problems ahead emerged one evening later in February, when I was to meet Keith for dinner to discuss important matters affecting Rank Kerby. He arrived late, as he had just been discussing a possible takeover of the GEC small appliances business, a move which would double the size of the Rank operation in Australia. He appeared so taken up with this prospect that he spoke of little else and Kerby affairs scarcely received any attention. Another portent.

When this move came about shortly afterwards it placed a

The new Board of Directors of Rank Kerby Pty Ltd.
From left: K. Russett, J Clark, AT Kerr, P Van de Velde,LJ Yeo.
At the Thomastown office.

very heavy load on the Rank administration which was not well equipped to deal with it. The former accountant who was inept and apparently a problem to Keith was moved sideways to become General Manager of Rank Kerby under me, to my dismay. Another Rank man was put in as manufacturing manager, responsible for planning production for all six branches, from Sydney. I had always followed a policy of making our branch managers rulers in their own domain, but with a good family feeling and maximum cooperation. Now there was a system of centralised control which caused growing confusion and resentment amongst Kerby managers. I had urged otherwise but to no avail as Keith had the concept of seven uniform factories centrally governed. So the year did not get off to a good start and the integration of Permarest and Kerby was slower than expected, especially in Sydney and Melbourne.

However, there were some good aspects and David Woods, Kerby Company Secretary, certainly appreciated having ample funds to meet requirements. Regretfully while all these changes were taking effect profitability fell and only a couple of branches were showing good figures. There was pressure to produce new lines and the development of these was slow and subject to too many opinions.

Life was going on much as usual on the home front. No. 51 Grandview Grove was still the centre of a good deal of activity, meetings and entertaining and the holiday home a welcome weekend retreat. Keith Russett had asked me if I would consider a move to Sydney to be closer to the centre of things but I declined. For one thing, I now had only a five-year contract. I preferred to travel up to Sydney weekly and still spend some time in my office at Thomastown, besides travelling to other branches. This had been pretty much my pattern for the past few years. My diary for 1978 showed forty visits to Sydney alone, virtually once a week excepting holidays and overseas travel. Now I was doing the same but spending most of each week in Sydney, it made me grateful for my membership of the Australian Club, which was like a home away from home.

In February Ada travelled to Sydney for a Renewal Conference held at the University of NSW . During the seventies Ada received much spiritual help and blessing, as did many others, through various ministries associated with the charismatic groups in the churches. For many Christians and some churches this movement of the Spirit brought a fresh touch from God with lasting blessing and joy. The following month we were visited by Jean Deeble and the two sisters went off to Tasmania, driving around the island sightseeing, besides calling on Howard and Andrea and children. At the same time I chaired a meeting which farewelled David and Jean Penman from St Andrews Hall. They had accepted an invitation to take up the incumbency of their former parish at Palmerston North in New Zealand. We were very sad to see them depart as they had contributed so much to the wider church as well as St Andrews during their stay in Melbourne.

In May Ada and I travelled with a number of Kerby executives to Germany for the Hanover Fair and also for the Interzum, the international furniture hardware fair held at Cologne. Following that we went to Zurich and met up with my brother Roy, his wife Muriel and son Mark They were enjoying a long awaited overseas trip and were to be our guests for a few days in Europe. From Zurich we travelled to Paris which we all enjoyed before going to London. A visit Ada remembers, because on an after dinner stroll past Buckingham Palace she received a nice wave from the Queen who was returning home from a function. The SU International Council met, and also held a conference, in Scotland at 'Carberry Tower' a lovely historic home at Musselburgh just outside Edinburgh. It was an excellent gathering and we appreciated the very long twilight when we could walk in the gardens after our meetings. We returned via the US and the Furniture Mart at High Point in North Carolina.

Regretfully the year was not going well for Rank Kerby and losses were being incurred. The intrusion of Permarest and its losses now showed up in Kerby results and it was not palatable. There were endless discussions, plan after plan, but somehow too many people were trying to do too many things and the desired changes did not come about rapidly enough. We could detect some encouraging signs but progress seemed all too slow and the Board was certainly not happy. I was finding it quite frustrating as my habitual style of management and control was not acceptable and I was probably not good at adapting and coming to terms with the new situation.

This was the background to the Mt Eliza summer holiday as 1980 dawned, a year that was to prove eventful for the Kerr family. While on holiday we enjoyed many visits to and from the Davis family at Flinders and the McCutcheon family at Hastings. A very happy occasion was a dinner party at the McCutcheon's with the Davis's, Ian and Beth Milne and Bruce and Honour Lumsden.

After a few days back at the Melbourne and Sydney offices Ada and I flew to Auckland to visit the Airest factory with the proprietor Cec Renwick. While there we enjoyed a weekend with Reg and Jean Deeble at Matapouri where we had much fun together in the surf and in long walks on the lovely beaches. After visiting another factory I returned to Sydney and Brisbane and Ada remained for a few more days with Jean.

In March we enjoyed a first Australian visit from two of our English friends, Derek and Ruth Warren. Derek, a lawyer with outstanding gifts of leadership, was founding chairman of the International Council of SU, and we had developed a firm friendship. After time at Rosanna we all participated in an SU Easter conference at Canberra which was a fine occasion. A few days after this I went to PNG for a quick meeting, then back to Sydney for the Furniture Mart arriving home in time to take Ada for a birthday dinner with Marcus and Barbara and her parents. Marcus was now General Manager of the Victorian branch of the company.

During this time heavier clouds were gathering over the

whole of the Rank organisation including the Rank Kerby division. The takeover of the General Electric appliance company had proved a major operation and Rank's organisation seemed unequal to the strain. They had also bought out one or two refrigerator manufacturers which were not going well. There was a lot of self-seeking amongst some of the executives and it seemed to me that the direction of the total enterprise faltered. This applied to Rank Kerby as well and some of our branch managers were leaving or wanted to leave. All of this meant that morale was low and many of the planned new designs and products seemed to be interminably delayed. In June Rank made the appointment of a General Manager to serve under Keith Russett. A man with a high reputation by the name of John Peile was the choice, at a very high salary. Shortly after he commenced he suggested to me that Rank Kerby should appoint someone to work under me, as the former accountant had been fired after a few months and not replaced. I agreed and was invited to interview an acquaintance of John Piele's by the name of Gary Reidy, a relatively young Brisbane barrister with business experience. With some reservations I felt that he could be a suitable person, but I realised that in any case John Peile and Keith Russett were planning to invite him. For Gary it would be a big step to leave his legal practice and to move back into the business world.

In mid-June Ada and I made a brief visit to Thailand to attend the second Lausanne Congress at Pattaya and whilst there received two important messages. One from Melbourne announcing the arrival of Marcus and Barbara's first son, Justin. The second from Peter Van de Velde in Sydney advised that Gary Reidy had accepted the position as General Manager of Rank Kerby.

On return it was made clear to me that Rank planned for Gary Reidy to fill the post of Chief Executive and it was suggested that I would become Chairman of Rank Kerby and play a lesser role in day-to-day affairs. This was set down in a lengthy memorandum by John Piele. I was to maintain contact with the branches and with Howard Silvers and overseas suppliers and would work less hours for a reduced salary. I would be provided with offices in Sydney and Melbourne, have secretarial help, car etc. I sought to insist that I should also have a voice in company policies whilst still a substantial shareholder. At that point Rank had acquired less than half of Lindsay's and my shareholdings.

Gary commenced work in Sydney on July 14 and relations seemed cordial. However after about three weeks he asked me one day why I was in Sydney and what I was doing. He was quite blunt and made it clear he did not wish to see me there as he was now in charge. I referred to the brief I had been given by John and also said that I was still a major shareholder and until my shares were purchased I had a right to watch company direction. These were not easy days for anyone in Kerby, which was already confused by major changes in management and policies, and now had further uncertainty brought about by new management decisions. Despite real abilities, Gary appeared impulsive and he had the disadvantage of not knowing the timber or furniture trades or markets. I was also confused as to how I could make any useful contribution and was coming to terms with a major change in my life. Further discussions with Rank indicated that the idea of being Rank Kerby Chairman was not a serious one and that I was really to see out my three-and-a-half remaining years of the contract as a consultant. An overseas trip focusing on Germany was already planned and I enlarged this at my own expense to include some time in the US, London and Tokyo.

On return I submitted my report on the German discussions which related chiefly to new agencies for Howard Silvers. A day or two later David Woods, Company Secretary, alerted me to the fact that no salary had been paid into my account since my departure. Enquiries from John Peile elicited the fact that this was an instruction from Keith Russett, who would not see me nor enter into any discussion. John told me that all of my arrangement with Rank was to be regarded as cancelled despite the existence of a firm contract. I was not to visit any of the plants or offices and the whole relationship was at an end. The matter of the shares would be dealt with by Rank in their own time. This was eventually negotiated with Lindsay Yeo and myself. We were offered only a tenth of the figure they had paid for the original shares. If we did not accept that, the substantial non-interest bearing loans which were still in the company would not be paid out. So we emerged at the end with very much less than we had once anticipated.

Over the previous two months I had been seeking to come to terms with the fact that my leadership of the enterprise which I had built up over forty-five years was at an end. However I had thought there would still be a relationship and interest in people and products, besides an income, at least for the next three or four years. Now I knew there would be none of that and my feelings were in disarray.

During this time there had been an interesting development on another level – the home front. Just prior to my departure overseas, on September 30th, Ada had noticed on a visit to Mt Eliza that a very desirable home at 37 Rosserdale Crescent was being put up for auction. I was most interested, although we only knew the house from the outside, so together we visited it on October 8th and again on the 11th and felt strongly that we should bid for it at the sale on October 18th. It has always been our habit to try and seek God's direction in issues great and small and the thought of a move from Rosanna was for us a major decision. By the date of the sale I would be away, however Marcus was willing to do the bidding and feeling it was right I duly briefed him on limits. Leaving for Germany I scarcely knew whether or not to hope that this fine home with its charming garden might become ours. Until Ada happened to see that 'For Sale' sign just two weeks earlier we had not entertained a single thought about leaving Rosanna. We did not know whether the Lord wanted us in Rosanna or Mt Eliza, and were happy to leave the issue in His hands. Nevertheless, when a phone call came from Marcus to me at the RAC in London to say that the home had been purchased, I felt a sense of elation as it seemed a gateway was opening to a new stage in our lives.

There had been another bidder at the sale but in a remarkable way Marcus had succeeded. We discovered quite some time later that the other bidder had been prepared to go to a lot higher price, whereas our limit had been reached. Somehow or other, because Marcus did not bid until the end and because of his youthful appearance the other man thought it was an auctioneers ploy, so refrained from making another bid thinking he could negotiate later. Apparently he was most upset not to secure the property. Ada had received a number of indications that the proposed move was the direct result of God's hand in our affairs and I shared her feeling on hearing these details, together with some of the Scriptures which had been impressed upon her.

It was November 14th before I arrived back in Australia and there was a family dinner party at Mt Eliza and general rejoicing over the new home, just three doors from our old holiday site on the cliff. Soon after that came the news from Rank referred to above. I felt the sudden termination of my employment by Rank very keenly and particularly the nature of it. There was no opportunity to say any farewells or even to speak to staff members with whom I had worked over the years and in many cases whom I had trained for their positions. I rang two or three of the managers but the conversations were uneasy and totally changed in tone from a few weeks earlier. I was left wondering what construction was being placed on my forced departure, and what was being said by Rank.

With the coming of Christmas and the holiday season, with many guests coming and going and preparations for the sale of No 8 to consider there was plenty to occupy my mind for the immediate future. Two or three years previously we had arranged a holiday for the eight adult members of our family when we spent a few days at the RACV country club at Healesville. A second 'get together' had been planned for early January and the four families set off for a chalet at Thredbo where we spent four summer days in the Alps. There were two infants in the party; Justin, who had arrived in June and Tom, Russ and Joan's fourth son, born a month later and they were the center of much attention. Needless to say, we all enjoyed a very pleasant time together. Shortly afterwards Ada and I travelled to 'Gilbulla' at Menangle NSW for an APCM Family Conference followed by discussions with Sydney friends about a new property project. After that it was back to Melbourne for the CMS summer conference and then to prepare for the sale of our still fairly new holiday home. At 2 pm on January 30th we took possession of No. 37 from the owners and at 3 pm the next day we had a lively auction which resulted in a good sale of No. 8. Thoughts now began to turn to what alterations would be made to the new home, because nice as it was, Ada and I could both see possibilities in some areas for really practical improvement.

The work of detailed planning was given to the architects who had built No. 8, with confidence that they would produce

Two glimpses of our new home at Mt Eliza.

the desired result. It was a very hot summer with a number of days over forty degrees and Ada felt the burden of having three gardens to water (with restrictions in force) and care for. Because of this most weekends were spent at Mt Eliza. We attended our final St James parish house party at Anglesea in March, shortly after welcoming David Powys, with Penny, as curate. Later in the year the parish entertained us at a very pleasurable farewell evening, when there were many reminiscences of our thirty-three years of happy fellowship. Soon after this we received a suitably inscribed album of delightful photographs.

After I returned from a visit to PNG, on April 11th our home at 51 Grandview Grove, which Ina and I had built in 1940 and which had been the family home for Ada and I since November 1943, was auctioned. It was a gracious house which had been extended and modernised four times in all, and with a fine garden, tennis court and wide views of the distant mountains. Facing due east, we had seen many a colourful and dramatic sunrise from its wide windows. Because of many indications, we felt certain that the hand of God was over these various moves and we had no doubts as to what we were doing. Nonetheless I felt the Rosanna sale sharply. Taken with the loss of Kerby, it seemed to be too much of a tearing-up of the roots of over forty years – almost all of my adult life. However this nostalgia did not persist for long.

The Rank issue was on my mind at this point because correspondence with them regarding the breach-of-contract had proved fruitless and I had moved to take legal action, despite Ada's urging not to adopt this course. The responses had all been negative. Now barristers had been briefed and were preparing to go to court in a matter of days when Russell, who was in Melbourne, called at breakfast time one morning to urge me not to pursue this matter any further. He said to me 'why are you doing this?' I replied that there were three reasons. First, I felt a strong sense of injustice, a contract had been broken and my rights disregarded. Second, my reputation was at stake, or so I felt. Third, quite a considerable amount of financial and other benefits were involved. Russ pressed the fact that as a Christian I should not be anxious about 'rights'. So far as money was concerned God had always looked after me financially and I should not allow that to trouble me. I concurred up to a point but made it clear that the biggest concern was my reputation. 'What are people thinking about me?' was my worry. 'What are all the staff saying' was the question which burdened me and I laboured that aspect quite forcefully to Russell. He said, 'Jesus made himself of no reputation and you should not be concerned about yours'. We broke off the conversation at that point, with me promising to give some thought and prayer to what had been said. I thanked him for coming and appreciated the fact that he had been prepared to speak so frankly.

At first my inclination was to leave things as they stood, but over the ensuing weekend God spoke to me through Russell's words and I decided to abandon the legal action. I was going to Sydney on the Monday morning and rang through a message to instruct the lawyers accordingly. At the airport a little later I received a message from Marcus that Peter van de Velde, a Rank Director, was anxious to see me. I met with him next day. Not knowing what I had just done, he wanted to tell me that Keith Russett had gone to the UK instructing him to resolve the matter as he thought best while he was absent. Peter graciously said that he thought I had been treated badly and he offered a fair sum of money and use of an office in Melbourne plus a few other benefits for the remaining years of the contract. Thanking him for his words I said that I would be very happy to accept the arrangement. I returned to Melbourne feeling ever so grateful for Russell's concern and advice and humbled by the Lord's goodness in the matter.

For a year or two after this I had an inward battle to feel forgiveness in my heart toward Keith, but the time came when the Lord enabled me to do so completely. Years later I have been able to see that there were many shortcomings in the manner in which I performed my duties after the takeover. At the beginning there was a certain sense of euphoria and I did not grapple firmly enough with the many problems as they began to emerge. I think my fundamental approach was wrong and it was not helped by the different philosophies Keith and I had about the branches and other aspects of management. Added to this was the near impossible task of breathing life into the moribund Permarest. I seemed to experience a kind of paralysis at the deepest level, despite hectic activities in the area of discussions, meetings and the rest. However that did not excuse my poor efforts and I could understand why Keith wished to dispense with my services and I experienced a sense of profound regret and shame.

Unfortunately the malaise which affected Rank Kerby was widespread throughout the Rank organisation. John Piele had apparently remained only one year. It was only another year before Rank closed down the Melbourne and Adelaide factories, and Roy, with all the other staff, lost their jobs. Marcus who had been managing both operations was quick to set up his own business as an importer of dining and occasional furniture. Chris Knudsen made a similar move in Brisbane. Roy was able to obtain some good agencies and became a successful 'free lance' representative. The remaining factories were either sold or leased and a year or so later I read in the financial press that the Rank parent company in England announced that the whole of their Australian operations had been closed or sold and that the total write-off was £30 million!

Lord, you establish peace for us, all that we have accomplished you have done for us.

Isaiah 26. 12 NIV

Christians tramp well worn paths; obedience has a history. This history is important, for without it we are at the mercy of whims. Memory is a databank we use to evaluate our position and make decisions. With a biblical memory we have two thousand years of experience from which to make the off-the-cuff responses that are required each day in the life of faith. If we are going to live adequately and maturely as the people of God, we need more data to work from than our own experience can give us.

Eugene Petersen,
A Long Obedience in the Same Direction

A Christian who has David in his bones, Jeremiah in his bloodstream, Paul in his fingertips and Christ in his heart will know how much and how little reliance to put on his own momentary feelings and the experience of the past week.

Ibid

- 14 -

1981

Unplanned Retirement

Just prior to our move from Rosanna to Mt Eliza Ada and I had both attended the second NEAC where some 600 delegates from all over Australia gathered for six days. Once again I had been chairman of the planning committee for this major event, perhaps because I was chairman of EFAC which was the body responsible for it. It was a demanding task and I worked closely with the Vice-Chairman, Bishop John Reid of Sydney, and a number of other splendid men and women on the planning group. The Reverend George Pearson was the one whose vision and enthusiasm had inspired the first congress and he was again a tower of strength. Profiting from our experience of the first congress, the program was far-reaching, arranged under four main headings. These were:

> The Gospel and the Kingdom.
> Life and Ministry of the Congregation.
> Christ and the Spirit.
> Marriage and Family in God's Purposes.

Over thirty speakers dealt with different aspects of these themes plus a most impressive array of workshop leaders. John Stott, John Gladwin, Colin Buchanan and Vinay Samuel were distinguished guest speakers from overseas. As in 1971 the major messages were published in a 220 page volume entitled *Agenda for a Biblical Church*.

These two large gatherings, ten years apart, did a great deal to bring evangelical lay people and clergy together, and also greatly helped relationships between those of Sydney and Melbourne and the smaller dioceses. This unity was to be fiercely tested a few years later in the debate over the ordination of women to the priesthood. The Congress program was widely praised and appreciated, but EFAC decided later that due to escalating costs of travel and accommodation it was better in future to maintain a program of smaller conferences for about 120 – 150 people on specific topics each second year, and this is the pattern which has prevailed since 1981.

Reverend Dr Vinay Samuel of India, one of the speakers at the Congress stayed with us at Rosanna afterwards whilst taking a mission at St James. It is always a privilege to receive ministry from Christians of another race and background and we learnt a great deal from Vinay.

At this time we had been hoping to move into the new residence at 37 Rosserdale Crescent but the various works, especially the painting, took longer than expected and it was time for me to travel to Canada and Europe for SU International meetings. My return on June 29 left only a week before the scheduled move to Mt Eliza which meant Ada had borne the brunt of the preparation for the move. This was a state of affairs in which she had often been placed, due to my frequent absences and heavy involvement in meetings. Her contribution to these various causes in this way may not have been always noticed but it was incalculable. In retirement this has gradually changed, not quickly at first but now we are able to do most things together and to share the workload at home.

Our eldest grandson Luke, now ten years old, was spending his holiday with us and one keenly awaited event was a League football match which happened to be Essendon versus Fitzroy at the old Junction Oval, St Kilda. It was a cold, wet day and not even hot drinks were available. We could only eat pies, which were just warm, in an effort to drive out the chill. We returned soaked and cold but very pleased with an Essendon victory. There were many trips in both cars to move household goods with the help of Luke, and finally the furniture vans came and went and we took up residence on July 7. The architects had done well in what was really a major rearrangement of the

Farewell function at St James, Ivanhoe. The Vicar, Reverend Howard Dillon making a presentation.

rooms and Ada's choice of colours, drapes and new furniture created the relaxed and inviting atmosphere we desired. For many months afterwards we shared a feeling of being on holiday in some remote location, as the new home seemed so secluded and the surroundings so delightful. It was quiet, with a wide outlook to the sea and the nearby headlands with the golden crescent of beach just below. The many moods of the sea plus the changing shades of clouds and water ensure that we never tire of this view. Whereas at Rosanna we saw the sun rise on many glorious mornings, we now face due west which enables us to revel in the extravaganza of colour frequently displayed by our Creator God as it departs. The few tinges of sadness felt at leaving Rosanna were quickly dispelled. These feelings of pleasure have continued and with them a deep gratitude to the Lord for leading us to a location and a home which provides such a deep sense of satisfaction and freedom.

This home was a busy place over the next few months. Besides picture hanging and all the settling-in jobs, the garden was making demands for replanning and planting to which Ada was responding with her skills and the help of Phil Stray. It was fun to have time for the stream of guests as family and friends came to visit us in the new surroundings. On August 10th I moved into the new office which had been provided for me by Rank at the GEC complex, Notting Hill.

For the next two years I was to travel there two or three days each week and by the end of August I had engaged a part-time secretary, Mrs Beryl Barter who worked with me on the various business and Christian projects in which I was involved. One reason why I had been able to cover a good deal of ground through my business years was the Lord's goodness in sending me a succession of superbly capable secretaries. Beginning with Ada in the early years of the war I had never lacked the assistance of a skilled, understanding helper in this role and I remember each one with gratitude. Alfred Stanway once said to me: 'A man without a secretary is only half a man, with an ordinary secretary he is just one man but with a good secretary, he is two men'. Now I was in a transition period and before long would be fending for myself, trying not to feel like 'half a man!'

A major task which I had just accepted was the leadership of a $1million dollar appeal for Ridley College, to build new lecture rooms, library and bookshop The College was growing in numbers and influence and these additions were prime needs. The plans called for a whole new block to house these facilities and that in turn would release space further down the line. When requested to take on this role I was at first inclined to say no. We had just been through long discussions on the APCM Council about a building project and found there was a body of opinion against overmuch investment in 'bricks and mortar', with strong feelings that our funds should be directed more towards people. Somehow I did not relish the thought of a large building appeal and as I was about to leave for overseas I said that I would defer my reply until my return. It so happened that soon afterwards I found myself in Cambridge with a few hours to spare and settled for a walking tour of the colleges.

Midway on this walk we crossed from Kings College to Clare and I remembered that this was the college where Nigel Sylvester and Michael Griffiths had studied. The college, founded in 1426, had been the gift of an Irish noblewoman and I was suddenly overwhelmed by the thought that her benefaction nearly six hundred years ago had provided the place for my friends to study and equip themselves for God's service. It gave me a new insight into the value of 'bricks and mortar'. It was clear to me that God had brought me to this place on this grey afternoon to teach me a significant truth and to provide my answer to Ridley's request.

Over the past ten years or so I had participated in two such 'Appeals' for Ridley but simply as a committee member. This one was by far the most ambitious and we were in a time of business recession. I was therefore glad that I now had the time to help and was particularly pleased to secure the help of Sir James Darling as Patron. He very graciously became an enthusiastic and helpful member of the Executive and developed a good friendship with us all as we worked together. This job called for multitudinous discussions, meetings and interviews besides much letter writing. I had already done quite an amount of fund raising, including the $100,000 appeal for the St James' renovations but this was the largest to date and I learnt a great deal in the doing of it. Once again I was working closely with George Pearson who was as usual an indefatigable secretary, and a constant source of inspiration. Given someone with George's enthusiasm and energy it was hard for the committee members not to be drawn into playing their part.

About this time I visited Russ and Joan in Queensland en route to PNG for Pasuwe meetings. We travelled down to the Gold Coast and this was a visit I later wished I had not taken. It was just past the peak of the boom in units and besides deciding I would like to buy one, I felt this whole scene offered a profitable form of investment. This led me over the course of the next few months to a series of investments, many of them unsuccessful which dissipated a significant proportion of the proceeds of the sale of the shares to Rank.

Looking back some time later, I was able to see that my reaction to losing the position with Rank had not been as good as I imagined. I think my feeling was that my business career had been cut short and that it should be possible for me to go out and build another one. I would use my money to make money. There may have been nothing wrong with that, but in the spirit I approached it, there was. As a young Christian in business I had asked the Lord to keep me from the love of money and throughout my business career had sought to keep money in a subordinate place. I believe that God answered that prayer. In fact my chairman used to tell me that my weakness was insufficient focus on the bottom line! He was probably right, business for me became an exciting adventure. The rewards were in seeing people being trained, factories expanded, and new products and territories opened up. Now, perhaps for the first time, abandoning the practice of a lifetime, I sought to do something simply with a desire to make money, and I look back on that fact with deep regret. Without really seeking guidance from the Lord and without obtaining proper commercial advice I made a number of decisions which proved unfortunate. As a result the family's circumstances were unnecessarily reduced. Good money was lost and the future made more difficult than it should have been, which I accepted as a consequence of some hasty and unwise personal decision making. Possibly in the overall purposes of God, I could be more useful with less money rather than more – so I wondered!

One occasion I enjoyed was the invitation from Bishop Stanway to join a small group to meet with Julius Nyere, then Prime Minister of Tanzania, and his wife in their hotel suite, during a rare visit to Australia. For an hour or so he talked of his country and its future and answered questions freely. What he had to say was consistent with the simple and austere style for which he was well known. Something of a rarity amongst African leaders.

Toward the years' end Ada and I made one of the first of many interstate trips by car, something which would be feasible now there was more time. First to Sydney and then to Burleigh Heads where we stayed for a week. Russell and Joan and family came down there to share our wedding anniversary with us. Then just before Christmas the ABC screened Zadok's film 'The Sunburnt Soul' made by our director David Milliken. Whilst controversial in parts it was a very good commentary on the Australian religious scene; being well received by most commentators. For Christmas 1981 and the New Year, Russ and Joan and family were down from Brisbane and joined us for our first Christmas together in the new home. Other members of the family came and went and there were lots of visitors.

When staying at our holiday house we used to worship at St Lukes, Frankston, which was a large and friendly parish. We were especially drawn there by the fact that John Stewart was the vicar at the time; his ministry was most stimulating. Now, as we were living in the area we decided to attend the small church of St James the Less at Mt Eliza, as it seemed right to worship locally. The incumbent had recently departed and a part-time *locum tenens* was looking after the small congregation. It was not a heart-warming scene but we began to make some friendships. We appreciated the ministry of the Reverend John Were, a naval chaplain, who was trying hard to stir a parish which had suffered some problems.

After several months there was still no appointment and another locum came, with some growth in numbers and interest. I was elected to the Vestry and sought to make some contacts with members of another congregation worshipping in the nearby Peninsula School under the ministry of the school chaplain. The existence of this group was a matter that was causing some unrest and reconciliation was called for. Eventually a new appointment was announced and during a visit to Canberra for Zadok I was able to meet the man selected, the Reverend Ray Gregory. Although from a different church background and tradition than mine I felt a rapport with him which I believed augured well for the days ahead at St James the Less. It was a different scene to the one we had left at Ivanhoe, nevertheless we shared a conviction that the Lord had placed us there and that it was right. With Ray's coming things began to change and so did we, there were many new lessons to learn, new ministries to discover and new riches to uncover. Today we look out on a very changed scene and are grateful that we have had the privilege of being made part of it.

A joint investment at Wentworth Falls in NSW planned some time before with the Steele-Smith and Knight families was now proceeding. It was a development of thirty home units plus two or three houses on an historic site in which the three families had equal shares. We had already completed one successful project, a block of three factory units at Homebush, largely helped by Phillip Knight's professional oversight. This one, in the mountains, was much more ambitious and difficult. From the outset we encountered problems, firstly with the Heritage Council which made demands costing money and reducing a lot of the effective area. Soon after commencing our dear friend Phil became seriously ill with cancer and as he was recovering he developed a brain tumour. God wonderfully intervened in this and he slowly regained a measure of recovery. However the building had to proceed without him and it struggled badly, beset with problems and with only the Steel-Smiths, both busy doctors, and the Kerrs, a thousand kilometres distant, to see it through. Eventually it was all finished and very well done, but the units were hard to sell and we all lost a great deal of money on the venture.

The SU International Council met in 1980 near Madras at a seaside resort about sixty miles south of that city. Camps have always been an important aspect of the work in India, and the Council had purchased land in a very suitable area which they hoped they would be able to develop as a permanent camp. The Indian Council, who were our hosts, had chosen a hotel on the beach, close to this land, as our venue for the meeting. Besides their natural desire for us to see it, I think they were hoping that it might prompt some gifts. What troubled me was the inability of the international body to assist projects such as this. The only funds we had were for administrative costs raised by a modest levy on the regions. We could see the strategy of certain proposals and warmly endorsed them but could not offer any practical help. Just occasionally, some of our members were able to interest individual donors or churches in sponsoring certain projects. Our Swiss friends were very good at doing this, but it was sporadic and unplanned.

As we travelled to the meeting I had some half-formed ideas in mind, that we as the International body might in some way be able to raise some funds for new projects. There was a major problem; any such move was inhibited by the fact that all the councils were autonomous and had the sole right to fund-raising within their boundaries. Already we had a plan in operation for the stronger national bodies to support the weaker, as England had done for India over many years. More recently the ANZEA region had undertaken the work in SE Asia, and was giving generously toward this. Such assistance was given on a regional basis and chiefly subsidised staff salaries.

During the meeting, as the regional secretaries reported, there was an emotional moment which made me feel that we must find a better way of developing our ministry. Paul Clark from Peru, our loved and respected regional secretary for Latin America, during the course of his report, suddenly burst out 'I don't see any use in being regional secretary. I see all the needs, I sit in my office and feel like climbing up the wall. What can I do? I don't have enough money even to visit these countries, let alone get staff for them!' The depth of feeling and frustration was clear to all and we were all aware that the Americas were perhaps our weakest region. I began a discussion on the possibility of seeking the approval of regions to us launching an International Development Fund, on the understanding that we would not interfere in any way with their fund-raising. Later in the meeting we set out some clear proposals for the formation of an IDF committee, preparation of a quality brochure, an approach to Christian trusts as well as significant donors and a determination that funds raised would be used only for development projects. I had always appreciated John Laird's concept of 'pump priming' and as with Pasuwe I put forward the maxim that the fund would seek to 'make things happen which would not otherwise happen'.

After much careful letter writing and diplomatic exchanges, all of the various national and regional bodies agreed, and we were able to proceed. Our first objective was to raise a quarter of a million US dollars. When that had been achieved and the money allocated we saw no reason why the appeal should not continue. We again approached the autonomous councils, seeking and receiving permission to make the fund a permanent one.

Nigel Sylvester, then International Secretary, fulfilled an important function for the fund, making some wonderfully helpful contacts and the Lord has graciously given it acceptance with some very large and consistent donors. The autonomy of the various national movements which make up the International SU movements is at the one time a strength and yet a potential source of weakness: it can inhibit strategic corporate action at the centre. Such an arrangement is typically British in style; most American movements are strongly governed from a central head quarters. Our method can make for better adaptation into different cultures, but calls for mutual understanding and a spirit of far-sighted cooperation. We follow the path of leadership by persuasion and example, rather than coercion. More difficult, but in most cases ultimately more fruitful.

As chairman of the IDF I had the opportunity of speaking about it to various councils and conferences and by the mid-eighties it was an integral part of the movement with an annual income of half a million dollars. When I retired from the committee in 1995 this figure was over $1 million yearly and I understand this is being maintained. This money has been of inestimable value in building up a stronger SU in many developing countries. It was pleasing that the Indian campsite at Mahabalipuram became a major beneficiary as well as many camps and projects in Latin America and Africa. Besides providing campsites it has built offices and staff houses, bought vehicles, trained workers and in latter years helped to fund the entry of SU work into Eastern Europe.

When I consider your heavens, the work of your fingers;
the moon and the stars which you have set in order,
What are we, that you should be mindful of us:
What are we, that you should care for us?

Psalm 8. 4-5 APBA

God allows creation, that is someone other than himself, to speak
for him. He lets those other things speak and causes them to
speak... eloquently of themselves. He obviously counts upon it that
they belong so totally to him, that they are so subject to him and at
his disposal, that in speaking of themselves they will necessarily
speak of him... He is so sure of them as his creatures... to be sure
at once of the service which the creatures will quite simply render
him in his self manifestation.

Karl Barth quoted from *Wisdom in Israel*

Through all his ancient works
amazing wisdom shines,
confounds the powers of hell
and breaks their cursed designs;
strong is his arm, and shall fulfil
his great decrees, his sovereign will.

And can this mighty King
of Glory condescend?
And will he write his name
my Father and my friend?
I love his name, I love his word;
join, all my powers, and praise the Lord.

Isaac Watts

- 15 -

1982 – 1986

Frequent Flyers

One of the very pleasant benefits of retirement was the ability it gave for Ada and me to do more things together and when we travelled to do so at a more leisurely pace. For the International Council meeting in 1982 in Lausanne Ada accompanied me first of all to Singapore where we visited ANZEA friends before we headed for Rome with Air India on a journey with a difference. Soon after leaving Delhi the plane was involved in a severe electrical storm and was struck by lightning. We heard a loud report but what had happened was not disclosed to the passengers; there was no communication system, no meal service, only an announcement that we would be required to change planes at Rome. On landing in Rome we discovered a large hole in the nose of the plane, the windscreen shattered and the radar out of action. We were eventually transferred to Swiss Air to complete the scheduled flight to Zurich.

At the conclusion of the various meetings we travelled to Lucerne and met up with Sydney friends George, APCM Treasurer, and Millie Turner, with whom we spent three memorable days. Derek and Ruth Warren had been at Lausanne for the meetings and we then joined them at the SU house at Locarno, again for three days, which included some adventurous driving by Derek as he probed to the very end, the lovely valleys. After leaving them we drove back to Lausanne over the Simplon Pass where the engine of our rented car failed and we had to roll on brakes only, all the way down to the nearest town at the foot of the mountain. Not to be recommended! There were then stops at the RAC, London and Epsom, before driving to Devon and Cornwall, staying with friends, Alan and Eileen Dyer in the Cotswolds, and Douglas and Betty Kahn at Cheam. We then moved on to the US to see Lister and Davidene Hannah, at Princeton, before returning via New Zealand, calling on our relations, the Deebles.

After a few weeks at home it was time to go to Port Moresby for Pasuwe by way of Burleigh Heads. While I was in PNG Ada was joined by Reg and Jean Deeble and we enjoyed a brief holiday. On our way home in Ada's Citroen we reached Moree where the car refused to go any further and we had a 48-hour wait for parts. It was 4.40 pm on Friday before the car was ready to get Reg and I to the VFL Grand Final, 1300 km distance, by 2.30 pm the following day. A long hard drive with four hours sleep at a motel had us back at Mt Eliza at 12.45 on Saturday and we were in at the MCG on time to see Richmond and Carlton come onto the ground, with Carlton ultimately Premiers. A concert in the new concert hall rounded off a hectic thirty hours.

October 2nd saw a wedding breakfast at our new home when Penny McCutcheon and Phil Stray were married in our charming old church by a family friend, the Reverend Dr Peter Adam. About forty guests gathered afterwards for the meal, conversation and speeches, and a pleasant time was had by all. November brought a very happy family event for the Kerrs when Barbara presented Marcus with his second son, Adam Thomas—another A.T. Kerr and our eighth grandson. Our next guest was Commodore Philemon Quaye from Ghana who had just succeeded me as chairman of SU International. A remarkable man, he had served his country as head of the navy, and then in the diplomatic corps, always bearing an unequivocal witness to his faith. When in the services he was one of the group of four or five who planned and executed the overthrow of the tyrant dictator Nkrumah. It was done, as he promised his mother it would be, without bloodshed!

In November, Melbourne received a visit from Lord and Lady Coggan. He had not long retired as Archbishop of Canterbury, and Ada and I were amongst the guests at a dinner at the Royal Melbourne Golf Club when Dr Coggan gave a never-to-be forgotten address. His quiet and convincing manner commended both the man and his message, perhaps the greatest tribute being the sense of absolute stillness when he finished speaking, no applause, no movement; it was a telling moment. Ada and I had been requested to entertain them for a rest-day at 37 Rosserdale Crescent, which was a privilege we much enjoyed.

Our next guests were also English, Douglas and Betty Kahn. Douglas, a retired chartered accountant, was treasurer of SU International and they had frequently entertained us in the UK. It was a great pleasure to show them some of the sights of Victoria and to have a dinner party for about twenty Victorian SU people one evening. As the year closed we were entertained by the McCutcheons who were shortly returning to live in the UK, after enjoying their twelve-month sojourn there.

At this time I often found myself reflecting back over those days which followed the takeover by Rank and brought about my demise from the business, wondering if there was anything I might have done or should have done which would have made any difference. Probably not, but the demolition in three short years of what had been painstakingly built over a life-time had left painful feelings of failure and disappointment which lingered as an unhappy finale to my business life. I had always been conscious of God's hand guiding the affairs of the company but I had to recognise that in some areas this had ceased to be the case. To what extent my personal fallibilities affected the overall events is imponderable, nevertheless the subject burdened me.

To some extent the failure of some of the other Kerramah (the Kerr family company) ventures and the heavy losses incurred, caused that feeling of errancy to persist for some time, although as has been noted earlier, there were direct spiritual lessons to learn from these later events. On June 28th, 1981, when I was in Manila I noted in my diary how God had drawn my attention to Psalm 31, verse 21 'Blessed be the Lord, who worked a miracle of unfailing love for me when I was in sore straits' (NEB). This verse had been given to me when I was reflecting on the incident of the previous month over the withdrawn legal action. Later I saw it as applying to God's hand in getting me right out of the company, in giving us a new home base, and in a sense a whole new way of life. Those darker days were in time put behind us. That Scripture continues to be true for me right up to the present day. Without the Lord we will always be in 'sore straits' and the wonder is that His love is unfailing, or 'constant' as other versions render it.

On the Diocesan Council it was a great pleasure for me to have a small part in an exciting move which brought our friends David and Jean Penman back to Melbourne with David's appointment as an Assistant Bishop. He was appointed to the Western Region, generally regarded as the most neglected and difficult of the four.

1983 was the year of the terrible 'Ash Wednesday' bushfires in Victoria and South Australia, when many hundreds of homes were destroyed and almost one hundred lives lost. Aireys Inlet, Mount Macedon, Cockatoo and many other well-known holiday locations were devastated. A number of churches were lost and a clergyman's wife burnt to death. David Penman in his position as Bishop of the Western Region was intimately involved with the suffering and trauma experienced by many of his clergy. It so happened that they had arranged to spend the Saturday of that week with us, which they did in part, and I observed at first hand the anguish he felt as he entered into the heartaches of his colleagues.

We had many interesting guests with us during the first half of that year. Ted Fletcher founder of Pioneers, one of the most effective mission leaders we have met, and his fellow board member Dr Will Miller, were outstanding for interest and humour. Os Guinness spent a few days with us without Jenny, who was at home but managed to wake us all up at 3 am one morning, having got her hours back to front. John and Jan Dean of SU Africa were old and honoured colleagues and it was good to welcome them. John spent many fruitful years devoted to his task as International Training Officer for SU International. To return to Ted Fletcher; he had left a career with *The Wall Street Journal* because of his great desire to preach the gospel to unreached people and had founded a mission which twenty years later has some six hundred missionaries amongst some of the 'hardest to reach' people on earth, and this continues to grow. Not only Ted, but his wife Peggy and their four married children and spouses are all involved in this dynamic ministry. Known as 'Pioneers', this mission has only recently merged with APCM bringing to Australian Christians the challenge of a worldwide commitment.

Scripture Union in the ANZEA region had a mid-year conference in the Phillipines which Ada and I attended. It spanned my 65th birthday and the program that night was a gala occasion in my honour. As I was not told about it, I was taken by surprise and was not particularly in the frame of mind or ready to respond when called on to receive a gift and to speak. It was a pity because a number of people had obviously been to a lot of trouble to make it a special time for me and I felt that I had let them down. The conference was held at a Philippine government training centre located in a rural area. The facilities were first class and it all went very well.

The SU International Council that year was held out of Philadelphia, in a Mennonite centre at Black Rock. I went on my own, journeying by way of PNG for Pasuwe and then into Irian Jaya for the annual missionaries conference at Karubaga deep in the highlands. The flight with MAF from Tari to Wewak was quite spectacular, across one of the most rugged parts of PNG. Next day I went on to Jayapura, which was Hollandia, the capital of Dutch New Guinea at the time of my first visit in 1956. On the following day I experienced quite a dramatic flight to the interior. After waiting all morning at Sentani airstrip for a plane to make the two-and-a-half hour flight to Karubaga, I was about to return to the house when the senior US MAF pilot said they would make an effort to get in as he was training one of the new pilots in bad weather flying. The first hour was OK, very beautiful over the jungle-clad mountains and wide rivers but then we encountered great billowing storm-clouds piled high and rain, rendering visibility virtually nil with 12,000-14,000 ft peaks all around. We probed one valley after another with startling glimpses of the rugged terrain and the pilot was about to turn back just as a sudden break appeared and we were almost over our destination, a little uphill strip carved out of the mountain side. The people on the ground were telling us on the radio to land quickly as the clouds were closing in and as we taxied down the strip a violent storm broke around us. The conference was great. It was a joint gathering of APCM and Baptist missionaries who were a wonderful group of dedicated and intrepid people and I was glad to be in their company. By contrast

*Early morning departure from the remote Mission post at
Mougulu, Southern Highlands, PNG.*

with the outward journey the return trip to Sentani was posi-
tively benign.

After that there was a flight to Biak, then Jakarta for a few
days, Singapore and London, before Black Rock, Pennsylvania.
in wonderful autumn colours. One day the SU group made a
journey out to the Amish country and we saw their beautiful
farms and barns with the Amish people appropriately clad and
riding in their black buggies and coaches. In what seemed to me
to be a rather bizarre concession to the contemporary age we
found an Amish information center complete with documentary
films, books, maps, etc.

Once again Russ and Joan and family were down from Brisbane for Christmas and spent a few days with us. It was always
a great delight to welcome them and to enjoy their lively company. Their affiliation with Outreach International was something of which we were all conscious and which in some areas
created inhibitions and barriers, nevertheless all concerned
were determined not to allow the family ties and mutual affection to suffer unduly. As I was in Pennsylvania on November
2nd, it had been agreed that the celebration of our 40th wedding
anniversary would be kept until later when all of the family
could be present, and so on January 4th, 1984 this special occasion was observed with about forty friends present. Howard

At a function at home to mark our 40th wedding anniversary.

and Andrea's gift to us was to call in a professional photographer to capture a family group, which we value highly.

Before January finished I had spent a week back in PNG. This was a special visit with Bob Callaghan, General Director, to discuss leadership problems in some of the Mission's most isolated jungle areas. Within the week we stayed at seven places, flew many trips with MAF and spent long hours listening to various aspects of the situation. We later reported to the Executive and the action taken subsequently largely put the matter to rest. This was the first of four PNG trips for the year.

In the parish the Reverend Ray Gregory had made a good beginning and many things had been done to improve the worship and the fellowship. More people were attending and there was positive discussion about building a new worship centre. This, despite the fact that some members were averse to any thought of moving from the picturesque but small and inadequate old church built over 120 years before. For quite some time Ada and I attended a Bible study conducted by Harry McDonald, headmaster of Peninsula school, at his home. The teaching was excellent and this was something we looked forward to each week. Firm friendships were forming and foundations being laid for a deeper and wider work.

It was not long before David Penman's presence was felt, not only in the Western Region but in all kinds of places. His energy and creativity knew no restraint, so that after only eighteen months, when Archbishop Robert Dann retired, there were many who thought of him as a suitable successor. On the other hand there were a number who differed and in a long drawn-out process the choice of the electoral committee of twelve was evenly divided between two other names. In the providence of God this deadlock ultimately led to the election of David Penman, which I am sure pleased the majority of the Diocese. He was to fill the post with great distinction but sadly only for five short years. After returning from a conference in Manila he suffered a severe heart attack and died after a few agonisingly long weeks in hospital. Public interest in his condition was intense and not for a long time had a church leader received such media attention. It was a grievous loss. Perhaps a good illustration of someone who never spared himself because he was so much in demand, he virtually tried to do the impossible. It is interesting to reflect that a person's influence is not measured by length of life or service.

Quite soon after his election David had been concerned to bring about a change in the diocesan electoral system for the appointment of an Archbishop, which had proved unsuitable more than once. I was one of a committee of three which he appointed to bring a recommendation to the Synod. Our plan, which was eventually accepted, was for a larger electoral committee to bring forward no less than two names for a final vote by Synod. I think this last factor was vitally important and gave a much larger and more representative group a voice in this critical process. At the time, it seemed rather early to be making such a change, but David's wisdom in the matter was manifest soon enough.

Before long I was setting off to my final SU International Executive in England. First of all there was a week's travel in Java with Bob Callaghan, calling on missionaries and discussing the future of APCM in that country. Then to Holland for an SU European Council where I spoke about the IDF. The executive meeting was held at the Kahn's home in Cheam, this being a rather critical one as it concerned the future leadership of SU International. I stayed a few days in London where I met for the first time with Roger and Mushie Simpson then on the staff of All Souls, Langham Place, to discuss their forthcoming trip to Australia. From there it was on to Singapore and then to

Alfred Coombe on his 90th birthday.

Kaoshung with a week spent in Taiwan seeking to do something in Marcus' interests before returning home.

In August I was asked to take the chair at the 20th anniversary of St Andrews Hall with which I had had a close connection for many years. It was good to know that the training college we had hoped and prayed for had proved its worth and was now a key element in the CMS program. Also in August I spoke at the Thanksgiving Service for the life of Alfred Coombe, one of my 'heroes', and a man who had influenced me greatly in Christian service when I was between the age of twenty and forty. Beside myself there would have been a great number of others who shared my feelings, as he was widely known and greatly loved. For the final twenty or more years of his life he was entirely dedicated to the growing ministry of Wycliffe Bible Translators which he had so largely helped to establish in this country.

When I first became associated with some of the Christian movements in Australia, apart from SU, I was a good deal younger than most of my contemporaries. Generally there was some five to twenty years difference, which meant that with the passing years we were to see many of our friends fail in health and then receive their homecall. At this time we found ourselves especially saddened as both Dulcie Davis and Jane Buck were seriously ill, which brought a deep shadow over the homes and lives of these loved friends.

Not long after returning from England that year I received a letter from Tony McCutcheon who was now living there, asking if I would be interested in managing a block of six factory units at Lakemba, NSW, which he owned. It would be necessary for him to get an agent to manage them and he wondered if I would like to undertake the task. This I was very happy to do; it gave me a business interest which appealed to me and I enjoyed the contacts which it involved. In addition I am always very much at home in Sydney. So began a new relationship with Tony, which continues still.

September in Melbourne is the month of the football finals and I always sought, if possible, to avoid being away at that time. The 1984 season brought a great deal of pleasure as Essendon performed well and there were some very exciting matches. In 1983 they had suffered an ignominious defeat by their keen rivals, Hawthorn. Now they met again in a semifinal, and in a brilliant match Hawthorn prevailed by just eight points. However, Essendon won the preliminary final which gave them the right to play Hawthorn again in the Grand Final. At three quarter time Hawthorn led by four goals, but in a dazzling final quarter Essendon kicked nine goals to one, winning the Premiership by four goals. No other passage of football will live longer in my memory and that is probably true for many who were there that day.

Early in 1983 I had composed a list of my various commitments by way of councils, boards, committees and the like with a view to considering how these might gradually be reduced over the next few years. In total there were more than thirty on the list. I had always sought to follow a rule of not accepting any appointment unless I felt it was a call from God and likewise I did not feel any task should be left unless the Lord's definite call was heard. I must say I like the spirit of Sir Francis Drake's prayer:

> *O Lord God, when you give to your servants to endeavour any great matter, grant us also to know that it is not the beginning but the continuing of the same until it be thoroughly finished, which yields the true glory, through Him who, for the finishing of your work, laid down his life, our Redeemer Jesus Christ.*

Having said this, taking into account my age, I knew that it was time to move in this direction.

The year 1984 did see the list of my responsibilities diminishing and some major tasks laid aside. However other smaller local ones emerged. The month of July marked the beginning of our fourth year of residence at Mt Eliza and we were now feeling very much at home in the environment. We had both become deeply involved in the life of the parish. A small Missionary Committee had been formed and the first major activity took place one night at our home when Dr Tim Linton spoke prior to departure with his wife for service with CMS in Nepal. The gathering was well-attended and marked a significant step for the parish as there was virtually no corporate missionary activity up to that time.

I had given quite a deal of thought to the financial policy in this connection and with the support of the Vicar gained first, I proposed to the Vestry that all missionary offerings should be paid into a trust fund and then divided equally between three Anglican societies, CMS, ABM, BCA and one other, the Scripture Union. This arrangement was to stand the test of time and was particularly valuable when the next step was taken, that of the Vestry allocating a percentage of the total parish income to missions. Beginning with a small amount this ratio was to grow steadily. Some years later, after I had retired from the Vestry, it was decided to include the South American Missionary Society and allocate the now considerable annual sum in proportion to the size of the societies' budget. This was a logical move and it was to the benefit of CMS. Many evangelical parishes give only to CMS and some parishes just to ABM. I formed the opinion that it was better to have a breadth of outlook and to provide for various loyalties.

In the APCM world Bob Callaghan had stepped down as General Director to be succeeded by an American, Doug McConnell who, with his wife, had served the mission with distinction. One of Doug's concerns was for work amongst the people in urban areas and I visited Port Moresby to discuss some initiatives with him. Our mission had traditionally worked in outlying and isolated places and our national pastors were trained with village work in mind. Now young people, and others too, were moving to the cities and towns to work and the Evangelical Church of PNG which had grown out of the Mission was setting up city churches. Its leaders were being forced to grapple with urban problems and needed skilled help. Our missionaries also had to learn to adapt to a very different environment, in fact the APCM as a whole, in common with most similar bodies, confronted change in several major areas. I was about to conclude my thirty years on the Mission Council, having served two five-year terms as Chairman, being succeeded by Graham Conway of Sydney.

The growth of the cities of PNG has brought with it new problems as thousands of village men and women seeking employment have moved into the urban areas. Crime and violence are unfortunately endemic in the main cities and towns. Whereas twenty years earlier it was possible to walk the streets of Moresby by day or night in safety it is now completely the opposite case. During the previous decade or so a growing tourist industry had begun to develop in PNG which promised good things not only for the towns but also for the interior. However the growth of crime and lawlessness over these years has largely destroyed it. It is sad to think that so much good work on the part of many can be nullified by relatively small lawless groups, and the inability of the authorities to control them. It is a common problem for hundreds of cities today, not only in the 'third world'.

Shortly after that time in Port Moresby I paid a visit to my old friend and associate in the work of the Mission, George Turner, who for many years filled the role of treasurer both for the Mission and Pasuwe. I have known no other treasurer who has taken such pleasure in voting to spend money. He saw the creative use of money as being an advance in the work of the Kingdom and rejoiced in every new opportunity. George was an independent thinker, very positive in his approach to all aspects of Christian enterprise. For a decade or more we saw a lot of each other, staying in each other's homes during meetings. We had a number of things in common, including the fact that we had both overcome some disadvantages in our youth, George more so than me as he had been born with a deformed leg and his early years were a great struggle against this handicap. He had become an accountant and built up a successful practice which enabled him to devote a lot of his time to various bodies within the Anglican church in Sydney and to missions, and was widely loved and respected. Now as we talked together he told me he knew he was dying and I came away knowing that George was at peace and ready for his 'translation'.

The time now drew near for what was to be a splendid occasion in the life of the SU movement – the first international conference open to all workers and supporters from around the world. Planning for this had commenced some years previously when I was International Chairman, and the location selected was the city of Harare, capital of Zimbabwe. The African continent was chosen not only for travel considerations, but also in view of the large numbers of SU members and movements in that part of the world. Harare was also able to offer suitable accommodation and facilities in a new teachers college at very reasonable cost. Nigel Sylvester had devoted much thought and hard work to this project for the past two years.

I decided to do some travel en route and flew by way of Moscow and Vienna. I had only four days in Russia but made good use of that time seeing as much as possible. I was put into a hotel in the heart of Moscow and enjoyed walking the crowded streets observing people and the fine buildings rather than the dreary shops. Performances at the Bolshoi Ballet, State Opera and Circus cost me only the equivalent of two or three dollars each. One afternoon I hired the services of an English-speaking lady guide who took me on a detailed tour of the Kremlin which I found full of interest. A feature was the number of ornate church buildings functioning as museums, all with carefully preserved exteriors and beautifully gilded domes and turrets. In visiting Vienna I was keeping a promise made to my nephew Mark who was spending a year there pursuing his piano studies. We enjoyed a fine time together attending many concerts, riding the 'underground' and looking around that handsome city and its parks, shops and buildings. From there I went down to Starnberg near Munich to spend a few days with Lister and Davidene Hannah, Lister being headmaster of the large international school there. After this I went to London before making my way to Harare.

From the opening day there was a heady atmosphere at the Harare gathering. It was the first time that such an occasion had taken place within the SU family, which alone gave the conference a special flavour. Added to that was the enormous excitement generated as the different nationalities converged and began to share their commitment and experiences. The program each evening was devoted to a report from one of the Regions and these were extremely well presented. The 'feeling' of the work in the various countries was vividly portrayed and brought home to the large assembly a new realisation of the life of the SU movement worldwide. For many, this was a revelation not merely of the work being done, but of the impact of the gospel on diverse races.

Dr John Laird, architect of the Old Jordans conference a quarter of a century earlier, though rather frail in health, was present, as were a handful of that original group. At 'Old Jordans' the Scripture Union consciously became an international movement but few then would have envisaged the rapid growth which had ensued. A great deal of this growth had taken place in Africa and the vigour and enthusiasm of the delegates from the various countries of that huge and vibrant continent permeated the whole of the conference.

During the week which followed, the International Council and Executive gathered at another venue on the outskirts of Harare for their annual meetings. This meeting marked the end of my association with the Executive and virtually my influence on the Council, although I was to remain for a further two years on the Council as Vice-Chairman. For a number of years I continued as Chairman of the International Development Fund. I was glad to be invited to the latter role, and to be able to play my part in encouraging the growth of SU in under-privileged areas of the world. Following the events at Harare there was a brief return to London. Accommodation had been arranged for a number of the delegates and I was fortunate to spend a pleasant few days as the guest of Noel and Fiona Tredinnick. Noel is the gifted music director at All Souls, Langham Place, London, also well known in many areas of Christian music.

Just prior to my departure for overseas I attended the first meeting of the Appeal Committee for the erection of a new church building within the parish of St James the Less, at Mt Eliza. The decision to proceed with the building project was the culmination of discussions going back over two years. The Vicar, the Reverend Ray Gregory, had seen the need for a larger place of worship from the beginning of his ministry in the parish, but there were only a few who shared this vision. This few, realised that there could be no growth whilst the present church building held only eighty worshippers at the very most. It almost seemed that some of the members were content for things to remain as they were, and not to expect or even want expansion, which they felt might end their worship in the lovely, but inadequate old building. However, gradually the Vestry came to the point of deciding to go ahead with the development, partly as a result of some new members being elected, and the arrival of some gifted new parishioners. The Vestry invited Stephen Bird to become chairman of the Building Committee, and me to chair the Appeal Committee. It was envisaged that we would need to raise between $400,000 to $500,000, which to the small group of parishioners at that time appeared to be a vast sum.

The committee had met to establish it's goals before I left for overseas, but now it got down to the serious business of planning the formidable task ahead. I had decided to use readings from the book of Nehemiah as a stimulus, being quite applicable to the situation, and to follow with a few words of encouragement. I was pleased there was a clear acceptance that the work could only be done in God's strength. The regular readings at each meeting, together with the brief commentary, reinforced this sense of dependence on Divine help and bound the members in a fellowship of faith and expectancy. Perhaps not all shared equally in this, but there was a good feeling of unity which I knew would be essential for the long haul. One of the early decisions was to invite Lady Southey, a parishioner, to accept the office of Patron of the Appeal. We were all delighted when she accepted, although we did not realise at the time just how fortunate we really were. Marigold Southey, daughter of the late Sydney Myer, became one of the most committed and inspiring members, in addition to being a generous donor. We quickly developed an excellent rapport and it lightened the load to have such a gifted colleague.

A major initial task for the committee was that of raising the sights of parishioners with regard to giving. Some were rather taken aback when we began to discuss the need for donations ranging from $1,000 to $20,000. Of course, smaller amounts were also needed but if the building was to proceed there had to be a lot of substantial gifts. Church statistics show that Anglicans are not usually good 'givers', that is the average parishioner, apart from those with missionary and charitable interests and strong biblical motivation. The main reason seems to be the lack of teaching on the subject. It is a subject rarely dealt with from the pulpit, as the clergy generally shy away from it. There is a feeling that it is not right for them to speak about giving because it looks as though they are pleading for their support.

To a point this sensitivity can be understood, but that again comes back to a lack of teaching, perhaps our theological colleges are at fault. In any case these feelings need to be overcome because of the importance of the issues involved.

Jesus spoke a lot about money in one way and another – it is said to figure in sixteen out of the thirty-eight parables. We are told that one verse in every six of the synoptic gospels has some reference to the theme. Why was this? because he knew it to be one of the central realities of life and also an acid test of character. He spoke a lot about stewardship and is recorded as teaching 'that it is more blessed to give than receive'. Paul's teaching on the subject was unequivocal and if our attention was focussed more often on chapters 8 and 9 of his second letter to the Corinthians, preferably in a modern version, our churches would not be so needy. It seems to me that tithing needs to be put forward as a model for all Christian people. Not as a formal obligation but because it is the biblical pattern. Some would protest that as we are no longer under the law this does not apply to New Testament believers. There are two brief responses to this. First, tithing precedes the law by centuries. Abraham gave one tenth to Melchizedek and Jacob promised God he would give a tenth. Second, should we as Christians, living with all the benefits of God's grace in Christ, give less than the Jews were taught to give?

Some teaching about tithing, in my opinion stresses far too strongly that financial blessings will follow for those who make it their practice. It is true that Jesus said 'give and it will be given unto you', this is part of God's general law. However the returns may not always be financial in nature and if our motive in giving is because it pays, then it may not pay. There is a great deal which can be said on this vital topic and this is not the place. However, it is worth considering that we would not think our teaching adequate if we failed to instruct new believers to read the Bible, to pray and attend a church. In my view it is of equal importance that they should be *taught* to give and we may rob them of much blessing if we fail.

To return to the Parish Appeal, late in September 1983 it was formally launched at a dinner in the Ansett Hall, when Archbishop David Penman together with Marigold Southey and I spoke. Some good gifts had been promised, so that we were in a position to announce that over $50,000 was already pledged. This function was highly successful, and in the goodness of God, established the Appeal on a high note.

Amongst a number of overseas guests that year were the Reverend Roger and Mushie Simpson from England, with their family of three, making the visit we had discussed earlier. Roger had come to Australia to take a mission in Sydney and was spending some time with us to consider the possibility of taking up ministry in Australia. Archbishop Penman had some proposals to make but as it happened, during their time with us they received a phone call from Edinburgh, with a request for Roger to take over the neglected and run down Parish of St Pauls and St Georges in that city. This they quickly discovered, was God's call for them and it proved to be a very fruitful ministry for Roger over the next decade.

In December 1985 our loved friend Dulcie Davis died after a long battle with Alzheimers disease. It had been a difficult path for Ralph and he felt the loss keenly. I felt most privileged to be invited to speak at Dulcie's memorial service and similarly, only a month later, at the funeral of Jane Buck. The home call of these two loved friends broke a circle of friendship which had existed for almost the whole of our married life and which brought Ada and me much spiritual enrichment and joy. Both Ralph and Len came to stay with us from time-to-time and Ralph brightened many a day with his spontaneous calls.

Parish activities commenced early in 1986 with two meetings of the Appeal Committee before January had run its course. Plans were going well for the building and it was hoped that the work could be started in a few months time. A very interesting architect had been commissioned and our discussions appeared to promise a rather striking but very practical design. Because the old church was listed by the National Trust we had to observe certain constraints in respect to the siting of the new building, also in matters of height and colour.

We were always glad to welcome old and new friends to 37 Rosserdale Crescent and in April enjoyed a lively time when John and Moyra Prince stayed with us for a few days. At the same time Professor Malcolm Jeeves, formerly a colleague on the SU Federal Council and his wife, now living at St Andrews in Scotland, spent an evening with us and Margery McCutcheon joined us as well. A few days later Russell and Morva Fountain of Christchurch, New Zealand, came to Melbourne and we had a delightful lunch with them. Russell had represented NZ at the SU 'Old Jordans' conference and over the years we had spent a good deal of time together with him at various gatherings. This was to be our last meeting as Russell passed to his reward in 1993. A perfect gentleman, a Christian of high integrity and a chartered accountant by profession, he worked in his practice until his death at the age of 88. Other old SU friends from another country who paid us a fleeting visit at Mt Eliza were Claude and Betty Simmonds. Claude was chairman of SU in Canada for many years and we first met in 1967 at the centenary celebrations in England.

The three churches then working in Mt Eliza – RC, Uniting and Anglican, were holding meetings in various homes for Bible studies and fellowship. These ecumenical gatherings sometimes took place in our home and were much appreciated. Unfortunately they lapsed after two or three years, but for us their place was taken by the study group which came together at our place. It began as a Lenten study meeting, then continued and, under the good hand of God, has become a significant factor in our lives and I believe in the lives of others also.

Meeting on Wednesday evenings we give about ninety minutes to a verse by verse study of whichever book we are working on, seeking chiefly to apply the Word to our own lives and circumstances, but also to better understand God's purposes for the Church and the world. In this manner we have studied virtually all of the New Testament and quite a lot of the Old. We also pray together and enjoy refreshments and much conversation. After the first few years I was most grateful to be joined in leading the studies by my close friend and colleague of many years, Ian Milne. More recently Dr Greg Perry from our parish has shared as well. I have no doubt that those who prepare the studies gain most from them.

Have you comprehended the vast expanses of the earth?

Job 38-18 NIV

Much have I seen and known; cities of men
And manners, climates, councils, governments....
I am a part of all I have met.

Tennyson, *Ulysses*

- 16 -

1986 – 1988

National & International
Events

On one of my visits to PNG in 1986 I went from Tari to Bosavi, one of the mission's most isolated areas on the slopes of the great Mt Bosavi. Here for a number of years Keith and Norma Briggs had built up a remarkable work amongst a primitive people who had never had any significant contact with the outside world. Because of this the Briggs had determined to keep their work as simple and natural as possible, preserving as far as they could the customs of the area, consistent with Christian beliefs. Their preaching of the gospel had made a striking impact on the tribe and by their hard work they had established not only a large and well-taught church, but a school, an excellent clinic, a Pasuwe trade store, plus workshops and other ancillary activities. It was their set policy to teach the people to look after themselves so far as possible.

I was particularly impressed that in this spirit of self-help and cooperation the work done in the store in the beginning was all voluntary. The school I also found to be most impressive, it provided simple accommodation for the two hundred children during the week, as many of them walked in from quite a distance, through the bush, returning home for the weekends. As the children came back on Sunday afternoon they brought with them food for the week ahead. The cost of this 'boarding school' was something in the order of twenty cents monthly. Norma taught infant welfare and hygiene and had also trained the women in sewing and domestic arts. Overall, I found this to be a most eloquent demonstration of applied indigenous principles and a testimony to the good sense of the Briggs and of the APCM. Apart from the work at Bosavi, Keith Briggs has made a significant contribution to the cultural life of the country with his magnificent photography and well-written articles published in various government booklets and airline magazines.

Shortly after returning from this trip, I was busy preparing for a major expedition with Ada. This was to last three months and would include a number of different facets. However just before setting off, on the 4th of May, the youngest Kerr grandchild made his entry into the world and we were all delighted to welcome Barbara and Marcus' third son, Trent. He brought the total number of our grandchildren to ten, nine boys and one girl. We are deeply grateful to our Heavenly Father for this precious heritage (see Psalm 127. 3). Like their parents, they are a source of unending pleasure and blessing to us both.

The new arrival made his first visit to Melbourne Airport a few days later when he accompanied his parents to farewell his grandparents on a journey to London where we stayed with the McCutcheon family at their residence in Tabernacle Street. After a few days we set out for a meeting of the SU International Council at 'Old Jordans' Conference Centre. Ada was in residence with the council party and enjoyed the atmosphere of this historic house, a centre for Quaker activities since early in the seventeenth century. It was from this home that the fathers of the Quaker movement were hauled off to prison during the years that their gatherings were forbidden by the government. It was also from this house that William Penn and his party set out in *The Mayflower* for their journey to the virtually unknown land of America, to find freedom to worship and make new lives. The mortal remains of Penn and others of his time lie buried in the graveyard alongside the Meeting House, which is still used today.

A few days after this we departed with Derek and Ruth Warren as their guests on a lovely expedition, which took us first to Edinburgh on a freezing afternoon in late Spring. There we had the opportunity of visiting Roger and Mushie Simpson, now into their task of breathing new life into the parish to which they had been called while staying at Mt Eliza. The following day we drove off across Scotland to Oban, taking the ferry to the Isle of Mull, where we were to holiday for the next four days. Derek, always a wonderful guide, drove us over every road of that beautiful island. Particularly enjoyable were the scenic drives taken in the long evenings after dinner at the hotel, when it was possible to take photographs as late as 10.30 pm.

One day we made an expedition from Mull by ferry to the island of Iona. Not only was this a delightful scenic treat but the visit to the ancient Abbey, now restored, and the story of George McLeod's ministry there were most interesting. The most significant thing for me especially, was the history of the early missionary, St Columba. With a small party of kindred souls he had arrived on Iona in the year AD 563 with the vision of carrying the gospel to Scotland and beyond. So determined was he they should not be tempted to turn back to their beloved Ireland that they burned their small ships to render a return impossible.

At the end of our stay on Mull we drove to the north of Scotland, through magnificent mountain scenery to the coastal town of Ullapool where we stayed with Derek's brother and his wife. A fishing port which had been laid out as a model town about two centuries ago, this is a focal point for many Russian fishing vessels to visit and it was interesting to learn that the Russian sailors come and go freely, without any formalities such as customs or visas. Many aspects of life in this remote corner of the UK were very fascinating to us. One day we drove to a west coast garden named 'Inverewe', where to our astonishment we found tropical plants flourishing in a manner akin to Sydney, apparently because of the warmth of the gulf stream which surges up that part of the coast. Such a contrast to the generally barren although rugged surroundings was most surprising in that chilly part of the world.

Another experience which remains in my mind was attending a Sunday afternoon service in a small stone church standing alone on a bleak hillside. From this church a group of men had once set off to walk to London in the cause of 'Bonnie Prince Charlie'. This service included a celebration of the Lord's supper, according to the pattern of that particular branch of the Reformed Church of Scotland. After the sermon we moved to sit at long tables, set with white linen and there partook of the elements in a very solemn atmosphere, heightened by the fact that many of the congregation, men particularly, remained in their original seats watching us but not partaking, apparently because they did not feel worthy to do so. We left with a strange mixture of feelings, admiration of their seeming honesty and sadness at the air of legality rather than grace which prevailed.

The varied interest of this beautiful Scottish experience continued even beyond the border, when on return the Warrens introduced us to some friends who were converting their heritage farm into a Christian conference centre, known as 'Blaithwaite Farm', where we spent the night. And so on to Keswick and then Berkhamstead, and next day back to our temporary home in London, full of gratitude to our friends Derek and Ruth for their generous gift of a unique holiday. The McCutcheons celebrated our return by taking us for a picnic tea at Kenwood, where we sat on the sweeping lawns by the lake listening to a symphony concert which concluded with fireworks. The orchestra was positioned on the opposite side of the lake and at one point the baton slipped from the conductor's fingers and flew in a graceful arc into the water.

We drove to Leicestershire to see our friends Jan and John Dean, formerly missionaries and SU workers in Nigeria, now serving on the SU International staff. From there we went through Oxford and into the Cotswolds to stay with Alan and Eileen Dyer. Alan had been for a time chairman of SU England and a member of the International Council. Our stay with them included a tour of many villages hidden away in the hills of Gloucestershire. Next we went on to stay with the Kahns at Dunsfold. Ruth Warren had kindly lent us her car with no time limit, a most generous gesture which enabled us to drive into Europe, crossing by ferry to Calais and driving across the north of France into Switzerland. There we stayed with Fritz and Heidi Hoppler at Winterthur. We had often visited this city before to see our late friend and colleague Armin, but now we had the opportunity of getting to know Fritz better. An engineer, he was later to serve as the fifth chairman of the International Council.

From a hill above the city he was able to point out to us various places where the Hoppler families had lived over the past four centuries and then, returning to his home, show us the family tree spanning all those years. Other friends have done similar things for us from time to time and coming from a new country with no great knowledge of my ancestors, I find myself fascinated by the richness of their family history, and desirous of leaving at least a foundation of information for our children and grandchildren to build on.

Leaving them, we drove across the Swiss Alps by way of St Moritz to Silverplana, a lake set amongst the encircling peaks, where we came across the world wind-surfing championships which were just beginning. We watched the opening procession which included a team of Australians bearing their national flag. After a night in the lovely town of Samedan we set off to follow a route along the Engadine Valley to Munich. We had been told that this was one of the most scenic roads in the country and it certainly came up to our expectations. All day long we followed the course of the River Inn, sometimes from high above, and then alongside, with the most magnificent panoramas continually unfolding as we drove. In the evening we arrived at Starnberg, an outer suburb of Munich, and enjoyed once again the company of Lister and Davidene Hannah and their family. For some years Lister was the headmaster of the International School there.

Following our time there, we drove by a route known as the 'Romantique Road' which makes it's way through some wonderful old walled towns of West Germany, seemingly untouched by recent wars, with the most marvellous atmosphere. Our destination was a town by the name of Marienheide, where SU Germany has its main camp site and head quarters office. Unlike England, most of the larger SU bodies in Europe own well developed camp sites or conference centres. Outside of school vacations, they use these as holiday destinations for their supporters from around the country. This enables them to maintain permanent staff and provides a nice facility for the Christian folk who give to and pray for SU. These centres become the focal point for much of their work.

Karl Schaffer, leader of the work in Germany had invited us to spend a holiday at Marienheide, which we enjoyed greatly despite the language barriers between us and the fifty or so others in residence. Returning to London we spent a week touring Wales before departing for Los Angeles, where the chief aim was to visit Robert Schuller's Crystal Cathedral, which was something Ada had long wanted to do. We were escorted on a private tour of the Cathedral on the Friday and went to a service and study group on Sunday. It was certainly well worth the visit and the whole place is a most impressive tribute to it's founder and his positive faith.

Auckland was our final destination where we were to stay for a few days. My brother-in-law, Reg, had some time before suffered a severe stroke and was in hospital, although he was driven home for a few hours at the weekend. It was distressing to see him so handicapped, although we were able to have some meaningful conversations with him. It was to be our last contact with Reg and we remember him as a faithful and serious-minded Christian, dedicated to the work of his church and to the APCM which he served for a number of years as New Zealand chairman. Before returning to Melbourne we had the pleasure of spending two nights with Alan and Ailsa Judkins, former members of Pasuwe Ltd staff in Pt Moresby, at their home and colorful garden at TePuna.

It was encouraging on return to see the new church building progressing and on Sunday 27th of September 1986 the foundation stone was laid by our former Archbishop, Frank Woods. He also braved a Spring shower to plant a gum tree which continues to make steady growth. In the months which followed we held two luncheon parties at home for Vestry members and spouses, one of these with thirty-eight guests was held on a most beautiful late Spring day enabling us to enjoy our meal in the garden.

Easter 1987 was a most joyful season for the parish when we were able to hold the first services in our new church building, including an exhilarating performance of 'The Messiah' which gave us all a deep sense of gratitude to God for His many mercies, spiritual and temporal. It was only on coming to this parish that we had been introduced to the tradition of the three-hour service on Good Friday. We found it most meaningful then, and still do, valuing it highly as a way of entering more fully into the significance of Easter; finding great benefit for our spiritual growth and understanding. A month after

Lady Southey points out in the architects model some of the features of our new church building to Archbishop Penman.

these services our new church building was dedicated, with appropriate ceremony, by Archbishop David Penman.

The unusual and artistic design, complemented by the attractive furniture created by Roger Putnam, formerly of our own Kerby Group, provides a relaxing setting for worship. This was subsequently enhanced by a striking stained-glass window created by Leonard French and a fine pipe organ, both gifts of groups of parishioners. It was 1862 when one of the pioneer families of Mt Eliza made the original gift of three acres of land on which the first church was erected. Surveying the whole complex, complete with the new vicarage, and car park set amongst the trees and the garden areas, we all experienced a deep sense of thanksgiving for God's blessing and his goodness as we reflected back over the past few years in the parish and to the commencement of the appeal in 1984–85, now successfully concluded. We were left at the time with a manageable debt to the Diocese, now virtually extinguished.

After this I left for my final meeting of the SU International Council, held in the fine new conference centre of SU France at Rimlishof. Prior to this meeting I attended the European staff conference to speak about the work being done by the IDF. This council meeting was Philomen Quaye's last as chairman and mine as vice chairman, after twenty-seven years of membership. Like me, Phil had been one of the early members of the Council and there were appropriate speeches and presentations. I enjoyed the meeting and being once again in the company of so many old friends, but I also remembered the words of the late Robert Menzies, former Prime Minister of Australia 'There is nothing more "Ex" than an Ex'. I then proceeded to London for a meeting of the IDF, a task which I was still charged with continuing, The fund was growing significantly and bringing much needed help and support to SU bodies in the third world.

It was at this time that I began to become involved with an enterprise which Marcus and Chris Knudsen had commenced in the UK, known as Birchgrove Furniture Ltd. The concept was to import furniture from Taiwan into England, supplying retailers from a central warehouse and assembly point. The idea was excellent and there was certainly a place in the market for the products, however the logistics and problems created by long distance management were formidable. Although at first I had not been keen on the idea, when I encountered it on the spot I found it presented a challenge and accepted a suggestion from Marcus to become involved.

On another level it was interesting to be in Britain during a General Election and especially on the actual polling day. Through the British system of 'first past the post,' most of the results were known within hours of the close and by midnight a great number of the electorates had already declared their polls and it was clear that Margaret Thatcher was to be Prime Minister for another term.

In August Ada accompanied me to Sydney as I went to attend a vital meeting of the Anglican General Synod at which a vote was to be taken regarding the ordination of women to the priesthood. Following some years of debate and seemingly endless discussions, demonstrations and the like, it was expected that this would be the Synod to finally resolve the issue and feelings were running fairly high. The whole occasion commenced on a low key with the traditional garden party on the Sunday afternoon at Bishopscourt, an event which Ada and other wives were invited to attend and enjoy. The handsome old stone home in its spacious grounds provides an expansive view of the harbour, and on a sunny afternoon made a pleasing setting. Later came a service of Evensong in the Cathedral.

Next day, the Synod proceedings began and Ada took a seat in the visitors' gallery. As the debate unfolded she began to feel that there was a biblical basis for women being in the ordained ministry, although previously having been somewhat doubtful. I had come firmly to this point of view some years earlier, my mind having been influenced by long experience of the ministry of women on the mission field and in SU, in addition to my own interpretation of Scripture. Voting in the 'Houses' of the Laity and Bishops was in favour; but ultimately the move was lost by a very narrow margin in the House of Clergy, to the enormous disappointment and chagrin of many of the laity and especially of the women present. A two-thirds majority was necessary in each house as the church guards itself well from sudden change. It was a very emotional time and the Primate, Archbishop Sir John Grindrod, who presided, handled the matter with great tact and sensitivity, adjourning the session and going outside to console the bitterly disappointed group of ladies who gathered there.

This difficult and divisive issue caused strained feelings between Evangelicals from Sydney and Melbourne in particular, as they found themselves on opposite sides in this debate. As Chairman of EFAC this was a matter of much concern to me and to others because of the implications it could have for movements such as CMS and BCA and for the evangelical cause in general. We therefore sought to arrange a residential gathering of General Synod members who were also EFAC supporters, at which the differences could be aired and the relevant Scriptures could be examined. To ensure a worthwhile conference it would be necessary to secure leaders from both sides of the debate, including the two Archbishops, and this was eventually achieved. The conference was held at Kurrajong, out of Sydney, and most of the proponents prepared and delivered papers supporting their viewpoint. Probably not many opinions were changed but certainly fellowship was strengthened and perhaps there was a greater degree of respect for each other's stance.

In October we hosted a large function at home organised by the Ladies Committee of Ridley College with a view to promoting greater interest in the work of the College. Jean Penman

Two views of Ridley College. Above, the main entrance gate, and at right a lecture in progress.

spoke and encouraged those present to reach out to new immigrants, especially Muslims, amongst whom she and her husband had worked for so long.

Once again we headed for Brisbane by car, this time with the objective of me catching a plane for Port Moresby and then on return collecting our English visitors, Ruth and Derek Warren and driving them down the coast to Sydney. Our overnight stops were Coffs Harbour and Forster and our friends enjoyed the trip greatly. Ada and I then departed, leaving the Warrens to enjoy Sydney for another week and journey down to our home later. Derek and Ruth then had twelve relaxing days with us. We made numerous excursions together but regretfully were unable to satisfy their keen desire to see kangaroos in the 'wild', where we had expected them to be. It was beautiful weather and the last four days of October were all over 30 degrees, enabling them to swim at the beach each day. We are sure that thereafter they retained a very favourable view of Melbourne's spring weather.

At the end of November Geoff and Anne Kells entertained the Bookhouse board members at a dinner party in their home at which I was thanked for my service as chairman over some twenty years. Back in Melbourne we enjoyed all the usual Christmas activities with the final day of the year bringing a rather special event when the whole fleet of tall ships sailed into Port Phillip bay as part of the festivities associated with Australia's bicentenary. The main celebrations were to take place in Sydney on January 26th, being the actual anniversary date, but this was a foretaste and one which Melburnians relished. We entertained a large party of friends on the cliff top from early morning and enjoyed the sight of these graceful ships making their way up the bay.

This was a nice prelude to a truly memorable week in Sydney marking the bicentenary of our nation. Tuesday, January 26th 1988 will live long in our memories, particularly the sight of hundreds of yachts and boats of all sizes attending the handsome sailing ships as they made their way up the harbour. The weather was perfect and from early morn till late at night the day was marked by a unique sense of euphoria which was shared by the hundreds of thousands who gathered in Sydney and in other cities and towns throughout the land. It was a day of shared good will, remarkably free from serious crime or accident.

We awoke early that morning to the sound of hundreds of family groups walking down Macquarie Street to the harbour and we later joined some of them in the Botanic Gardens. After lunch we were able to view the whole extensive panorama from the roof of the Club building. Late afternoon saw us on the harbour in a ferry and for quite some time we were unable to proceed, because of the crowded conditions on the water. This gave us an unrivalled view of the ships and the harbour in carnival mood. At dinner in the Club we met some friends and went with them to the gardens to watch the extended fireworks display, rounding off a notable day. In one sense ours is still a young country and as a people we lack the strong feeling of history enjoyed by citizens of the 'Old world' At this point in time I had lived for a third of the life of Australia as a nation, a concept which comes as a surprise to my friends on the other side of the world. I believe that these celebrations did a lot to strengthen our feeling of nationhood.

Returning home from that exciting week in Sydney we continued the 200th Anniversary theme by attending a special cricket match between England and Australia at the MCG with English-born Stephen and Rosemary Bird as our guests. Another major bicentenary event took place on May 9th when Her Majesty the Queen opened the new Federal Parliament House at Canberra, a notable building erected at a cost in excess of $1 billion.

During this time we had the great pleasure of the company of our friend from SU in Peru, Paul Clarke. He spoke to a large gathering in our home on the Saturday evening and preached at the morning service in church next day. Both of these addresses lived long in the memory of many who heard them. Paul, and his wife Marty, stand very high on the list of remarkable Christian people we have been privileged to know through the Scripture Union. One week later another group of friends were invited to join in celebrating my 70th birthday. It was a warm and friendly occasion which the guest of honour greatly enjoyed. On the following Wednesday we had a total of fifteen present at the Bible study, the highest number to date. The next weekend was the parish house party at Kallista when thirty-five parishioners enjoyed a splendid time of fellowship despite cold and wet weather. These gatherings have continued through the years and have done much to draw people into a closer fellowship with the Lord and with each other.

The second half of the bicentennial year also provided us with an array of interests. We flew to London via Hong Kong and made our way to the University of Kent at Canterbury where we joined with six hundred delegates to a conference conducted by the Anglican Renewal Fellowship. Dr Terry Fulham of New York delivered a masterly series of Bible studies and Graham Kendrick, the hymn writer, led the worship sessions, amongst numerous other features, altogether a fine gathering. From there we moved to Oak Hill Theological College, north of London, where the English EFAC movement had arranged a one week pre-Lambeth programme for bishops from around the world. We had kindly been invited to join with them as I was Australian chairman and a member of the international executive of EFAC, and we especially enjoyed meeting a number of the African bishops. Some of them were to play a major

EFAC, International Executive 1988.
Back row, from left: Bishop David Evans, Bishop Gideon Olajide,
Alan Kerr, Jill Dann, Bishop Michael Nazir Ali, John Rodgers,
Ruth Etchells.
Front row: Dr John Stott, Bishop Donald Cameron, Dr Vinay Samuel.

role in the Lambeth conference a few days later and, I gathered, in the initiative for the 'Decade of Evangelism'.

Later that month we had a very satisfying executive meeting of the EFAC international body, enjoyable too, as we were guests of a family which generously made its centuries-old home 'Highmoor Hall' available for such meetings. We met in a specially built conference room, ate in the panelled dining room with members of the family, slept in the huge bedrooms and strolled and chatted in the spacious grounds and gardens. It was as well that we made the most of these luxurious surroundings as the following year we held our meeting at Oxford and were accommodated in a small and rather cheerless college. A good opportunity to put Paul's well known advice into practice.

That 1989 meeting marked the retirement of Dr John Stott, on the grounds of age, from the executive of a movement which he had so carefully guided over the years. For the same reason it was also my final meeting, having exceeded the set retirement age by one year. I was succeeded as Australian chairman by Bishop Peter Chiswell, and Canon David Claydon became the international delegate. It is encouraging to see EFAC playing an increasingly influential role within the Anglican church worldwide.

Derek and Ruth Warren had offered us the use of their home while they holidayed and we enjoyed a month of country living at 'The Potteries', visiting friends and sightseeing. I was also involved in the affairs of Marcus's business, Birchgrove, which was growing, but in the process creating certain problems, chiefly of management.

Soon after returning, we travelled to Canberra for Bookhouse and took the opportunity of inspecting our new Parliament House, a vast and unusual building. Much of it lies underground, but we found the interior most impressive. I was due for a meeting in PNG and drove Ada to Brisbane to stay with Russell and Joan and then on return had a good look at the Brisbane 'Expo', another aspect of the 200th anniversary.

Having attained the age of seventy years it was necessary for me to retire from membership of a number of different bodies. CMS was one from which I parted with real regret. I had been a member of the Federal Executive and associated committees for thirty-seven years and it had occupied a significant and inspiring place in my life. It has been a source of pleasure to me that one of my final contributions on the nominations committee, was to have a share in the appointment of David Claydon as Federal Secretary. After leaving SU he had been seven years in parish ministry and was well equipped for this global role. The intervening years have seen him widely acclaimed as a distinguished missionary leader and strategist.

Melbourne diocesan Synod and the General Synod were also on the retirement list. Archbishop David Penman made a typically generous gesture one evening by entertaining another member and me with our wives at an Afghan restaurant. There we reclined Eastern fashion on cushions, as we partook of our meal and conversation and then received gifts from David. It was a typically kind action from a man whose life was already far too crowded.

Jesus said ...
When you enter a house, first say, 'Peace to this house'.
Luke 10-5

To be happy at home is the end of all human endeavor.
Samuel Johnson

- 17 -

1989 – 1995

At Home and Abroad

When invited, many years ago, to submit some personal details for entry in *Who's Who* I named travel as one of my recreations. Since then, maybe the passage of the years and another two million or so miles have dulled the keen edge of my enjoyment a little, but it remains a source of delight. In my boyhood days of reading, travel was one of my favorite subjects. My grandfather had given me an old volume of *The Swiss Family Robinson*, and it became one of my most treasured possessions. It was a large book, profusely illustrated. I read and pored over it until I completely identified with the family in their castaway adventures. R M Ballantyne, Daniel Defoe and similar writers fueled my imagination and with them I traveled to many countries, saw natural wonders, walked the streets of famous cities and visited the haunts of men and women who were leaders in the arts or deeds of the day. All of this built up within me an intense desire to experience these things at first-hand and encounter history for myself.

Only over the last two or three decades has overseas travel become so widely available and feasible for thousands of young and old as it is nowadays. In the forties and fifties this was not the case and it was not until I was thirty-eight years of age that it became possible for me to travel beyond Australian shores, when visits to Papua New Guinea and New Zealand made a great impact on my mind and senses. A year later when I was able to circle the globe, touching all continents, it came as a superb climax to all the years of reading, dreaming and longing.

My mind was stretched and challenged at so many different levels that it was difficult to process all the new thoughts and ideas. It developed within me an appetite for background knowledge to better understand the peoples and places I was encountering. Whilst travelling I read quite large histories of America and Great Britain which leapt into life before my eyes.

On that initial journey I was blessed in having new and old friends awaiting me because of my associations through business, or SU and CMS. This has increased over the years and in so many places there have been helpful people able to interpret for me the significance of what I was seeing. How much more enriching this might have been if only one could speak other languages! I envied some of my European friends who had three or more at their command. Essentially, it is a humbling experience for an Australian to meet other cultures and traditions and to appreciate the value as well as the limiting aspects of a long history. The older world has so much to teach us, but this can be balanced by the more invigorating liveliness of spirit and enterprise which is part of the Australian ethos.

So, for many reasons travel became part of my life and I have been fortunate that it has been a large element in both my business and Christian interests. Always there has been the delight of exploring something new as I used to make a practice of trying to fit in at least one unknown city or country on every journey. There is also much to sadden one as well, the poverty, oppression, injustice and wickedness, which are rarely out of sight for long, are sometimes overwhelming. These serve to emphasise the value of the work of Christian missions.

As time has gone on Ada has been able increasingly to share these travels and the experiences they give. We have also been able to see more of our own country, travelling by car instead of by plane, as time demanded in busier days. Now there are no business imperatives or council meetings we travel less but with greater leisure. Our own Mornington Peninsula has provided much unsuspected treasure.

Early in 1989 it appeared that the troubled state of Birchgrove might be settled when Chris and Mary Wharmby of Hobart nobly agreed to spend some time in the UK undertaking the task of managing this company. With our knowledge of their splendid record with Kerby (Tas), Marcus had every confidence that their presence would be effective in establishing it in new premises and making it efficient and profitable. Marcus was with them at the beginning, being greatly encouraged and in March 1989 I travelled to London to try and lend some help. I was amazed at the progress which had been made, and to see the new factory functioning most effectively, having responded to the expertise of the Wharmbys. Now the problems to be dealt with remained in the areas of sales and distribution. In addition to the imported products, the company was now manufacturing recliner chairs, under license to an American firm, and I returned home via Detroit to confer with the people there. On the outward section of that trip the plane experienced an engine failure, resulting in a twenty-four-hour stop-over at Dubai which provided a good opportunity to see something of this flourishing city, a fascinating mixture of modern glitz and the ancient East.

A month after my return from the sophistication of New York and Detroit found Ada and I in one of the least developed regions of PNG. To mark the twenty-fifth anniversary of Pasuwe Ltd, the directors had invited the two previous managers to join with us in a special board meeting at Tari, in the Southern Highlands, and then to travel to Balimo in the remote Western Province for the opening of our new store in the area where the APCM had its beginnings. Whilst at Tari we visited the Teachers College at Dauli, one of APCM's fine achievements in the educational sphere, where hundreds of trainees prepared for their lifework as schoolteachers. Then with Charles Horne, veteran retired missionary, and the former managers we flew to Kawito, our supply base for the Western region to prepare for our visit to Balimo. There we shared in a meal by the riverside with thirty staff and families present, and made a presentation of a watch to an employee for twenty years service. The number of mosquitoes to the cubic metre of atmosphere in this lowland area is high, even for PNG. Some of our party waged an unequal battle with them through the night.

Next morning we travelled up the Aramia River, three hours in open boats with rain teeming down on our umbrellas, to finally cross the wide lagoon to Balimo. The opening ceremony was postponed because of the rain and we toured the excellent Mission hospital meanwhile. The new Pasuwe store was the first building in Balimo to be built in brick, or rather, concrete block. Even the sand for the mortar had to shipped down from Moresby. The rain eased, the edifice was declared open with due ceremony and we proceeded to a grand feast for the whole township provided by Pasuwe, and so back down river to Kawito. Another world, so utterly different from our busy modern Melbourne, and yet how close we can be in the bonds of Christ to our Papuan brothers and sisters.

Later that year Ada and I were invited to attend the Lausanne II Congress at Manila. The church as a whole, and mission hearted Christians in particular, owe a great debt to the Lausanne movement for articulating in clear and convincing fashion, the ongoing task of world evangelisation. Building on the success of the first congress at the location which gave the movement it's name, the Manila occasion was much more comprehensive in its composition. The 4300 in attendance were drawn from no less than 173 countries, almost certainly the most representative gathering in the history of the Church. I suppose for many of the delegates this was one of the most significant features. Each day brought us all such a rich variety of contacts, dedicated men and women, old and young, from countries and churches we had scarcely heard of or encountered. A noteworthy aspect of this splendid gathering was the music, under the direction of the blind pianist and singer, Ken Medema. Quite often at the end of an address he would play and sing something which he had just composed in response to the message.

The purpose was well expressed in the title 'Proclaim Christ Until He Comes' and the focus was on the two billion people yet to hear the gospel. While we found encouragement in the dynamic growth of the churches in the developing world, we were sobered by the fact that for Christianity to maintain equality with population growth it would need a thousand new churches every day of every year. A remarkable array of speakers presented a program of great breadth and diversity, making a profound impact on the thinking and caring hearers.

Not long after our return from Manila I received a visit from three senior members of the Victorian Council of Scripture Union, Bruce Johnston, chairman, Ken Sleep, treasurer and Tom Slater, director. The organisation had moved from its previous headquarters in Richmond having found it inadequate for the growing work and was renting portion of a large building in Fitzroy. The Council had reached the decision to make the move with the intention of buying this space and fitting it out to suit their needs, knowing that this would involve a major appeal to their supporters. At the same time they wished to raise funds for the provision of a new accommodation block at the Toolangi camp site and if possible some funds for work at Coolamatong. Over the past few months I had responded to requests for advice as to how they might best approach this task, now they came expressing a united desire for me to accept leadership of such an appeal. They were aware of the fact that I did not wish to be involved but felt they were unable to find any other suitable person. I was probably more aware than they of just how much work would be called for in seeking their objective of two million dollars. However, the Lord made it clear to me that this was a task I should accept and so we began to plan.

It was the last week of September when the call came and two weeks later we held the first planning committee, deciding to publicly launch the New Building Appeal in the following March. So began a period of intense activity, forming committees, designing and printing promotional material, assembling lists of names and writing hundreds of letters. It was difficult for a movement which already relied heavily on generous giving for its day-to-day work, to seek large gifts for capital purposes. In our approach it was essential that we should be very sensitive to the fact that many of our loyal supporters already contributed to the point of sacrifice. We especially sought to involve the senior members of our constituency, beside charitable trusts and business houses.

The Appeal was formally launched at a dinner held at the Melbourne University Union in March. The function was well attended and a good spirit prevailed, the needs were well presented by four speakers and the brochure distributed. Following that the gifts and commitments began to flow in. The main burden of the work fell on the small executive which functioned with a fine enthusiasm throughout 1990 and well into 1991. During this time the Council of the movement reduced our goal for actual cash contributions to $1.5 million as there were many gifts of materials and services. One very large donation from a Trust provided for the new building at the Tallawalla camp, which was erected and opened on February 24th 1991.

View of the corner section of the building in Fitzroy which was purchased for the offices and meeting rooms of SU Victoria.

The work at Fitzroy was being done as the funds became available and from the bare walls and floors of the building emerged a most attractive, flexible and serviceable set of offices and meeting rooms. Those who helped with design served us well, in my opinion; the final result looked quite handsome without being lavish. The new headquarters were officially opened with a typically joyous SU-style celebration on Saturday, October 12th, 1991. At that point the amount raised in cash and promises was about $1.25 million and it was necessary for the movement to borrow some of the funds. However, about four years later a very substantial legacy was received. It came from the estate of a lady who was present at the dinner in March 1990 and who responded at the time with a large gift. I like to feel that this bequest was the completion of the appeal and that the prayers and faith of the executive and others were, in God's time, fully answered, providing the movement with a valuable resource and asset.

On the personal front, the year 1990 tended to become very crowded. It was not planned that way but illness and the advent of the SU appeal were not part of the early thinking. The year had a pleasant beginning with our friends Douglas and Betty Kahn spending ten days with us in February, after them Alan and Ailsa Judkins from New Zealand and then our niece Robin from England. In March the Reverend John Stott came to Melbourne for some meetings and spent two days with us, during which he spoke at an EFAC dinner held at Trinity College and delivered a memorable address on 'Evangelism in the Local Church'.

Soon after this came the SU appeal launch and a few days later I had a bad cold which worsened to bronchitis. This was not unusual for me but perhaps because I kept going a bit too hard I found myself quite unwell and confined to bed. My doctor diagnosed double pneumonia and said I was to stay in bed for at least two weeks. It was my longest spell for some years and it actually became three weeks before I was able to get slowly back into action. This played havoc with lots of commitments, but of course my fears were groundless and everything went perfectly well without me! Now our attention turned to Ada who was finding arthritis in her hips increasingly painful. This was not a new condition but one which demanded attention, so we consulted a surgeon regarding a hip replacement. He advised that this should be done but not until we returned from overseas, as we had made arrangements to attend the 'Passion Play' at Oberammergau.

I went to PNG for a Pasuwe meeting, followed by a splendid parish house party and an EFAC conference at Monash University. It was time then for the vital meeting of Synod which had the task of electing a successor to the late Archbishop David Penman. Five names were put forward under the new system; three were eliminated and in a ballot late on Saturday afternoon Bishop John Reid very nearly gained election. The meeting adjourned, and when it resumed on the Monday the final result was the election of Archbishop Keith Rayner of Adelaide. Both were excellent candidates and Melbourne, together with the wider church, has been splendidly served by Keith Rayner.

Although, because of arthritis, Ada was now quite limited in her walking we decided to continue with our plans for the overseas journey. We arranged with the airline for help with a wheelchair, which made it all feasible. In fact it provided 'royal' treatment, wafting us like a breeze through immigration and all other queues and ahead of other passengers on to the plane each time. At Hong Kong airport the plane parked on the tarmac and

"The Passion Play", Oberammergau, Germany.
Looking beyond the stage to the Bavarian Hills.

we were taken down on the catering elevator, rather than asking Ada to walk down the gangway steps. At another stop I fulfilled a long-standing ambition to ride down the long walkway on the airline's electric car. We stayed at the Hong Kong Hotel, on the waterfront and close to the ferry so that we could see and do quite a lot with little walking.

At Frankfurt we hired a car and drove for the next two days, across Germany, through Hungary to Budapest. Here again we were located in the centre, overlooking the Danube and with the hotel wheelchair I was able to take Ada on short city walks. We took some tours and especially enjoyed a ferry trip on the river at night with many of the magnificent buildings and bridges illuminated. Leaving this lovely city with some reluctance, we drove through the southern part of the country, stopping for a night or two and enjoying enchanting scenery in Austria, and so to Oberammergau.

The history of the 'Passion Play' dates back more than 350 years to when, during the plague in 1663 the village council vowed to perform it every ten years and from that time there were no further deaths. All the performers and musicians, numbering about two thousand are drawn from the five thousand in the community, which has a deeply rooted Christian tradition. The Play begins at nine in the morning with an interval for lunch, continues until about six in the evening. We found it a profoundly moving experience. The very reverent and authentic presentation makes an unforgettable impression, heightened by the most beautiful singing between scenes and also the incidental music. I had not realised that music played such an integral role in the performance and this was a pleasant surprise.

Looking back now, after eight years, what do I remember? A great deal; in fact it would be true to say that whenever I read or meditate on those portions of Scripture which tell of the betrayal and trial of Jesus, that portrayal of these events forms a backdrop in my mind. The meetings of the Sanhedrin, the discussions with Judas, his remorse and the crowd scenes were most powerful and are vivid still in my mind, likewise the depiction of the taking down of Christ's body from the cross.

Leaving picturesque Bavaria we drove to Frankfurt to resume our journey to London and to Dunsfold where we stayed with Douglas and Betty Kahn. They kindly lent us a very comfortable car, making it possible for us to tour Scotland and stay for a weekend with the Simpsons in Edinburgh where Roger's ministry continued to flourish. Returning home we spent a few days in Perth with our friends John and Moyra Prince who kindly took us on a tour of the wildflower areas. We also had opportunity to meet other friends including Des and Fay Kenna, our first contact with them since Kerby days.

Two days after arriving home Ada entered hospital for hip surgery and this was attended by a good deal of pain and discomfort during her stay over the next three weeks. As the weeks went by after returning home, it became apparent that the operation had not been successful. Ada suffered sharp spasms of pain which left her helpless and quite unable to leave her bed. The specialist, whom we visited often, simply counseled patience, saying the new hip would 'work in'. Her sister Jean came from NZ, originally planned so that I could go to PNG, but this visit was out of the question and the two of us were fully occupied trying to find ways of easing Ada's condition and caring for her. It was suggested that the advice of a leading neurologist might be sought in case the pain had some other source. This we did but he said it was not the case. All of this led to six days in the Royal Melbourne Hospital for further X-rays and scans. One of the senior surgeons there was known to us and he expressed to me his strong opinion that the surgery had not been properly done and 'would never work'. It was Christmas Eve when Ada returned home and armed with this knowledge we knew that consideration should now be given to re-doing the operation.

Russell and Joan had returned to Melbourne to pastor the Outreach church at Ringwood so that it was nice that we were all able to gather at their home to celebrate Christmas together. Howard and Andrea had also been back in their home state for a year or so, living at Alphington, relatively close to us and we appreciated the opportunities of seeing them quite often, and sharing with our whole family once again.

In the New Year Ada had a measure of recovery and was walking more freely with the help of a crutch and with less pain. This being the case, we decided to do some regular swimming at a heated pool at Mornington, checking on progress and continuing monthly visits to the doctor, before deciding on further surgery. Ada had begun driving a little in my 'Prelude', and one day on her way to the pool she had a collision at an intersection near home, a lady coming on her left failed to stop. My car ended up on its side, badly damaged, and Ada was lifted out through the sunroof, in the goodness of God, suffering only from bruised ribs.

Soon after this we received a strong recommendation regarding a surgeon who had helped a lady in a similar plight to Ada's. We had an appointment with him, and feeling a sense of assurance, arranged for the surgery to be re-done in July. This was an entirely different experience and before long Ada was using her limb freely and without pain. However there was arthritis in the other hip so we accepted his suggestion that he should do that as well and by Christmas 1991 Ada was well, free of pain and beginning to enjoy normal mobility, for which we gave grateful thanks to the Lord for His guidance and help throughout that difficult period.

In February of that year Russell and Joan were spending a few days with us and Russ made a timely suggestion. He noted that even when Ada overcame her immediate problem, it was clear that the present garden would be too much for us to manage. Swimming was likely to be a continuing need for exercise. Why not sell part of our land and build a good indoor pool? Although we hated the thought of losing the very attractive area we called 'The Orchard' with its many trees, we agreed with the logic, had a survey done and put the land on the market.

By June it was sold and plans were drawn up for an extension which would include a ten-metre heated pool. It was an involved exercise, because of the steep slope and the need to make it look right. However, with the combined efforts of architects, engineers, builder and pool builders, by March of the following year it was completed. We were delighted with the appearance and it has been a highly valued facility ever since. For a large part of the year we use it almost daily, friends living locally and needing exercise are able to avail themselves of it and it is a popular feature with family members when they visit. For about four years nothing was built on the land sold. Now there is a home and attractive garden. We are so grateful, as we realise that keeping all that ground even looking just tidy would now be beyond us, and swimming in the sea mostly too chilly for our aging bodies.

The chairman of the Ridley College executive, Dr John Upton died suddenly whilst playing squash at the end of January 1991 and a few days later I received a telephone call from the Principal, Maurice Betteridge saying that the executive would like me to become the chairman. I found there were a number of issues to be considered. There was the fact that the College was facing the need for some major changes, the Principal was about to retire and a suitable new appointment was crucial to its whole future. For my part, Ada's condition at that point made me uncertain, also I was seventy-two and had served on the executive for about half of those years. However the new appointment coming up weighed most in all of these issues and I was glad to say that I would accept.

I was a keen supporter of the College and all that it stood for and I had enjoyed working on the various appeals over the years. To me it seemed that meetings of the council tended to be stiff and formal, rarely engaging in frank debate and I hoped that in becoming chairman, it might be possible to bring about a change in the 'atmosphere' of the meetings. I set out with this objective and was encouraged to feel that we did experience a move to a different ethos, more in keeping with the biblical and evangelical tone of the college itself. The man who had been responsible for so ably maintaining those standards in the College over the past twelve years, the Reverend Maurice Betteridge, together with his charming and gifted wife Jacqueline remained with us until April 1992. I was pleased that it fell to me to plan a farewell function at the Royal Auto Club when the Archbishop unveiled a portrait and with others paid tribute to them both and wished them well.

The task of seeking a new principal provided the executive with an excellent opportunity for working together as a team, and that is what happened. We advertised the position widely, scrutinised references closely and when the short list was drawn up the search committee of eight gave two or three full days to an intensive interviewing process. Four candidates were flown in from interstate and one from London. The President, Archbishop Rayner, was kept well informed and personally met some of them. When the appointee was announced by the council, we all shared a sense of confidence that he, Graham Cole, was the man of God's choice. The progress in the life and standing of the College in the intervening years bears that out, as Ridley has developed strongly in many areas and has clear plans for the future. It gave me much pleasure that Mrs Beryl Coombe was elected to succeed me as Executive chairperson. We have enjoyed a long friendship and I knew her to be extremely capable, with a commitment to church and mission, at home and worldwide. The College was fortunate that someone with the ability was willing to to give so freely of her time and energy.

Strangely, not long after concluding the Ridley search I was involved in a somewhat similar exercise as a member of the incumbency committee at St James-the-Less. The Reverend Ray Gregory's very effective ministry was drawing to a close, as he had reached the age for retirement. He had been assisted in the final year by a curate, the Reverend Lydia Saunders, a lady with a most attractive personality, deep faith and a gift for preaching. After the deadlock over the ordination of women at the 1983 General Synod, the issue was partially resolved at the next meeting four years later, by agreeing that individual Dioceses could make their own rule on the matter. Melbourne was one of the first to do so and about twenty dioceses are now ordaining women for both the diaconate and priesthood. I think there were some of our parishioners who had reservations about this, however I fancy very few doubts remained after Lydia had been at Mt Eliza for a few months. She had a really beautiful ministry amongst us for the three years of her curacy.

Our committee did its work carefully and well, guided I believe, by the Holy Spirit, and eventually we were all very pleased when the Reverend David Powys accepted nomination. Ada and I were delighted, as David, with his wife Penny, had begun a curacy at Ivanhoe in the last few months of our time there. I had also had the pleasure of working with David's mother, Mary Powys over many years in CMS on state and federal councils. The parish planned a major dinner function to mark the day of Ray's retirement. Five days before that his wife, Lesley, suffered a heart attack and died within a few hours, so that sadly we gathered for a memorial service rather than the dinner.

Within the space of one week in mid-1991 I lost two people who had figured largely in my life. Ralph Davis died on June 30th. As Bruce Redpath, his friend and successor as chairman of Mayne Nickless noted in his address, he died like a good accountant, at the end of the financial year! For forty-eight years I had been the fortunate recipient of his friendship, and there were hundreds of others around the world who, like me, loved him for his warmth and generosity, his steadfastness of spirit and his zeal for Christ. I had the privilege of speaking, with Bruce and the Reverend Peter Corney at the thanksgiving service, saying something about Ralph's life of faith and prayer and the gifts which God had given him.

Five days after Ralph's death my brother Roy died suddenly after collapsing in the doctors' surgery. He was more than four years my junior and since the war our lives had diverged somewhat. Nevertheless we shared a strong affection for each other and a mutual love of music. He also worked at Kerby for the last decade or so of its life. Apart from work, his interests were bound up in his home and family and his grandchildren. Roy's wife Muriel, who had been his constant helper and companion, accepted his passing bravely and with composure, strongly supported by her family. I was very grateful that I had the opportunity of paying my tribute to Roy when asked to deliver the eulogy at his funeral service at St Andrews, Rosanna.

Following on the highly successful conference at Harare in 1985, SU International planned for the next one to be held at the De Bron Conference centre, Holland in 1992. We planned to attend and set off on May 14th, stopping for a few days in Singapore. Whilst there I became unwell and on the day of departure had a temperature of 103 degrees. It did not help that on arrival at Amsterdam we had two trains to catch and when we reported at the conference centre I could only collapse into bed.

After missing the first two days of the program I began to enter into things without much energy but sufficient to enjoy some of the richness of all the good things available. We were blessed with most beautiful Spring weather, a delightful location beside a splendid river, seven hundred delegates from ninety different SU movements, many of whom were old friends. In addition there were some fine speakers and national presentations, Bible studies and stimulating discussion groups. My only task was to chair and speak at a Sunday afternoon program about the work of the International Development Fund. This attracted a much greater number than expected, speakers from the receiving bodies gave first-rate accounts of how the money had helped their work and I felt very happy about the occasion.

I think most of those present felt sad when it came to the last day of this great conference and it was time to part. We certainly

At the De Bron SU conference: seven nationalities were represented in our study group shown here.

did. However it was nice to get to London and have a few days rest as I had not really recovered my strength. Returning to London two years later I could not help feeling amused at the surprise shown by some people at how much younger I looked. One friend told me that he had thought my days were over when he saw me at De Bron!

After some time with Tony and other friends it was just great to have a few days with Russell and Joan who were enjoying a holiday trip, Joan's first overseas journey. We visited Bath together, later driving through Devon and staying at Dartmouth, finally leaving them at Bristol as we went on to Scotland. A highlight was a brief stay on the Isle of Skye, and the memory of that interlude has remained with us. Then something more. Our friend Douglas Kahn was in the habit of arranging church house parties from time to time, much more elaborate than our parish weekends at Kallista! This year he invited us to join with some members of his parish and others for a ten-day stay at a hotel in Lenzerheide in the Swiss Alps which turned out to be a most agreable time. It included two wonderful all-day coach trips, inspiring after-dinner talks from the Reverend John Salter of Guilford, beautiful views, short walks and new friendships.

Before leaving England we had already heard from Russ and Joan, now back in Australia, that they had been asked to transfer to the Outreach church in London. We had so enjoyed having all the families back in Melbourne that this was disappointing news, although we were pleased with their readiness to do whatever they felt God wanted. They would probably leave in the middle of the following year. We now set out to return home, at least pleased that we had recently acquired a fax machine! Since they had returned from Brisbane we had greatly enjoyed the company of Russell, Joan and their boys. The constraints on spiritual fellowship remained, but we felt much closer than previously. Our Christmas party that year was at Marcus and Barbara's home in the hills at St. Andrews, about fifty kilometres from Melbourne, and we made the most of all being together.

In the parish our lady curate had made an interesting suggestion to some of the men. She felt that as the ladies had numerous meetings amongst themselves, why not start a mens' breakfast fellowship? She was warmly supported by the vicar and so it was decided to try it out. We settled for 7 am one Saturday morning a month; an informal meal, costing two dollars, discussion with occasional addresses and finishing sharp at 8.30. It began a little uncertainly, we found it hard to get the hoped for younger men but had surprising interest from the older age bracket and some non church goers. The winter months caused a change in time to 7.30 and we found speakers to be more acceptable than discussion. The usual pattern is that speakers share something of their life-story, their vocation and their faith. Occasionally there is a strong evangelistic note, if so it is usually incidental. I am sure the example and the quiet testimony of some of our speakers have proved to be most welcome and the most telling, and the monthly gatherings are now a much appreciated feature of our Parish life.

In the month that our breakfasts began it was stimulating to have David and Robyn Claydon both preaching in our parish for CMS and staying with us for the weekend. David has taken his place as one of the most articulate leaders in world mission, with the ability to helpfully analyse global trends and events. Robyn, who is also a gifted speaker, has left the teaching profession and is working with the Lausanne movement, encouraging and training women for ministry, particularly in undeveloped and oppressed countries. We have seen 'overseas' mission change enormously in our lifetime.

That same week I attended the memorial service in Sydney for Dudley Deasey, one of the pioneers of UFM work in Papua. It was an absorbing time. After the formal addresses, those present were given the opportunity of speaking, which brought forth stories moving and humorous. It is not often that funeral services end with peals of laughter but this was most appropriate for Dudley, who was himself a noted story teller. He with his wife Marjorie had spent fifty years in what is now PNG. They, together with two other old friends of ours, Charles and Shirley Horne, began their pioneer work as an absolute grassroots ministry amongst head-hunting tribes of the lower Fly River area. The spiritual impact of their lives on those primitive people has been incalculable. It was in many ways a complete contrast to the style of ministry which David Claydon and other leaders are promoting today, which is however an equally valid expression of 'going into all the world'. As a footnote on the pioneer spirit, Marjorie Deasey stayed with us shortly after this and spoke of obtaining her driving licence at the age of eighty-three, apparently an Australian record. As I write she is back in her old territory in PNG helping with translation of the Scriptures.

The battle to put the Birchgrove business in England on a sound footing a year or so earlier had regrettably been lost. Chris and Mary Wharmby had worked wonders in moving the factory into a new building and the whole enterprise was beginning to look very businesslike, but the combination of growing stocks and debtors and lack of adequate capital plus distribution problems brought about its demise. If the Wharmbys had been thought of one year earlier I think the story could have been very different. The fact that it was so near to success made us all the more unhappy to admit defeat. For Marcus and Chris it was an exceedingly costly episode in their business careers and it took its toll on their individual companies back in Australia. For me also there was a financial downside.

In the meantime Howard, who had with Andrea and family returned from Tasmania because of the steady building up of his business in shredding machines and other engineering items, was now thinking of moving further north. He was finding that his main markets tended to be in territories where large timber mills were concentrated, in northern NSW and Queensland.

The time for Russell and Joan's departure drew near and on June 5th we had a family party at home to say farewell, which also served to celebrate my 75th birthday. It provided a good opportunity for a family photograph, with all eighteen members present, maybe the last such occasion. The following weekend we spent at our parish house party when former colleague Bishop Dudley Foord and his wife Elizabeth gave the Bible studies. In July I went to another of the excellent smaller EFAC conferences, this time held in Sydney.

I returned on the Friday evening to witness what was becoming a new feature in the world of League football, a Friday night match. Essendon were playing old rivals Collingwood and a crowd of 87,750 was in attendance to see a handsome Essendon victory, which needless to say I found vastly enjoyable. 1993 was a vintage year for the 'Bombers' and they went on to win the Premiership in convincing fashion against Carlton in September. In between those two matches Ada and I drove by way

*Our Golden Wedding year, 1993, when all family members were
present at Mt Eliza in June for these photographs.
Top left: Howard and Andrea with Ondine, Fraser and Andrew.
Top right: Russell and Joan with Tom, Ben, David and Luke.
Bottom: Marcus and Barbara with Trent, Justin and Adam.*

of Port Augusta to the Flinders Ranges to spend a few days in what was for us a very different environment. On the return trip we travelled by way of Broken Hill which provided us with a few surprises, and all told we relished the change of scene.

That year also marked a special anniversary for Ada and me, being the fiftieth since that wartime day when we were united in marriage at Holy Trinity church, Hampton. I always love celebrating birthdays and anniversaries, and this was an especially good opportunity to remember November 2nd, as it was Melbourne Cup Day holiday. About forty friends and family gathered at home for lunch, followed by a service of thanksgiving. After hymns and readings then some talks and prayers, we shared together in a celebration of Holy Communion led by our vicar, David Powys. Ada and I were grateful that the program captured the spirit of thanksgiving to our loving God which was the focus of the day.

In June 1994 we flew to London to be met by Russell and taken to the home which they had bought at South Croydon. After a year they had adapted well to English life. We had been keeping in touch by fax, Joan especially being a splendid correspondent, but it was nice to once again be in their company. Tony McCutcheon graciously lent us his car, as he had on previous trips, and we enjoyed travelling far and wide, staying at B&Bs and visiting friends. With the family we found it easier than ever before to discuss matters relating to Outreach and spiritual issues in general. Tony Kostas the director of OI was living in London now and it seemed to us that there were signs of strains in the relationship, although Russell was very loyal to Tony. For our part we felt that the demands which Tony was making on his followers were totally unreasonable and could not be justified by Scripture in any way, and before leaving we expressed some of these concerns to Russ and Joan.

A few weeks after returning I was working in my office when a message began to come through on the fax machine. It was in Joan's writing and as usual ran to the welcome few pages. I began to gather it together when five words seemed to leap out from the rest 'that we have left OI'. I quickly took it to Ada and read to her the whole letter, which detailed the thinking, praying and discussions leading up to this decision. It is hard to describe our emotions at that point; paramount was an overwhelming sense of relief and gratitude to the Lord that this bondage to Tony had been broken. Excitement that the barriers between us would be removed and that our prayers of twenty years had been answered. Then we began to wonder; what would Russell do? What about the boys, how would they react? Luke was in Canada, returning shortly to Australia, David was working in Manchester and in the OI church there. All of these queries were answered in due course but for the moment exhilaration ran high and we had to share the news with the rest of the family.

There were indeed many consequences and it was instructive for us to see God at work even in small details of this situation. Russell was a schoolteacher but it was twenty years since he had taught. He applied to an agency and was sent to a school associated with the church of St Martins in the Fields. Most of the pupils were black and the work was difficult. The Christian lady principal said to Russ after a few days 'You are the answer to our prayers'. Later he was to get a permanent appointment in an excellent school much closer to home where he remained until they returned to Australia in September 1998.

As a family they were guided first to a Vineyard church in Croydon, then later moved to one at Wimbledon. These charismatic churches grew out of the ministry of John Wimber in the US and later in the UK. During the final year or so of their stay they worshipped in a number of churches closer to home. Dave returned from Manchester and seemed to fairly readily accept the changes and appreciated the worship at the Vineyard. Ben, at University, was already encountering other Christians and as he had been close to the events he had a good understanding of the issues. He also moved to the Vineyard with his parents, as did Tom. For Luke , the eldest son, it was much more difficult. The news reached him when he was in Canada staying with OI friends, just as he was about to leave for Australia. He had a partly formed intention to enter into full-time ministry with OI in Canada.

Luke was returning because his visa had expired and he had to come here to apply for a Canadian visa. He planned to stay first with us and then with OI friends. We met him at the airport and the conversation soon turned to the topic of OI, and recent events. Luke is a man 'in whom there is no guile', dedicated, earnest and intensely loyal to Tony Kostas. He was greatly distressed and stated his firm intention of remaining as he was. Many things were to happen over the next few weeks to influence him, but crucial was his deep sense of shock at the way the OI congregation in Melbourne were thinking. At his second Sunday visit a very lengthy letter from Tony was read out containing many untrue statements about their former pastor Russell, and saying that he had turned his back on Tony and therefore, on God. Luke returned to our home in tears and confusion, we did our best to put things in perspective and he had lengthy telephone talks with his parents. He did not return to any services, although he had long sessions with OI people. Slowly, through his reading of Scripture and prayers and in talks with us he came to see the issues in their true light, and made it clear that he too was withdrawing from the church. In the weeks that followed he found that there were other members who were unhappy and he was able to counsel them, some leaving but many fearful of the consequences.

After a happy Christmas with all the local members of the family, Luke agreed to accompany us to a CMS summer conference being held in the mountains at Rawson. For someone with virtually no knowledge of other churches or of mission, this was ideal. There were lots of young adults, plenty of missionaries, and Bible studies from Archbishop Harry Goodhew of Sydney. Luke's spiritual nature responded and subsequently we all had an enriching time over the next few weeks. He came quite often to church with us as well as attending other churches, and also to our Bible study group and to a family camp. His friendly personality ensured that he was remembered by many people for a long time afterwards. He remained with us until March, then renewed his visa for the UK and returned there to continue teaching and to join with his family at the Vineyard church.

The historian friend who encouraged me to write this book specifically urged that I should give an account of our experience with Outreach International, because of the fact that exclusivist, authoritarian groups are on the increase and beguiling many believers. This is why I have dwelt on the topic at some length. One aspect of them which appeals to many is the emphasis on the body life, the love which members have for each other. Alas, it lasts only so long as one remains within the circle. Russ and Joan have been deeply pained to find that loved friends of twenty years, with whom they shared so many experiences, no longer wish to talk with them and even pass them by in the street. From the spiritual viewpoint, the worst aspect would seem to be the teaching that God will speak to them only through the leader; so that in OI every major issue in the life of the members had to be submitted for Tony's approval. He terms himself an apostle. Next to that is their disapproval of any other spiritual bonds, a rigid exclusiveness which totally isolates the group, sometimes even from family members. On the material side, no account is given of the leader's stewardship. There are no committees and no treasurer, although the members give generously, often sacrificially. The reply to any query about this aspect of things was simply 'we trust each other', but too often in situations like this trust may be abused.

Before the events described above, in our parish it had been decided by the Vestry to conduct a stewardship campaign as our giving was not keeping up with the growth and the needs of the parish. Asked if I would be willing to act as chairman of the appeal, I felt that I had done my share of fund-raising and was inclined to refuse. On the next day I was trying to tune-in a radio program for Ada when 'by chance' I came across the voice of Eva Burrows, former World Leader of the Salvation Army. She was preaching and referring to the widespread use of calculators and went on to speak of a 'calculating' generation. 'God is an uncalculating giver' she declared 'what about you, do you stop to calculate everything you give and do? Learn to give like God, without calculating'. I had to move on , but that was all I needed to hear. God was saying, 'that is for you!' I shared this with two colleagues who were somewhat opposed to the campaign, and they agreed to lend it support and I took on the leadership. It is interesting that quite often God guides us with this type of intervention.

In April came the time for a family party to farewell Howard, Andrea and Ondine. They had sold their home at Alphington and were making a move to Laurieton on the NSW central coast where Howard had already established an office. We were sad to be losing them again, but pleased to think it might give them a more settled lifestyle with less travel for Howard. The pace had been unrelenting over recent years and we hoped this move might mean a more relaxed lifestyle for them both. Andrew was remaining in Melbourne but Fraser had already been working in Sydney for some time. Jean Deeble was with us at the time and after the farewell we made a very pleasant trip with her to the Grampians for a couple of days.

Our good friend in Singapore, Dr Khoo Oon Teik was critically ill, he had suffered a massive stroke whilst having some surgery. As we were on our way to Europe and UK in June 1995 we called at Singapore, where David Chan took us to the hospital to see him. We found it very saddening to see this great man of God, who had been used in the healing and blessing of so many, inert and unable to speak. We said a few things and prayed, grateful to receive some signs of his cognisance. Since that day, his wife Adeline has received her home-call and we hear that Oon Teik is somewhat improved and able to converse.

We continued our flight to Zurich, then travelled by rail to Locarno where we planned to stay for ten days at 'Casa Lumino' the new SU guest house and conference centre on the familiar site at Monti, overlooking Lake Maggiore. After a delightfully relaxing time we went on to London to be met by Russell and Tom, collecting Joan from a meeting on the way home. It was just great to be with them after all the trauma of OI and we had some lovely times together. We made two visits to their church and went to some other local ones, also to All Souls a couple of times. We were invited to a most enjoyable lunch at John Stott's home with a fascinating group of overseas guests and Tony McCutcheon. We did a good deal of our usual touring and spent five enjoyable days with Alan and Eileen Dyer, and a weekend with Robin.

Back at Mt Eliza there were further echoes of old SU times when Kevin O'Sullivan from NZ spent two days with us. Then later a similar visit from Colin Becroft with Bruce and Honor Lumsden down as well. Two trips to PNG were still part of the annual routine, where Pasuwe affairs proceeded steadily. On our wedding anniversary we departed for our NSW holiday at Hallidays Point, now a welcome and regular feature, thanks to the kindness of Geoff and Ann Kells. This location now became very appropriate for us as it is less than an hour's drive from Laurieton, providing the opportunity of spending some times with Howard and Ann.

It was on October 9th that I attended my final Vestry meeting at St James the Less and it was a nice surprise when we all adjourned to the vicarage for supper to find that Ada was also in attendance. Some kind words were spoken and I was presented with a copy of the complete new Australian Prayer Book, a most welcome gift. It was sixty years since my first Vestry meeting at St Andrews, Rosanna. There had been a break for a few years when we began attending at Ivanhoe, so that it was not continuous, nevertheless it was still a lot of meetings.

In December my old colleague and former factory manager, Alan Johnston died after a long battle with illness and I was quite moved when his family requested me to conduct the funeral service, which I did gladly. The only other time I had done this was a year or so earlier when my lifelong friend Brook Hannah went to his reward. Held in the Chapel at St Pauls youth camp, on Phillip Island, that was a rather unique occasion when those attending were invited to bring items which reminded them of Brook. Then his son Digby with his wife Lyn said something about Brook which related to each of the items, ranging from a dish mop, an apple, a gum leaf to a Bible and more.

It gave us much pleasure to have Tony Mc Cutcheon staying for the weekend before Christmas 1995. He joined us for our regular visit to the Melbourne Town Hall for carols with the Victoria Chorale, this was preceded by dinner in honour of Marcus' birthday, with a few other guests. The observance of Christmas with church services, carols, family parties and gifts has always meant a great deal to us, as to countless others, carrying, as it does, special significance for members of the household of faith. A beautiful way to close the year.

Remember your leaders, who spoke the word of God to you.
Consider the outcome of their way of life and imitate their faith.
Hebrews 13.7 NIV

A few, very few, have magic.The magic of personality, which
demands attention and escapes detailed analysis.
W. Wyatt speaking of Aneurin Bevan

At its foundation, true leadership is the authentic outward expres-
sion of the inner character of the individual. True leaders listen to
a deep inner wisdom, speak from their heart, and act with integrity
and courage. They inspire others toward extraordinary achieve-
ment by the strength of their vision, the clarity of their purpose,
and their unswerving commitment to personal integrity. It is not
what visionary leaders do that makes them extraordinary; it is who
they are as human beings.
Charles Kiefer

- 18 -

1932 – 1999

Heroes and Friends

Example is a powerful factor in our lives. It has been a rich blessing to me in that God brought certain people into the orbit of my life at different stages when I was most likely to benefit from their example. These were people who had given their all to God and were living for Him in such a fashion as to light the way ahead for me in my struggle to become a better person. This is one way in which the Lord instructs His children and such tuition is common to us all, because He knows we sorely need such inspiration if we are to persevere.

For years I have thought of a group of these people as my 'heroes'. Men and women whom I have admired because of the quality of their lives and deeds, who have been the means of encouraging me to press on in times of failure and difficulty. Now seems to be the point in this story to acknowledge my debt to at least some of them. There is a sense in which all one's close friends are heroes, however I have selected six names to write about here. Obviously they will have appeared in these pages already and I seek forbearance for this burst of nostalgia as I relate how they each made a profound impression on me, chiefly during the first half of my life.

Without doubt, the earliest influences become the most deeply rooted and outside of my family, the figure who loomed largest in my teenage years was Horace J Hannah. Already in middle age when I came to know him, he was a man of slight stature, with grey hair, slightly bald and with his gold-rimmed spectacles and somewhat severe countenance he had exactly the appearance I would have expected for a chief inspector of a large bank. With a State school education which ended at the age of fourteen, he had risen to that position through his diligence and natural gifts. It was as a Christian layman that he displayed his greater gifts of theological scholarship and administration, and supremely as a teacher and preacher of the gospel. He was a voracious and discriminating reader and possessed a library which was the envy of many scholars. His large study was lined with books on all sides from floor to ceiling, tables were piled high with them, hallways and other rooms of the large family home were crammed with books and theological journals. If the Scriptures were his lifeblood, books provided the oxygen; they were the very air that he breathed. From them he drew his great learning of men and events, of doctrine and heresies, of history and the church and above all, the towering figure of Paul, the apostle to the gentiles. After Christ, Paul was the predominant figure in all of Horace Hannah's thinking and teaching. He interpreted him and his epistles with exceptional insight and understanding, which he conveyed to his hearers with all the force at his command.

I was in my thirteenth year when I began regularly attending church services at St Andrews where Mr Hannah was accustomed to preach, both morning and evening. Only occasionally did we have the vicar of the parish of St John's Heidelberg, the Reverend W T C Storrs with us. By the time I made my personal commitment as a Christian I had already absorbed a great deal of Pauline theology, had a good understanding of justification by faith, and a firm conviction as to the reliability of God's word, particularly the latter. It was central to all of Mr Hannah's preaching. 'The first three chapters of Genesis are the seed bed of the Bible', was one of his constant affirmations, likewise 'the New is in the Old concealed, the Old is in the New revealed', as he sought to drive home the message that the whole of scripture was important for us. He also possessed an intimate knowledge of the Psalms and loved to dwell on the statement that 'the Word of God was more to be desired than gold, yea, than much fine gold, sweeter than honey and the dropping of honeycombs'.

Although of 'low church' convictions Mr Hannah took his position as a lay preacher in the Church of England seriously and all of our services were conducted carefully in accordance with the Book of Common Prayer. Some of my fondest memories of those days are of evening prayer, sharing in the canticles and sung responses, then listening to the sermon from Mr Hannah. In his cassock, white surplice and black scarf, with the light shining on the gold rims of his spectacles, his earnest face alight with the burden of his message, he was, it seemed to me, at times like an angel of God, as he spoke to us of the grace of God in Christ, with all the intensity of his being. The little wooden building indeed became like the gate of Heaven and we, the congregation stood before it, hushed and uplifted.

There was another side to Mr Hannah's activities which I did not know about then. His missionary interests as a Council member of the China Inland Mission, also CMS and BCA, as founder in Australia of the Mission to Lepers, and as one of the founders of Ridley College, all provided a pattern for me in later life. Nevertheless, it is as a devoted servant of Jesus Christ that I remember him most. I recall how often in a sermon as he paced up and down the platform that served as a sanctuary in our little church he would quote from F W H Meyers' great poem 'St Paul'; the first stanza:

Christ! I am Christ's! and let the name suffice you,
Ay, for me too he greatly hath sufficed:
Lo with no winning words would I entice you,
Paul has no honour and no friend but Christ.'

Then the last;

Yea thro' life, death, thro' sorrow and thro' sinning
He shall suffice me, for He hath sufficed;
Christ is the end, for Christ was the beginning,
Christ the beginning, for the end is Christ.

I fancy Horace Hannah may not have been a popular figure in the wider church of his day because of his outspoken criticism of commentators, teachers and ecclesiastical leaders who put forward 'modern' or liberal views of the Bible. He was unrelentingly conservative in his theological values, but with a mind informed by the greatest biblical scholars and teachers from the reformation onwards. I do not know what side he would have taken in the debate on the ordination of women, but I do know he had a fine understanding of the place of women in the ministry of Jesus and Paul. I can recall clearly a sermon he gave on the verse from Romans 16; 'Greet Mary, who bestowed much labour upon us' and I also treasure a book he once gave me entitled *Those Women*. A little rule which he frequently quoted has become a lifelong guide. It ran "In all things natural, be spiritual; in all things spiritual, be natural". More than sixty years later I remember so much of what he taught me and I wonder what direction my life may have taken, if I had not been granted the blessing of growing up under the ministry of this devoted man.

As Mr Hannah's health failed, in the late thirties he called increasingly on the services of his friend, the Reverend CH Nash to preach at St Andrews and for a period in 1942-3 Mr Nash was officially appointed as curate. So in this way I became acquainted with the man who was to become my second hero. Already Mr Nash was a hero to many, as his recently published biography tells, and I will refer simply to his impact on my life. When I attended the Upwey Convention at Christmas time in 1935 it came as a great surprise to hear 'our' Mr Nash addressing that great assembly. Over the next few years I was to learn a great deal more of his stature, but at the beginning I knew him as a warm-hearted, wise and godly preacher. He had a wonderful gift for friendship and as long as he lived, whenever we met his eyes would light up as he voiced his greeting, 'Ah, Alan' and clasped my hand. This was also the experience of hundreds of others but none the less meaningful for any one of us, simply evidence of his care for people.

As the years went by I became aware of the breadth of his thinking, his interest in world affairs and his understanding of contemporary events. I was just twenty years of age when the British prime minister, Mr Neville Chamberlain flew to Munich for talks with Hitler in 1938 and returned, announcing dramatically, 'peace in our time', hailed as a triumph by press and populace. On the following Sunday I was startled when Mr Nash devoted his sermon to this statement and thundered from the pulpit, 'He is crying peace when there is no peace' and quoting from the passage in Ezekiel 13 he compared the prime minster to those who paint over an unsound wall with untempered mortar to make it look strong. He warned us to expect war, assuring us that the whitewashed wall would be brought down and the faulty foundations discovered. I had been brought up to treat the words of British prime ministers with much greater respect, but we were soon to learn the accuracy of our preachers' prophecy.

Although both he and Mr Hannah were at one in the essentials of the gospel, Mr Nash evinced a more moderate, slightly gentler outlook. He was more tolerant of people whose views differed from his own and showed more sympathy for those whose faith was weaker. Whereas Mr Hannah preached most often from the words of Paul, Mr Nash was always greatly drawn to the writings of John. I think his background of English public schools and Cambridge made him more irenic and strangely enough, more loyal to the church as an institution, although he suffered greatly at the hands of some of its hierarchy. He certainly instilled something of this loyalty into me, for which I have been grateful.

During the year in which he spent most weekends in my home we conversed over a wide range of topics, it was in a sense, compensating for the education I had missed. One Sunday evening, after church, he began reading to me from a volume of Tennyson which was in my bookcase. He read most movingly, for a long time. I was enthralled and as he came to an end the book slipped from his hands, tears ran down his cheeks and we both sat, silent.

I always thought he was at his best when he spoke in an informal fashion to groups such as Campaigners conferences. He had time then to develop large themes and to deal with them in depth, bringing his marvellous knowledge and understanding of the Scriptures to bear on his chosen topic.

One year he based his talks on the Book of Revelation and I believe we all felt that we had been spectators of a number of epic biblical events. We had seen the Lamb breaking open the seals of the book, we had watched as the prayers of the saints ascended, mingling with the smoke of the incense upon the golden altar before the throne, and had been briefly admitted to the holy of holies. I think it was because he had the gift of helping people to understand deep spiritual truths and of leading them into the presence of Christ, that our various differences faded into insignificance. As I said earlier in these pages we were a mixed group in Campaigners, but as we shared in his ministry we were truly all one in Christ Jesus.

One weekend he came away to a gathering for beach mission

leaders run by SU. On the Saturday evening as we sat around an open fire, just about twelve young men, he began to speak of his early days as a leader on the beaches in England. He went on to speak of the Cambridge Seven, then of men and leaders and their lives in church and mission, shedding light from Scripture on different aspects of both as he progressed. He began to speak at about 8.30 and ended close to midnight, leaving us with a wealth of memories and inspiration.

My association with Mr Nash, with his breadth of outlook, caused me to question some of the more rigid views of some of my 'low church' Anglican friends and I did a lot of thinking and reading to try and find a satisfactory balance. This has proved to be a lifelong pursuit. I remember the remark of Ernest Aebi, Swiss SU staff member, to John Laird about certain colleagues, 'You know John, I think they are just a leetle bit under the law'. I have to confess that over the years I have had reason to feel that is the case with some of my fellow Anglicans, particularly in regard to modes of worship, ornaments and matters of that nature. I think we need a certain amount of freedom in some of these areas so that we might more effectively bear witness to the central facts of our faith. The oft repeated advice given by Mr Nash, that we should 'keep to the broad stream of undisputed truth' is always helpful. After more than half-a-century I remain aware of my debt to these two men who instructed me in the faith. They helped me to become a convinced Anglican whilst retaining the freedom to minister and worship with men and women of differing viewpoints.

A Presbyterian layman of the same era was my third hero. Alfred Coombe has already been mentioned several times in this story. His example greatly influenced and instructed me. He was a man of warm spirituality, a born administrator, charged with the highest ideals of service. Working alongside and watching him I was always impressed with his calm and methodical approach to conducting meetings, stimulating discussion whilst gently guiding emotive committee members and bringing about a spirit of unity and aspiration. He was a role model for me in so many ways. I well remember an early occasion when Ada and I went to Port Melbourne to farewell Alfred and Sabina on one of their many voyages overseas. He sat with me in the cabin and said 'Just let me check my list of things to do'. After a minute or so he looked up saying, 'yes, all done', and gave me a glimpse of a long closely written list, each item neatly ruled out. It established me in a similar lifelong pattern of list making, goal setting and crossing off which has been of immense value. It is one thing to make lists, another to see them achieved and to follow through, so that once noted down nothing can be overlooked.

Alfred was a busy man with heavy responsibilities yet he always had time to help me, a very junior associate in the early days of our friendship. When I accepted the leadership of a youth group for the Australian Nepalese Mission and we wanted to have a house party, I was not sure where to begin. He offered to drive me up to the hills and spend a Saturday looking for a suitable place, which he did most graciously, giving much wise counsel as we drove. Many times I needed to consult him on Campaigner matters and invariably he not only heard me out and gave help, but took time for a chat and a few words of encouragement. With his wife Sabina he exercised a ministry of hospitality in their home which extended widely. Sometimes there were dinner parties, at others they gathered their fellow workers for tennis days or group evenings and we shared in these, always 'special' occasions, enhanced by the charming courtesy of our hosts.

Another biblical precept he fulfilled was that of generosity. He contributed freely and regularly to many movements and as I became involved in SU and other causes I sometimes sought his assistance for particular needs and my requests never failed to elicit a ready and cheerful response. Whatever he did was done with such a spirit of wholeheartedness and grace that his participation was a benediction. In one or two areas it was my privilege in later years to succeed Alfred and it was a blessing and a help to follow in such clearly marked footsteps.

Alfred Stanway, Bishop in the Anglican church, was a hero to thousands, men and women, Australian, African and American. What a wonderful influence for good this positive and practical disciple of Christ exercised. How many, like myself, were inspired by his prayerful example. As I have made clear earlier, I thought the world of him and here I want only to set down one or two typical instances of his help. When I was Chairman of CMS Victoria in the 1950s it troubled me that we did not have the money to properly finish our camp site at Belgrave Heights.

We did, however have a considerable sum set aside in a fund for a city office building. This was a 'dream' that was past it's time, but my efforts to convince the committee that this money could be used for the completion of the Belgrave Heights buildings were unavailing.

At that point of time the Bishop returned from Tanzania on furlough and I put the problem to him. By carefully marshalling all the facts and by a clear presentation of scriptural principles to the committee, under the good hand of God, he brought about a change of mind and a great forward step was made at Belgrave Heights, later sadly destroyed by bushfires. Alfred said to them 'the best guarantee of God's supply for the future is the right use of what He has given you today'. He showed them that they were asking God for money that they actually had already, and the spiritual logic won the day. This became a most helpful rule for me, learning how to rightly use what God has already given.

On another occasion a member of a committee queried the wisdom of his building a hospital where no observable spiritual results had been achieved. He responded that he too was disappointed, but he did not regret the move, 'to do good is always right', he said. No doubt this statement would sometimes need to be qualified, however it was another Stanway principle that has remained with me, often providing timely guidance. Alf's aphorisms were legion and we probably all have our favourites: 'You cannot pray one way and expect another', is one of mine and encapsulates much of his positive outlook and firm belief in God's promises. On another level I loved the way when, confronted by a problem, he would say a day or so later, 'Well, I put my mind to it and this is what I think'. Invariably, the result would be sensible, logical and helpful. Quite often, during the early days of 'Church Scene', board members would be feeling rather downcast by some of the problems we encountered and Alfred's practical advice, encouragement and prayerful guidance saw us through.

The fifth spiritual leader to loom large in my life was Dr John Laird and I have already given evidence of this. We first met when I was in my mid-twenties and over the next twenty years I spent quite a deal of time in his company and we corresponded with each other extensively. A gentle Scot, he was a

Dr JM Laird, circa 1950s.

doctor of medicine who never really practised his chosen profession because God called him to another. In his first months as a ship's doctor he found himself plunged into the aftermath of the fearful earthquake in Napier, New Zealand, as his ship docked there in February 1931. Over 250 people died and there were many casualties. Working amongst them he made contact with Christian people involved with the Crusader Union in schools. Before this he had met others in Auckland and they decided he was just the man needed to become their first full-time worker amongst the young people of New Zealand. So it was that he left the ship at Wellington and in due course came to head up the rapidly expanding work of SU and CU in that country for the next fifteen years. It was 1945 when he was called to the joint secretaryship of the movement in London.

Spiritual wisdom and leadership were the outstanding impressions most people carried away from their first contact with John Laird. Later they would come to value the warmth of his personality, his orderly mind and the excellence of his talks and sermons, his zeal for souls. When he moved to London and found that his new work involved much more by way of administration than his former post, he set himself to study the principles of business management by reading widely and carefully from secular books on business management, a course some of his conservative friends were inclined to regard as dubious. So well did he imbibe the principles at the heart of the matter that he became quite a doyen in the field of organisation and not only did the SU benefit from his knowledge but also many other areas of Christian work. I was one who sought counsel from John about organising staff and situations and I also received great help in my business life from books he recommended. With humility and skill he was able to identify issues and problems and help one toward getting things right.

So I come to the final hero in this list, my friend and fellow worker of more than fifty years, Leonard Buck. I once read of an army report on Lord Mancroft that said of him 'his men would follow him anywhere – even if only out of curiosity', and this often came to my mind as Len set off on some new adventure of faith. We would follow, half fearful, yet expectant and certainly curious, because something always happened. What were the qualities that drew so many of us to him and quickened in us such a strong love for him? He was a very vibrant person, fully alive. Time spent in Len's company was never dull, he had a good sense of humour and was always stimulating in conversation. He possessed a strong sense of the reality, the power and the holiness of God and God's sovereignty was paramount in his thinking. He would say with all the assurance of the Psalmist 'Our God is in Heaven and He does whatever He wills'. All of his thinking was shaped by that truth. Faith in God's power was uppermost in his praying and work for the Kingdom. At the same time he was acutely conscious of spiritual conflict and frequently called on God to 'bind the strong man' as he sought in prayer and faith to tread down the powers of darkness.

It was this faith that fuelled his vision for the remarkable work amongst the troops during the war, and for the early work of the UFM in Papua New Guinea. That also sent him with Gil McArthur, criss-crossing the Highlands of that same country to find a location for the Christian Leaders Training College, and that caused him in his seventies to play a leading role in establishing Prison Fellowship in this country. This vision was accompanied by an admirable breadth of outlook and generosity of spirit. There was never anything narrow-minded or petty about Len's activities. His contributions to the Convention movement and the Bible College of Victoria were also outstanding. But perhaps his most lasting memorial will be in the hearts and lives of hundreds of individuals whom he led to a personal faith in Jesus Christ. I am reminded of the passage in the book of Daniel 'Those who are wise will shine like the brightness of the heavens, and those who lead many to righteousness, like the stars for ever and ever'. This is surely true not only of dear Leonard but of all those of whom I have written in this chapter, devoted servants of the living God.

Soon after I became chairman of CMS Victoria in 1954 I had my one and only conversation with a person whom I had sensed was rather a legendary figure in that Society. It was a lady by the name of Sophie Dixon, who had gone as a missionary to Africa in 1903, and in her retirement had commenced the Diary of Prayer, still circulating each month to members. When we were introduced she said: 'So you are Alan Kerr; well I pray for you every day'. Being still quite young, this was the first time anyone had said this to me. I was at the same time startled, humbled and then deeply grateful for support of this kind from someone I had never met. Later in life, with wider involvement in Christian service one was aware of many faithful helpers, friends and family whose regular prayers lay behind much of what was being attempted. How thankful I was, day by day, for the intercession made for me and for the work I was doing. I would not care to think about the way my life may have gone if it were not for such prayers. 'We should all be priests for one another' I once heard Gottfried Osei-Mensah say, in a study of a passage in Exodus. How true this is and how great our debt to our priestly friends.

This thought leads me to speak further of friends and friendship, and to express a concern which has persisted throughout the writing of this personal record. Every phase of the journey I have been describing has involved friends. Just a few have been mentioned, many have not. Some of you who read this may wonder why there is no reference to things we did together which were significant for us both. I have had to accept a limitation as to the size of this book and remind myself constantly that I could not hope to recount all the stories I would wish. Alluring bypaths have presented themselves on almost every page and it has been necessary to resist the urge to launch into other tales. Rightly or wrongly there has been a limit to the cast of players and many close and dear associates do not appear which causes me much regret and some embarrassment and I can only trust for their understanding.

Hopefully, readers will sense the fact that there are many other heroes from whom I have learnt and friends to whom I am indebted. In every sphere, whether of business or Christian activity, in different places and countries, there have been friendships which have made things possible, caused them to happen and given them significance. Friendships are the warp and weft of the fabric of life and by them I have been empowered and enriched.

When morning dawns and evening fades
you call forth songs of joy.

Psalm 65-8b

One must wait until the evening to see how splendid the day has been.

Sophocles

Now as they walked in this land, they had more rejoicing than in parts more remote from the Kingdom to which they were bound, and drawing near to the City they had yet a more perfect view thereof.

John Bunyan, *Pilgrim's Progress*

O may we soon again renew that song,
And keep in tune with heav'n till God erelong
To his celestial consort us unite,
To live with Him, and sing in endless morn of light.

John Milton, At a Solemn Music

You will ask where I find my ideas: I hardly know. They come uninvited, directly or indirectly. I can almost grasp them with my hands in the open air, in the woods, while walking in the stillness of the night, early in the morning, called up by moods which the poet translates into words, I into musical tones. They ring and roar and swirl about me until I write them down in notes.

Ludwig van Beethoven,

in Alexander Wheelcock Thayer's *Life*, 1866

- 19 -

1996 – 1999

'Drawing Near to the City'

Besides friends and heroes of the sort which I have written about in the previous chapter, we all have a host of others in different spheres of life. These may be in literature, art, music, sport or other fields of human endeavour. Ada and I find that music plays a large part in our lives and how grateful we are for Beethoven and Bach, Mozart, Schubert, Brahms, Hadyn and Handel and all of the great company of composers through the centuries and for the heritage they have left us. What heroes they are! How music can lift our spirits if we are burdened, or stir us to endeavour, comfort us when sad and delight us when glad. It is very interesting and true to our own experiences that we read about Elisha, when confronted with a grave problem saying: 'Now bring me a harpist', and then we read that, 'While the harpist was playing, the hand of the Lord came upon Elisha'. So as the music stole into his ears he felt the touch of God and found the answer to his problem (2 Kings 3-15).

Likewise we have our heroes amongst the painters, poets, and writers who have inspired us, but these are not our concern here, save for this fleeting reference. One often wonders about the part played by the Spirit of God in the lives and work of these artists and composers. Did their masterpieces flow simply from the gifts inherent within them or was there a divine influence at work? And if the latter, to what extent and in what manner were they led by God?

When it comes to hymns, perhaps the ground is clearer. John Wesley affirms that: 'When poetry keeps its place, as the handmaid of Piety, it shall attain a crown that fadeth not away'. So many hymns have inspired and blessed believers through the ages by giving us the means of praising Almighty God in exalted terms, that we feel sure they have come to us from a Divine source. Regrettably, as in all human endeavour, there are many that appear to fall short of this high standard. It seems quite possible to me that some of the current rejection of traditional hymns is due to the poor quality of much hymn writing, especially many from the nineteenth century, as well as the music which accompanied them. Archaic and flowery language, diffuse spiritual expression, and lack of clarity fail to stir the spirit of worship. As B L Manning has said of one particular example, they 'choke us with metaphorical confectionery'.

We welcome our first great grandchild Chloe Victoria Jane, 1996.

If we go back a century or two earlier we find that as a general rule the sentiments are much stronger, and the verse simple and direct. To quote Wesley once again 'we find the purity, the strength and the elegance of the English language and at the same time the utmost simplicity and plainness'. He was speaking chiefly of his brother's compositions but the same might be said, perhaps even more so, of Watts, Cowper, Newton, Montgomery and a host of others. This is not to mention the treasures of the early church to which we are indebted for some of the loftiest hymns of praise and supplication.

As one who sang, taught and enjoyed CSSM choruses with a generation of young people, I know the worth of simple, short devotional songs. There are many modern songs which convey spiritual truth and offer praise in most beautiful fashion. Also some fine new hymns in the traditional style. However, should they supplant entirely the use of the older hymns in some places it will be a sad loss, as we need both. For me, the earlier hymns have been a means of instruction and have also provided a great source of inspiration stored within the memory. From them I have absorbed doctrine and found practical help and strength in Christian living. 'I will sing of the love of the Lord for ever', says the Psalmist and a mind well-furnished with good hymns and songs enables us to do that in a worthy manner, until the time comes when we shall join our voices with angels around the Throne.

When Mr Nash read and reflected upon Psalm 128 at our wedding service, he made reference to verse five and expressed the hope 'that we might live to see our children's children'. In the kindness of God we have been granted this blessing, and more. Not only have we seen them but we are enjoying the great pleasure of knowing them as adults. We are frequently involved with them in various activities and increasingly of sharing with them in the things of God. We have seen some of them married and in 1996, Chloe Victoria Jane Kerr was born in Launceston, daughter of Fraser and Sarah, becoming the first of the next generation, making our eldest son, Howard and his wife Andrea, grandparents, and giving us all great delight.

One morning in March 1996 I was in my office preparing for the Pasuwe Ltd board meeting to be held in Port Moresby the following month. Whilst writing I was suddenly assailed by very sharp pains in my chest and was forced to lie down. As the pain increased I realised it was necessary to call for medical attention. Ada was in the garden and I went out to ask her to phone the doctor and quickly returned to my bed. The pain had now become so crushing that I knew it was serious, if not life-threatening and felt it likely that I may be about to die. I wanted to be sure that I would be ready to meet the Lord and my thoughts centred on the Cross. I remembered reading about a famous English author who was greatly moved by a church service which concluded with the singing of Isaac Watts hymn, 'When I survey the wondrous cross'. 'Yes', he said afterwards, 'the Cross remains and in the straits of the soul retains its ancient appeal', and with those words he collapsed and died. Recalling this brought me a sense of great comfort.

It seemed strange to be inwardly calm although sweating profusely and feeling scarcely able to breathe. Then I was violently ill, my doctor entered the room and immediately said 'Alan, you are having a coronary' and gave me an injection. The ambulance arrived and I was soon being swiftly conveyed to the cardiac section at Frankston Hospital. The sense of calm and clarity remained for a while but as we reached the hospital events became blurred. A doctor was telling me that he thought I would be allright in a few days. Later he reappeared through the 'mist' to say that I was having a severe attack and that I might be there for a while but they would look after me. The rest of that day was a rather confused pattern of nurses and medical hardware, with Ada sitting beside my bed. During the next day or two, the effect of the drugs passed and I was able to think very clearly. I have always been fond of John Donne's poem 'Hymn to God my God, in my sickness'. I could not properly remember it but felt that I was in, 'that holy room, where,... I tune the instrument at the door' (Note 1).

Just recently I read Henri Nouwen's account of a time when he was gravely ill after an accident and he spoke of it as being at the portal of death. That describes very well how I felt at that time. After a few days it became clear that I had been close to death but that I was now stable and beginning to recover. Five days after being admitted however, I had another seemingly milder, attack and we went through the intensive process again. From then on I made a slow but steady recovery. Surgery was debated, but ruled out by the specialists because of my chest condition and the severity of the attacks. The answer was to be careful management of diet, exercise and medication. During my hospitalisation I attended rehabilitation sessions with talks and videos about heart attacks and their characteristics. These all identified the crushing pain, sweating and vomiting which I had experienced. They gave as a fourth element, severe mental distress and turmoil, which interested me because I had found myself so unusually calm and focussed, which undoubtedly is God's provision for His children.

However, there were spiritual ills that needed attention also. As my condition stabilised I experienced a deep sense of concern as I thought over some of the many shortcomings in my life. I knew there were failures for which I had not sought forgiveness, and there were sins which had been confessed, yet I could not obtain peace about them. I mentioned this to my minister, David Powys during one of his visits. That night the

Lord gave me a dream, or vision, in which I saw two or three large, heavily bound books, like family Bibles, which were opened as though ready for reading, and then they were suddenly engulfed in flames and disappeared. I knew immediately the meaning of this vision and accepted it as God's message of forgiveness. He not only forgives but promises that He will remember our sin no more. This brought me a true sense of peace and gratitude for the grace and loving kindness of my Heavenly Father. Altogether this time in hospital became a great blessing to me. I read and pondered on the Epistle to the Romans which we were about to study in our home group. I re-read *Mere Christianity* by C S Lewis, with great profit and also some other books.

Whilst in hospital my vicar, David, had suggested a time of anointing and prayer for healing, and the day after returning home he came with four of my friends from our church and conducted a simple service. I believed the promise in the Epistle of James, on which this service is based, 'that the prayer offered

Luke's wedding to Jane Burgess, in the UK, 1996. From left: Tom, Ben, and David with the Bride and Groom.

in faith will make the sick person well; the Lord will raise him up', and this has been the case. After two or three months of weakness and uncertainty I regained strength. Since then until the time of writing, two-and-a-half years on, I have enjoyed virtually my normal measure of health, taking age into account. Activities have been gradually reduced and exercise increased. I look back on the experience with deep thanksgiving for several reasons. For the personal touch of God's love and care as

257

recounted above. For the devotion and help of Ada and family throughout. Also because I have emerged from it with a different perspective on the affairs and values of this life, and hopefully better prepared for the issues of death and eternity, as we 'draw near to the City'.

One evening, just before leaving the Frankston Hospital I was able to visit another ward where Leonard Buck was a patient. We had a brief talk which proved to be our last. He was moved to another hospital where he died a few weeks later. My first formal outing after my illness was to the service of thanksgiving for his life. This was held, it so happened, at the very church in which some seventy years earlier Len had responded to the call of the gospel, as evangelist W P Nicholson preached Christ. Family members spoke, as well as others, and Marcus Loane former Archbishop of Sydney, paid the major tribute to a great man of God. It was a fitting and heart-warming occasion.

Just a few weeks later Ada and I attended another funeral service, following the sudden death of my cousin and life-time friend, Joyce Findlay. She suffered a heart attack similar to mine and died a few hours after admittance to hospital. I was asked by her husband, Ron, to give the address at the memorial service in the church at which she had been a member for many years, and I was grateful to have the opportunity of paying tribute to her steadfast faith.

A few months after this, in October, there was an important family event in England which we were not able to consider attending because of my illness. Our eldest grandson Luke was united in marriage with Jane Burgess an English lass whom he had met at the Vineyard church they both attended. Dave made the journey to act as best man at the wedding and Marcus was fortunately able to fit it in with a business trip, so that there were some Australian family members present at what proved to be a splendid and very happy occasion. It was very real compensation for us when the happy couple made Melbourne part of their honeymoon holiday.

After about six months I resumed my attendance at meetings of Pasuwe Ltd in PNG. I confess that I was reluctant to step down from this commitment. However it did appear wise to relinquish it and the second half of 1997 seemed to be an appropriate time. So that after thirty years, I chaired my final board meeting in October. At the invitation of the board Ada was able to be with me and we both enjoyed to the full the excellent farewell function which took the form of a dinner at a leading hotel. Bob and Val Callaghan happened to be in Port Moresby at the time and also some other missionary friends were with us. It was an occasion which touched me greatly, particularly because of the affection and the tributes from the national members, besides my long-standing Australian colleagues. It turned out to be a good time to leave as some capable new nationals were joining the board and the whole enterprise seemed in good shape and nicely profitable.

With the approach of my 80th birthday I had now divested myself of all council and board responsibilities. Apart from a few minor roles my activities now centre on parish and home and maintaining contact with friends around the world. The monthly men's parish breakfast begun in 1993 continues to be a useful focal point for fellowship and witness; an outreach to be commended. The weekly Bible study group in our home is something which Ada and I value greatly. It is a privilege to enjoy Christian friendship centred on the Word of God and the more we learn, the more we realise how much remains to be learnt.

In November 1993 we enjoyed the relaxation of a holiday on the north coast of NSW at the quiet seaside town of Hallidays Point. Our friends, Geoff and Ann Kells had kindly lent us their holiday home there. Situated virtually on the beach, it looks across the water to a crescent of golden sand, backed by green hills and headlands, a delightful retreat. Whilst there we took the opportunity to search our diaries and our memories in order to set down a few snippets of family history for the benefit of our children and grandchildren. The following year found us once again in the same pleasant surroundings and we took up the task we had begun twelve months before; another year later the work continued. By this time we had received a deeper sense of purpose regarding the memoirs, as we had reflected on the fact that in many places in God's Word we are clearly told not just to teach our families about the Lord, but to share our own experiences of His guidance. Deuteronomy 4-9 is a good example, it says:

> Only be careful, and watch yourselves closely so that you do not forget the things your eyes have seen or let them slip from your

heart as long as you live. Teach them to your children and to their children after them.

So the work broadened out and we came to see that it should be in a form which could be shared more widely. Earlier I had resisted this thought, but after my illness in 1996 and with the advice and encouragement of some helpful friends, I came to believe that this was what we were meant to do. Looking back over my journey of eighty years, with all of its mistakes, wrong turnings and hesitations, I realised that nevertheless the pillars of cloud and fire had not failed me and that it had indeed been a 'Guided Journey' All of this due to the kindness of God.

When Joshua, led by God, took the people of Israel across the River Jordan he was commanded to set up twelve stones from the river bed as a sign among them. God said to him: 'In the future, when your children ask "What do these stones mean?" tell them that the flow of the Jordan was cut off'. They were to explain to their children that Israel crossed through the river on dry ground, and that God did this in order that all the peoples of the earth might know that the hand of the Lord is powerful and so that Israel might always fear the Lord their God.

This book is my little pile of stones.

Note 1.

To do justice to the verse of the great John Donne, here is the first stanza from his poem 'Hymn to God my God, in my Sickness'.

Since I am coming to that holy room,
Where with thy choir of saints for evermore,
I shall be made thy music; as I come
I tune the instrument at the door,
And what I must do then, think here before.

Epilogue

I turned on my bed and by the grey light of dawn studied the details of the hospital room, pondering the events of the past forty-eight hours. On Monday we had celebrated our fifty-fifth wedding anniversary and on Tuesday, Melbourne Cup Day holiday, together with Marcus and Barbara we had visited Russell and Joan in the home they had purchased recently on the waterfront at Mornington. After spending time on the beach, and climbing some steep steps I was visited with a heart attack. It was not the same violent kind as my last attack but none the less quite unmistakable and clearly demanded hospital attention. Frankston Hospital had no cardiac beds available so that after several hours in emergency I was transferred in the small hours of Wednesday to a hospital in the foothills of the Dandenongs.

During that day I received excellent care but the doctors expressed the opinion that surgery was called for, and that I should be moved to Epworth and be advised by my cardiologist. Now, that time had arrived and I felt in my spirit a chill sense of fear: overnight the only other occupant of my ward had died. Although there were screens I had witnessed the sad drama; the efforts of the medical staff, hurried visits by the family and finally removal of the body. The atmosphere of death was palpable and in the half-light of morning seemed to reach out to embrace me. At Frankston I had been heavily dosed with morphine and that probably heightened my trepidation.

With the coming of day I reached for my Bible and read two or three strengthening Psalms, then as I turned to the daily SU reading my eye fell on a verse in 2 Timothy, Chapter 1 – 'God did not give us the spirit of timidity, but a spirit of power, of love and of self-discipline'. I remembered it better in the old version – 'God hath not given us the spirit of fear, but of power, and of love, and of sound mind'. It was a word from the Lord for me at that moment and it brought liberation from the shadowy feelings of apprehension which had been clouding my mind.

At Epworth an angiogram indicated that surgery was imperative and a quadruple bypass was successfully performed.

Epilogue

In due course I was moved to a rehabilitation centre but unfortunately developed pneumonia which kept me there for a further month. This had been the concern of my doctors and it proved a more difficult episode in some ways than the heart surgery. We were grateful for the attention of skilled physicians and nursing staff and through the goodness of God I was granted recovery, returning home on Christmas Eve. How thankful Ada and I were that Russell and Joan had come back from England a few weeks prior to all of this and had decided to live nearby. The support they were able to give was invaluable.

Once again the hospital experience was lightened by knowledge of the Lord's presence which gave me a remarkable feeling of repose. There were trying times during that seven-and-a-half weeks and emotions tend to fluctuate with illness. I needed help frequently, and it came. Almost daily the Spirit conveyed quickening messages from the Scriptures. The love and prayers of family and friends were effective not only in the physical realm but also in the spiritual. One morning, back at home, I came across a verse which not only summed up that section of the journey but also gave promise for days ahead. It is found in Zephaniah, 3.5: 'Every new day He does not fail'.